中 共 上 海 市 徐 汇 区 湖 南 街 道 工 作 委 员 会
上 海 市 徐 汇 区 人 民 政 府 湖 南 路 街 道 办 事 处 编

陈世东 主编

200031

一個歷史街區的文化記憶（2）

汪觀清

上海教育出版社
SHANGHAI EDUCATIONAL
PUBLISHING HOUSE

湖南街道

《200031——一个历史街区的文化记忆》

编委会

主　　任：陈澄泉　董　伟

委　　员：郭艳楣　祝　恽　吴　思　张正海　卢　芸
王　华　陈世东

主　　编：陈世东

副 主 编：刘　烨

编　　委：（按姓氏笔画排序）
刘宁路　孙玲弟　邬海佳　严　岷　陈　苏
钱定华　隋淑光

编写人员

撰　　稿：（按姓氏笔画排序）
马信芳　王为松　王伟杰　石纯如　刘光清
刘　烨　朱毅琳　李　卫　陆其国　陈世东
周　楚　徐　达　袁龙海　淳　子　章慧敏

翻　　译：范祥涛　李　健

绘　　画：汪观清　杨宏富　齐亚明　何祖明　叶　雄
刘为民　忻秉勇　桑麟康　吴耀明　陆小弟
戴晓明　钱定华　王　药　邬海佳

摄　　影：（按姓氏笔画排序）
马信芳　陆　杨　郭　良　谢云健（部分照片由家属提供）

顾　问

编写顾问：包南麟

艺术顾问：汪观清

建筑顾问：钱宗灏

翻译顾问：朱亚军

统　筹

中共上海市徐汇区湖南街道工作委员会
上海市徐汇区人民政府湖南路街道办事处
上海梧桐画社

200031—Cultural Memories of A Historical District

Painters: WANG Guanqing, YANG Hongfu, QI Yaming,
HE Zuming, YE Xiong, LIU Weimin,
XIN Bingyong, SANG Linkang, WU Yaoming,
LU Xiaodi, DAI Xiaoming, QIAN Dinghua,
WANG Di and WU Haijia

Photographers: (Sorted by surname strokes)
MA Xinfang, LU Yang, GUO Liang and XIE Yunjian
(Some photos provided by family members)

Consultants

Writing Consultant: BAO Nanlin

Art Consultant: WANG Guanqing

Building Consultant: QIAN Zonghao

Translation Consultant: ZHU Yajun

Co-ordination

Hunan Road Street CPC Working Committee of Shanghai Xuhui District
Hunan Road Subdistrict Office of Shanghai Xuhui District People's Government
Shanghai Wutong Painting Society

前　言

上海市徐汇区湖南路街道地处上海市衡山路—复兴路历史风貌保护区，属于邮编为 200031 的区域。这片仅有 1.73 平方公里的社区集中了上海近 15% 的老洋房，是上海花园洋房住宅最集中、优秀历史建筑数量最多、建筑类型最丰富、风貌特色最鲜明的地域。在高大的梧桐树掩映下，一幢幢满布岁月沧桑的西班牙式、英国乡村别墅式、法国文艺复兴式，以及少数地中海式的花园洋房住宅，营造出浓郁的异国风情，东西方文化在此无声地交汇，显现独特的人文特色和深厚的文化底蕴。

这片“花园街道”始于清末，历经民国，迎来中华人民共和国成立。众多政治人物、金融巨头、实业大王、文化名流先后居住于此。晚清重臣李鸿章、辛亥革命先驱黄兴、民国第一任总理唐绍仪、中国社会主义改革开放和现代化建设的总设计师邓小平、中华人民共和国名誉主席宋庆龄、中华人民共和国元帅陈毅、金融奇才周作民、钢铁大王朱垣清、纺织巨头郭棣活、面粉大王孙多森、丝绸翘楚莫觞清、商界女杰董竹君、文学大师巴金、漫画家张乐平、金牌导演汤晓丹、影坛“雄狮”张翼、“电影皇帝”金焰、昆剧泰斗俞振飞……曾在此居住的这些人物，给这片社区的一条条弄堂、一幢幢洋房留下了一个个让人回味的故事，充满戏剧的张力，为湖南路社区赢得了“典雅湖南”和“文化湖南”的美誉。

然而一百多年来，这片宁静的社区也有过无奈和苦涩，穿越历史的尘埃而繁盛起来的街区，见证了人世的沧桑流变，演绎出近现代中国曾经的风云际会，向世人展示具有悠久历史的中华民族如何从沉沦中奋起。

上海自 1843 年开埠，各色外国人纷至沓来，践踏中国主权，形成“国中之国”。殖民者的野心无休无止，到 1914 年法租界第四次扩界（东至沙恩桥，西至徐家汇，南至徐家汇浜，北至大西路一带），覆盖了现在整个湖南路街道区域，使这块土地蒙受了最大的耻辱。一条条马路以洋人名字命名，虽然早已成为历史陈迹，觉醒的中国人却不能忘记这段沉痛的历史。

这里曾响起救亡的号角。1935 年 4 月聂耳在霞飞路（今淮海中路）1258 号为电影《风云儿女》谱写了主题歌《义勇军进行曲》，这首后来成为中华人民共和国国歌的歌曲，轰动了整个中国，唱遍了大江南北，吹奏出中国人民抗日战争的激昂号角。一大批爱国知识分子为了国家存亡，“以笔代戈”不惜牺牲生命。革命烈士郁华、郁达夫兄弟就是千千万万知识分子的代表。

这里还传递过增强国人抗战决心的时代最强音。1938 年，毛泽东《论持久战》英文版从霞飞路 1754 弄 9 号经过中共地下党员杨刚、美国记者项美丽、翻译家邵洵美翻译成英文而走向世界，不仅让外国友人尽快了解中国共产党的抗战方针，更鼓舞国人投入持久抗战的勇气，激励国人争取民族解放的最后胜利。

这里还留下抗日战争胜利结束时的一段秘闻。1945 年，蒋介石通过军统设在福开森路（今武康路）117 号周作民住宅内的秘密电台，电令冈村宁次赴芷江何应钦处接洽投降事宜，有关条款内容以及冈村宁次回复蒋介石的电报等均从此处发收。这是自 1840 年鸦片战争以来，中国人民在反抗侵略斗争中第一次取得完全彻底的胜利。

为了这个时刻的到来，中国人民经历了艰苦的历程。曾居住在这片花园街道的工商业者目睹国家贫弱、民族工业落后的局面，立志实业救国。他们创办各类企业，苦心经营，奋斗多年，为国家发展、民族振兴作出了积极的贡献。

企业家包达三秉持民族气节，拒绝汪伪政府的官职，不顾全家生命安危为新四军捐钱、筹粮、采购药品，支援抗战。出身贫寒的女商人董竹君把以毕生精力创办的锦江饭店，无私地奉献给国家。人称“钢铁大王”的朱恒清，宁愿关厂甚至坐牢也不跟日本人做生意，实现“肉烂了，也要烂在汤里”的诺言。纺织巨头郭棣活为了刚解放的上海的经济发展，不顾个人安危和长辈劝说，毅然决然留在上海，支持国家工商业的发展。中国民族工业的杰出代表、爱国人士、社会活动家刘靖基，在上海解放后积极响应社会主义改造的号召，带头申请纺织行业公私合营，为全国工商业作出表率。1979 年，78 岁高龄的他以“老牛明知夕阳短，不用扬鞭自奋蹄”的精神，带动民建中央和全国工商联骨干，以民间集资方式创办爱国建设公司，为中国工商界的继续发展奉献自己的全部力量。

从沉沦到奋起的历程中，众多文学艺术名流不甘人后。入住于此的他们，抢救历史文献、弘扬传统文化、倡导社会文明、吸取文化精华，为海派文化从孕育、成长走向进步，为中国文化事业的发展作出了不朽贡献。

1942 年，郑振铎先生为抢救沦陷区中国古代文化珍籍，蛰居高邮路 5 弄，虽生活清苦，却不遗余力搜寻整理有珍藏价值的历史文献，在战火纷飞中延续中华文脉。

1949 年，张元济先生为保住合众图书馆，不顾生命危险，以衰迈之躯，坐镇图书馆大门。

一代文化巨匠巴金，用自己的智慧和勇气，回顾个人和民族经历的风风雨雨，挥动如椽巨笔，在武康路 113 号创作《随想录》《再思录》，成为中国文坛上的不朽之作，成为中国人民精神宝库中一份珍贵的财富。

漫画大师张乐平先生，用半个多世纪塑造经典艺术形象——翘鼻、噘嘴、额上飘着三根头发的可爱“三毛”，述说着人世间喜怒哀乐，传递对人生的感慨和美好未来的向往，引得无数人一起品味世态炎凉，共同寻找和创造新的生活，半个多世纪以来始终散发着璀璨光芒，教育影响了几代中国人。有人说看三毛的整个故事，就好像是在看一部中国现代史。

翻译家草婴倾 20 年光阴，译完托尔斯泰的全部小说，成为以一己之力将托翁作品带给中国读者的第一人，完成了我国俄罗斯文学翻译史上的一大壮举。

中国电影一代骄子——电影艺术家郑君里，以独树一帜的艺术实践为我国电影事业的发展作出了重要贡献：他对戏剧、电影理论的执着探索，为后人留下了一份宝贵的遗产。他和蔡楚生联合执导的《一江春水向东流》成为中国电影史上不朽的经典。

电影表演艺术家赵丹，在近半个世纪的艺术生涯中，孜孜以求现实主义的创作风格，不断探索中华民族的表演艺术体系，他那鲜明的艺术形象成为闪烁在中国银幕上的璀璨明珠。

德艺双馨的艺术家张瑞芳，始终把个人命运与民族、国家的命运联系在一起，她主演的影片《李双双》家喻户晓，轰动全国。

昆剧泰斗、京剧大师俞振飞，数十年如一日，为昆剧的延续和发展殚精竭虑。在任上海市戏曲学校校长期间，不仅培养了数以百计的昆、京、沪、越、淮等剧种的演员和评弹演员，还培养了戏剧舞台、化妆、音乐、服装、武功等专门人才。

越剧改革先行者袁雪芬，率先在中国戏曲中建立了编、导、演、音、美齐备的艺术机制，为越剧走向全国乃至世界作出了不朽的贡献。

作曲家、音乐教育家贺绿汀，他创作的歌曲《游击队歌》《垦春泥》《嘉陵江上》，在抗日战争期间流传海内外，对抗日救亡歌咏的大规模发展、对社会音乐生活都产生了至为重要的影响，是中国电影音乐文化中的宝贵财富，至今仍是音乐会和歌咏活动中经常演唱的曲目。

铭记历史，面向未来。我们挖掘整理这一批人文历史资料，目的是更好地传承历史文脉，弘扬核心价值，培养城市精神，增强社区归属。我们认为，优美的环境需要文明的人相协调，温馨的区域需要良好的社会风气相融合，典雅的地段需要高素质的居民相匹配。我们希望，通过品味跨越世纪浮沉的人物及建筑，体验上海梧桐树下的老房子蕴含的文化积淀，更系统地关注和重视我们的城市历史文脉，唤起更多的人参与到整理和保护历史文化资料的工作中，进一步凸现湖南路街道人文环境浓郁，社会秩序和谐稳定，整个社区充满生机活力的新风貌，努力建设彰显海派文化特色的国际化街道，为上海城市文化建设作出有益的贡献。

我们的工作微不足道，我们的心意是真诚的。

Preface

The Hunan Road Residential Subdistrict of Shanghai Xuhui District is located in the Historic Conservation Area along Hengshan Road and Fuxing Road in Shanghai, belonging to the district with the zip code of 200031. This community area has only 1.73 square kilometers, but pools nearly 15% of the old foreign-style houses in Shanghai. In this sense it is an area where the foreign-style garden houses in Shanghai are mostly concentrated and there are the largest number of outstanding historical buildings, the most extensive architectural types and the most distinctive features. Against the tall plane trees, various residential buildings of foreign-style garden house are weather-beaten with years of vicissitudes of life—some are of the Spanish style, some are of the British country villa style, some are of the French Renaissance style and a few are of the Mediterranean style—all these constitute characteristic architectures with features of rich exotic flavor, where the Eastern and Western cultures gather together in a silent communication, showing a unique cultural characteristics and profound cultural heritage.

This "Garden-like Residential Subdistrict" traced back to the late Qing Dynasty, went through the period of the Republic of China and ushered in the establishment of the People's Republic of China. Many political figures, financial giants, industrial kings, cultural celebrities have lived here successively. They embrace such big names as LI Hongzhang, minister of the late Qing Dynasty, HUANG Xing, pioneer of the 1911 Revolution, TANG Shaoyi, first premier of the Republic of China, Deng Xiaoping, the general designer of China's socialist reform and opening up and modernization, Song Qingling, the honorary president of PRC, and Chen Yi, the marshal of PRC. In addition there are still the financial wizard ZHOU Zuomin, the steel king ZHU Yuanqing, the textile giant GUO Dihuo, the flour king SUN Duosen, the silk leader MO Shangqing, the outstanding female merchant DONG Zhujun, the literary master BA Jin, the cartoonist ZHANG Leping, the prestigious director TANG Xiaodan, the "Lion" in the movie circle ZHANG Yi, the "Movie King" JIN Yan, the leading authority in Kun Opera YU Zhenfei ... they once lived in this community area, leaving behind them memorable stories in those alleys and foreign-style buildings. All these stories abound with dramatic tension and win the Hunan Road community the good reputation of "Elegant Community" and "Cultural Community".

However, for over a hundred years in the past, this quiet community has also experienced helplessness and bitterness. Passing through the dust of history and flourishing gradually, this community has witnessed the vicissitudes of life, perceived the gathering of the talented in modern China and demonstrated to the world how the Chinese nation with its long history went through the ups and downs and finally rose to the occasion.

Shanghai started opening port since 1843 and mixed varieties of foreigners came over one after another to trample on China's sovereignty with the result of the formation of "states within state". The ambitions of colonialists were endless. By 1914 the French Settlement expanded its boundary for the fourth time (Schaan Bridge in the east, Xujiahui in the west, Xujiahui River in the south and the Great West Road in the north), covering the entire Hunan Road area with the result that this piece of land suffered the greatest humiliations. Roads were named after the names of foreigners. Although they have already become historical traces, the awakened Chinese people can never forget this painful period of time in the history.

Here the horn of salvation once rang. In April 1935 NIE Er wrote the theme song *March of the Volunteers* for the film *Children of Trouble Time* at No. 1258 on Xiafei Road (now Huaihai Road). Later this song became the national anthem of the People's Republic of China and turned into a sensation throughout China. It was once popular across the whole country and blew the heated horn of the war of resistance of the Chinese people against Japanese invasion. A large number of patriotic intellectuals "used pens as weapon" and did not hesitate to sacrifice their lives for the survival of the country. The brothers YU Hua and YU Dafu, two revolutionary martyrs, are the representatives of tens of thousands of these intellectuals.

Here the strongest voice of the era was also passed around to strengthen the people's determination in the War of Resistance against Japanese Aggression. In 1938, the English version of the booklet *On the Protracted War* by MAO Zedong made for the world from No. 9 in Alley 1754 on Xiafei Road by means of YANG Gang, the underground member of the CPC, XIANG Meili, the American journalist and the translator SHAO Xunmei. This not only enabled foreign friends to understand as soon as possible the guidelines of the war of resistance of the CPC, but also excited the courage of the Chinese people for the lasting war and inspired them to fight for the final victory of national liberation.

Here also a secret has remained uncovered after the victory of the War of Resistance against Japanese Invasion. In 1945, JIANG Jieshi ordered Okamura Yasuji by telegraph to go to HE Yingqin at Zhijiang County for the affairs of surrender. The telegraph was sent by means of a secret radio transmitter stationed by the Military Statistics Bureau in the residence of ZHOU Zuomin at No. 117 on Ferguson Road (now Wukang Road). The contents of the relevant provisions and the replies from Okamura Yasuji to JIANG Jieshi were all sent and received from this transmitter. This is the first time since the Opium War in 1840 that the Chinese people achieved a complete victory in the struggle against aggression.

For the arrival of this moment, the Chinese people have gone through a tough and bitter course. Those businessmen who once lived in this garden community witnessed the situation of a poor and weak country and the backwardness of national industry so that they aspired to save the country with industry. They set up various types of enterprises, made painstaking efforts and struggled for many years, dedicating positive contributions to the national development and national revitalization.

The entrepreneur BAO Dasan upheld the national integrity and refused to take official positions of WANG Jingwei's puppet government. Regardless of the life safety of the whole family, he donated money, prepared grains and purchased medicines for the New Fourth Army to support the war against Japanese invasion. DONG Zhujun, a woman merchant born in a poor family, selflessly dedicated to the country the Jinjiang Hotel which she constructed with her lifelong energy. Known as the "Iron and Steel King", ZHU Hengqing would rather shut down the factory and even wear the stripes than do business with the Japanese invaders, realizing the promise that "rotten meat must stay in the soup". The textile giant GUO Dihuo resolutely decided to stay in Shanghai regardless of his personal safety and the persuasion from the seniors in order to support the development of national industry and commerce, and the economic development in Shanghai after its liberation. As one of China's outstanding representatives of national industry, a patriot and social activist, LIU Jingji positively responded to the call of socialist transformation after the liberation of Shanghai and took the lead in applying for public-private partnership of textile industry, setting a good example for the national industry and commerce. In 1979 when he was at the age of 78, he still encouraged himself and brought along backbones of the central committee of China Democratic National Construction Association and All-China Federation of Industry and Commerce to found Patriotic Construction Company in the field of industry and commerce on the basis of civil fund-raising, devoting all his strength to the continuous development of Chinese industry and commerce.

In the course from decline to rise, many literary and artistic celebrities also cherished the desire to overrun others. Those who lived here rescued historical literature, upheld traditional culture, promoted social civilization and absorbed the essence of the world, making invariable contributions to the breeding, growth and progress of Shanghai culture and also to the development of Chinese culture as a whole.

In 1942, Mr. ZHENG Zhenduo lived in seclusion at No. 5 on Gaoyou Road for the rescue of the invaluable books of ancient Chinese culture from the occupied areas. Although his life was full of hardships, he still spared no effort to search for and tidy up historical documents which deserved precious conservation. In this way he was protecting and preserving the Chinese culture in the flames of war.

In 1949, Mr. ZHANG Yuanji braved against the life-threatening danger at the gate of the library with his declining body in order to protect the Public Library.

BA Jin, a great cultural master for a generation, made use of his own wisdom and courage to review the ups and downs of personal and national experiences and waved his giant pen to create *Random Thoughts and Afterthoughts* at No. 113 on Wukang Road, which have become monumental works in Chinese literary world and precious wealth in the treasury of spirit of the Chinese people.

Mr. ZHANG Leping, a master of cartoon, spent over half a century to shape a classic art image—the lovely "Three Hairs" with a tip-tilted nose, sucking mouth and three floating hairs on her forehead, telling about all the sufferings and happiness of the world and passing on the understandings of life and longing for a better future. This image has attracted countless people to taste the fickleness of the world together and find and create new life accordingly. It has always been radiating bright light and educated and influenced generations of Chinese people. Some say that reading the whole story of the "Three Hairs" is just like reading the history of modern China.

The translator CAO Ying poured 20 years of time in translating all the novels of Tolstoy. In this case he became the first person to have translated all of Tolstoy's novels only on the basis of his own efforts, accomplishing a great feat in the history of Russian literature translation in our country.

ZHENG Junli, a film artist and a pride in Chinese film, has made important contributions to the development of China's film industry with his unique artistic practice—his persistent exploration of drama and film theory has left behind a valuable legacy for future generations. The film *A Spring River Flows East* co-directed by him and CAI Chusheng has become a permanent classic in the history of Chinese film.

ZHAO Dan, a film performing artist, industriously pursued the realistic style of creation and constantly explored the performing art system of Chinese nation in nearly half a century of artistic career. His distinctive art images have become bright pearls glittering on the screen in China.

ZHANG Ruifang, excellent both in virtue and art, has always associated her personal fate with that of the nation and the country. The film *LI Shuangshuang* which she starred has become widely known among the audiences and become sensational across the country.

YU Zhenfei, a leading authority of Kunqu Opera and master of Beijing Opera, exerted all his strength and wisdom for the continuation and development of Kunqu Opera for decades like one day. During his tenure as president of Shanghai Opera School, he not only trained hundreds of actors in such opera fields as Kunqu Opera, Beijing Opera, Shanghai Opera, Shaoxing Opera and Huaiju Opera as well as actors of Suzhou Pingtan, but also trained specialists in such spheres as drama stage, make-up, music, costumes and martial arts.

YUAN Xuefen, a pioneer in the reform of Shaoxing Opera, took the lead in establishing the artistic mechanism of the Chinese opera with everything ready including screenwriting, direction, performance, music and artistic decoration, and made monumental contributions to help Shaoxing Opera spread across China and the world as a whole.

HE Luting, a composer and music educator, created such songs as "Guerrilla Song", "Spring Plough" and "On Jialing River", which spread at home and abroad during the War of Resistance against Japanese Invasion and exerted significant impact on the large-scale development of salvation singing against Japanese invasion and on the social life of music. Therefore they are valuable treasures of the Chinese film music culture and are still incorporated in the repertoire of songs often performed at concerts and singing activities up to now.

Bearing in mind the history and opening up the future, we have sorted out and compiled these cultural and historical materials with the purpose to better inherit the historical context, promote the core values, cultivate the city spirit and enhance the sense of belonging of the community. We believe that the beautiful environment requires civilized people for their coordination, that the warm district needs a good social atmosphere for their blending, and that elegant sectors need high quality residents for their matching. We hope that the taste of the ups and downs of the characters and architectures across centuries, the experience of the cultural accumulation implicated in the old houses under the plane trees in Shanghai and more systematic attention to and recognition of the historical context of the city—all these will serve to arouse more people to participate in the compilation and protection of the historical and cultural documents and to further highlight the facts that the Hunan Road is characterized with rich cultural environment, that the social order boasts harmony and stability, and that the whole community is full of vigor and vitality. By doing this, we mean to make great efforts to build an internationalized community area which intensifies the characteristics of Shanghai culture and further make instructive contributions to the construction of urban culture in Shanghai.

CHEN Shidong

湖南街道

目　录

湖南街道

200031

陈传熙
（1916—2012）

祖籍广西南宁，出生于广西龙州县，音乐指挥家。毕业于上海国立音乐专科学校，主科为钢琴，副科为双簧管。1946年加入上海工部局交响乐团，任双簧管演奏员，并任教于国立音乐院常州少年班、国立上海音专和上海交响乐团。1958年调任上影乐团指挥，开始其电影音乐指挥生涯。为近600部影片配乐并指挥演奏，代表影片有故事片《林则徐》《聂耳》《红色娘子军》《李双双》《天云山传奇》等，美术片《牧笛》《渔童》《金色的海螺》《大闹天宫》等，被誉为在银幕上名字出现次数最多的指挥家。2005年被授予“当代中国电影音乐特别贡献奖”，同年被授予“中国音乐金钟奖终身荣誉勋章”。

为电影音乐“打补丁”

中国电影银幕上名字出镜率最高的，就是那位幕后指挥陈传熙。正是在他那根榆木指挥棒的“统领”下，交响乐队奏起了曾让无数观众着迷的难忘的乐曲。

陈传熙有着惊人的听觉，能听辨100个由乐队奏出的和弦。1958年，为支持电影配乐，他被调到上海电影乐团任指挥。从面向观众的音乐舞台转到了银幕后面，自此他进入电影新天地，而这一干竟是40多年。

电影音乐和交响乐最大的区别，是电影音乐要跟着画面走。在一秒钟里，音乐只有几个音符，而电影胶卷要转过24格之多。两者要完全匹配，这全在指挥的掌控之中。

电影《聂耳》中，有一场戏表现“义勇军进行曲”诞生的情景：聂耳满腔的激情像火山般爆发于笔端，突然，聂耳站起来把笔兴奋地一掷，表示乐曲的完成。这时选用的正是义勇军进行曲的音乐，按要求掷笔的同时乐曲必须戛然而止，于是乐曲何时开始成了问题。陈传熙的做法是：先计算出乐曲的长短，然后倒转电影胶片，找到乐曲应该进入的位置。

电影《红日》主题歌《谁不说俺家乡好》已先期录音，审查时有关方面提出要改动歌词。重录歌曲既要对长短，还要对演员前期演唱的口型，这又有相当难度。陈传熙凭着几十年的经验，调动好乐队和独唱者的情绪，极富感召力地喊了一声“跟着我的指挥棒，实录！”，竟一遍通过。

译制《简·爱》《巴黎圣母院》等影片时，由于当时还没有多轨录音，为配音把原来的对白去掉时，同时把衬托在对白后面的音乐也一起抹掉了。重新配乐的任务交给了陈传熙，如何“还原”再次考验这位指挥。陈传熙反复观看原版影片，先听旋律，再听和声、布局、声部的走向与变化，把乐曲分解到各种乐器、声部上，再重新组合并指挥乐团演出。陈传熙以其扎实的音乐基础、过人的音乐听力，把“补丁”打得天衣无缝。影片上映时，观众丝毫也没有意识到其中的音乐有一部分是上海电影乐团重新录制的。

建筑简介：五原路212弄16号

陈传熙旧居位于五原路212弄16号。五原路212弄大华新村，为新式里弄，1947年建造，共有17幢，占地面积5420平方米，总建筑面积7226平方米。建筑略具现代派风貌，三层砖混结构。平屋顶四周设置女儿墙，立面简洁，极少装饰。南部二层设有悬挑的阳台，下部为底层门廊。素色水泥砂浆外墙面均布钢窗，窗裙板仅以网格细槽略作装饰。楼内布局紧凑，功能齐备，原用锅炉水汀供暖。大华新村居住过的社会各界名人，有国民党将领张发奎、大新公司创始人蔡昌、画家汪观清、大中华橡胶厂经理洪念祖、歌唱家周碧珍等。

CHEN Chuanxi

CHEN Chuanxi (1916–2012) has his ancestral family from Nanning in Guangxi province. Born in Longzhou County, he is known as a music conductor. He graduated with the major of piano from Shanghai National Institute of Music with a minor of oboe. In 1946, he joined Shanghai Municipal Council Symphony Orchestra and served as an oboe performer and also worked as a teacher at the Changzhou Juvenile Class of National Academy of Music, Shanghai National Institute of Music and Shanghai Symphony Orchestra. In 1958, he was transferred to serve as orchestra conductor in Shanghai Film Orchestra and since then began his career of film music conductor. He produced soundtrack and conducted for nearly 600 films and his representative works include such feature films as *LIN Zexu, NIE Er, Red Detachment of Women*, *LI Shuangshuang* and *Legend of Tianyun Mountain*, as well as such animated films as *Pastoral Flute, Fish Boy, The Golden Conch* and *Uproar in Heaven*. He was known as the conductor whose name appeared on the screen for the most times. In 2005, he was awarded the “special contribution award for contemporary Chinese film music”. In the same year he was awarded the “Lifetime Medal of Honor of China Music Golden Bell Award”.

“Patching” for Film Music

The name which most frequently appeared on the film screen in China was CHEN Chuanxi, the conductor behind the curtain. It was under the direction of his elm baton that the big symphony orchestra played pieces of music which were fascinating and unforgettable to countless audience.

He had an amazing sense of hearing and was capable of distinguishing 100 chords played by the band. In 1958, in order to support film soundtrack, he was transferred to Shanghai Film Orchestra to serve as conductor. In this case he switched his work from the music stage in front of the audience to behind the screen and he entered the new world of film ever since, where he worked for actually 40 years.

The biggest difference between film music and symphony lies in the fact that film music must follow the pictures on the screen.

指挥家陈传熙
Conductor CHEN Chuanxi.

In one second, there are only a few notes of music, while the film must turn around for over 24 bars. To match the music and the pictures entirely relies on the control of the conductor.

In the film *NIE Er*, there was a scene which depicted the birth of the "March of the Volunteers", where NIE Er's passion erupted at the end of his pen like a volcano and he suddenly stood up and threw the pen excitedly, indicating the completion of the music. At this time what was selected was the music of "*March of the Volunteers*". According to the requirements, the music must stop short at the same time when the pen was thrown, so when the music should begin became a problem. CHEN's approach was like this. First the length of the music was calculated and then the film was reversed to find where the music should enter.

The theme song "Whoever Doesn't Say Our Hometown Is Good" of the film *Red Sun* was recorded at an early time, but when it was time for the censorship, a proposal was made to change the words. If the song was to be recorded again, not only the length of music must be the same, but also the actor who was singing the song must be be lip-synced. This was quite difficult. With decades of experience, CHEN mobilized the mood of the band and the soloist, speaking aloud to them with great emotional appeal "follow my baton and make realtime recording!" The whole process was finished at one stroke.

When foreign films like *Jane Eyre* and *Notre Dame de Paris* were translated and produced, there was no multi-track recording. Once the original dialogue was removed by new dubbing, the music behind the dialogue was also erased. The task of new soundtrack was given to CHEN Chuanxi, which was quite a challenge for the conductor. He repeatedly watched the original film, listening to the melody first and then the chord and layout as well as the direction and change of sound. Then he broke the music down and distributed all pieces to a variety of musical instruments and music parts. In the end he reorganized the music, which was performed by the orchestra under his conduction. With his solid foundation in music and extraordinary music listening, he made the "patching" of music seamless. When the films were released, the audience did not realize at all that part of the music was re-recorded by Shanghai Film Orchestra.

The former residence of CHEN Chuanxi is located at No. 16 in Alley 212 on Wuchuan Road, which was Dahua Village, a new-style alley. Built in 1947, it has a total of 17 buildings, covering an area of 5,420 square meters with a total construction area of 7,226 square meters. With a touch of modern style, it has three stories of mixed structure of brick and cement. Around the flat roof are constructed parapets with a concise facade of very little decoration. On the second floor of the south, there are cantilevered balconies and under them is the ground floor porch. The outside walls coated with plain cement mortar are evenly covered by steel windows and window skirts are only slightly decorated with grids of thin grooves. The layout in the building is compact with all functions available, which was originally heated with steam from water boiler. Dahua Village once accommodated celebrities from various circles of the society, including ZHANG Fakui, the KMT general, CAI Chang, founder of Dah Sing Company, painter WANG Guanqing, HONG Nianzu, manager of Greater China Rubber Factory and singer ZHOU Bizhen.

陈传熙 （何祖明画）　　CHEN Chuanxi （By HE Zuming）

陈家泠

（1937— ）

祖籍广西，出生于浙江永康，原名陈家麟，国画家、陶艺家，新海派水墨画领军人物。1963 年毕业于浙江美术学院。初习人物画，20 世纪 70 年代师从陆俨少学山水、书法，后攻花鸟。80 年代起吸收中国古代壁画和外国水彩技法，创造出具有中国哲理性，兼有印象派、抽象派及表现主义特点的现代国画新流派，对海派绘画的发展起到引领和推动作用。1983 年起任教于上海大学美术学院。现为上海大学美术学院国画系教授、中国国家画院首聘研究员。作品曾获第六届全国美术展佳作奖、第七届全国美术展银质奖，多次在欧美、东南亚等地举行个展和群展。其策划组建的上海半岛美术馆和“泠窑”陶艺工作室致力于弘扬传统文化，推进艺术创新，为海派艺术精神的一面旗帜。2014 年，纪录片《陈家泠》在意大利罗马国际电影节首映。

“我只是玩一玩”

在中国美术界，陈家泠不乏美誉：新海派水墨画领军人物、海派艺术精神的旗帜。他成立了上海第一家民间美术馆——半岛美术馆；创立了将水墨语言与瓷器创新相结合的“泠窑”；探索将瓷器与红木家具结合，甚至用瓷器创作出独一无二的麻将牌；还尝试将水墨在旗袍上加以表现。登完三山五岳，又用山水技法画了罗汉观音，并涉足佛学艺术创作。要问他哪来这么多创造力，他回答：“我只是玩一玩。”

1979 年，42 岁的陈家泠如痴如醉地“玩”起了“水墨的实验”，几乎每天晚饭过后都要画一幅水墨肖像。如此数月，其中的一幅《鲁迅》入选华东六省一市肖像画展，他的实验得到了认可。

画家的最高境界，是走向自由王国。而通向这个王国的途径，在陈家泠看来，就是会玩。所谓玩，就是在创作时心态放松，没有条条框框，没有功利，不急于求成，顺其自然。

1984 年，陈家泠以一幅表现荷花的画作《开放》在第六届全国美术展中获得佳作奖；1987 年同类题材画作《霞光》被美国艺术史专家琼珠恩编著的《新中国绘画（1949—1986）》选作封面；1989 年同类题材画作《不染》获得第七届全国美术展银奖。荷花是他由人物画转到花鸟画创作首先找到的突破口。究其缘由，是陈家泠为“好玩”，而在个人艺术道路上走出的具有划时代意义的创新之路。陈家泠认为，前辈大师所达到的艺术高峰，后人可望而不可即。只有在前人的基础上，不断求新求变，自成一格，才有光辉前途。于是，他做出两大改变：一是弃擅长的人物、山水画，改攻花鸟；二是弃规范的用笔用墨，探索纸、墨、笔、水、色之间相互作用的关系，也就是绘画材质的变化。陈家泠的创新，既是传统的，在浓郁的画意中，分明看到了灵动的线条、古典的情趣；又是现代的，那构图、墨色十分地简洁、典雅，符合现代人的视觉要求。

以荷花为代表的探索获得成功后，陈家泠的手更痒了，他“玩”了一个回马枪，将探索的主题转回山水画，选择的是桂林山水。读他的作品，只有两个字：惊叹！笔墨不多，意趣连连。朦胧的山，清澈的水，飘浮的云，飞翔的鸟，给予人的都是静和美。

陈家泠说：“我感到自己在绘画上已进入一个自由和灵动的状态，每天作画都无羁无绊，非常开心。”陈家泠的好玩，是对艺术本质的一种认识，更是文化人的一种理想和境界。他，玩出了境界。

建筑简介：武康路280弄1号楼

陈家泠寓所位于武康路280弄兴国花园1号楼。兴国花园为上海市第一批外销房，建于1992年。院内共6幢房屋，砖混结构，1梯2户，总高4层。陈家泠寓所位于花园北侧，外立面采用淡黄色涂料饰面，南侧阳台外墙面为暗灰色涂料，四层阳台有弓形拱券，阳台上方为屋顶露台。红瓦双坡屋面，硬山搁檩，南坡屋面布置有老虎窗。入口位于北侧中部，入口门厅及楼梯地面和踢脚线均有灰白相间的马赛克瓷砖装饰。房屋一层南侧设有庭院。

CHEN Jialing

CHEN Jialing (1937–) has his ancestral family from Guangxi Zhuang Autonomous Region. Born in Yongkang in Zhejiang province, he had a former name of CHEN Jialin and is known as an artist of Chinese painting, pottery artist and ink painting leader of the New Shanghai School. In 1963, he graduated from the Zhejiang Academy of Fine Arts. At first he learned figure painting. In the 1970s, he took LU Yanshao as his teacher to learn landscape painting and Chinese calligraphy and later specialized in flower-and-bird paintings. Since the 1980s, he drew inspiration from ancient Chinese frescoes and foreign watercolor techniques to create a new school of modern Chinese painting with the characteristics of Chinese philosophy in addition to impressionism, abstractionism and expressionism, which played a leading and promoting role in the development of painting of the Shanghai School. Since 1983, he has been teaching at the Academy of Fine of Arts Shanghai University. Now he is a professor of the Department of Chinese Painting of Shanghai University and one of the first researchers of China National Academy of Painting. His works won the Sixth National Art Exhibition for best works and silver award of the Seventh National Art Exhibition. He held personal and group exhibitions for many times in Europe, the United States, Southeast Asia and other places. The Shanghai Peninsula Museum of Art and "Ling Kiln" Pottery Studio which he planned and set up are dedicated to promoting the traditional culture and artistic innovation, and have been a banner of the artistic spirit of the Shanghai School. In 2014, the documentary *CHEN Jialing* had its debut at the Rome International Film Festival in Italy.

"I Just Have Fun"

In the art circle in China, CHEN Jialing is well-known with many titles—ink painting leader and banner of the artistic spirit of the New Shanghai School. He founded the first folk art museum in Shanghai—Peninsula Museum of Art; he created the "Ling Kiln" which combined the ink language and porcelain innovation; he explored the combination of porcelain and mahogany furniture and even the use of porcelain to create a unique set of mahjong; also he tried to use ink on cheongsam for artistic creation. After climbing mountains and peaks in artistic creation, he also made use of landscape techniques to create paintings of arhat and Guanyin and involved himself in Buddhist art creation. When asked how he was so creative, his reply was "I just have fun".

When he was at the age of 42 in 1979, he was drunk in the "fun" of "ink-wash painting experiment" and painted a portrait of

陈家泠在创作
CHEN Jialing at his creation.

ink almost every day after dinner. A few months in this way, one of the paintings *LU Xun* was selected for the East China Six Provinces and One City Portrait Exhibition, which meant that his experiment was recognized.

The highest state of an artist is to enter into the kingdom of freedom. In his opinion, the way to the kingdom is to have fun. The so-called having fun means a relaxed state of mind in the time of creation and there is no rule, no material gain, no hurry. What is needed is to let nature take its course.

In 1984, he won the prize for outstanding works in the 6th National Art Exhibition with the painting of lotus *Blossom*. In 1987, his painting in the same vein *Morning Rays* was selected as the cover of the book *New Chinese Painting (1949-1986)* edited by an American art historian; in 1989, the painting of the same subject *No Dyeing* won silver award in the Seventh National Art Exhibition. Lotus represented the first breakthrough he found to shift from figure to flower-bird. The reason was that his "having fun" led to an epoch-making road of innovation in his personal artistic pursuit. He thought that the peaks of art reached by artist predecessors could only be appreciated from afar. Only on the basis of predecessors, constant innovation and change as well as a unique style could an artist have a bright future. So he made two major changes. The first was the discarding of figure and landscape he was good at and shifting to flowers and birds; the second was the abandoning of standardized pen and ink to explore the interaction between paper, ink, pen, water and color, which meant the change of materials for painting. His innovation was both traditional and modern. Being traditional meant the classical taste and smart lines in rich paintings; being modern meant that the composition and ink were very simple and elegant, which was in line with the visual requirements of modern people.

After his exploration with lotus as the representative was successful, he was more eager to do experiments and went back to explore the theme of landscape painting with the choice of Guilin landscapes. Viewing his works only generated one word—amazing! Not much ink radiated charm again and again. Obscure mountains, clear water, floating clouds and flying birds—all these impress viewers with silence and beauty.

Once he said, "In the painting I feel like entering a state of freedom and agility. Every day I paint without any restriction or binding. So I'm very happy." His having fun is not merely a kind of understanding of the nature of art, but an ideal and realm of professionals in art and literature. He created a realm by having fun.

The apartment of CHEN Jialing is in Building No. 1 in Xingguo Garden in Alley 280 on Wukang Road. Built in 1992, the apartments of Xingguo Garden were the first for sale in Shanghai. In the garden there are a total of 6 buildings with a structure of bricks and concrete. They have four floors and each floor has two families. His apartment is located in the north side of the garden. Its facade adopts a veneer of pale yellow paint finishes and the south side has a balcony with outside walls of dark gray paint. The balcony at the fourth floor has an arch with the shape of a bow and above the balcony is a roof terrace. Its roof has double slopes of red tiles and hard gables with purlins. The southern slope of the roof has the tiger window. The entrance is located in the middle of the north side and the entrance hall, the stairs floor and the baseboard are all decorated with gray and white mosaic tiles. There is a courtyard on the south side of the first floor.

陈家泠 （邬海佳画）

CHEN Jialing （By WU Haijia）

陈烟桥
（1911—1970）

广东东莞人，笔名李雾城等，版画家。毕业于上海新华艺术专科学校，后加入中国左翼美术家联盟。1933 年后，在鲁迅先生鼓励与支持下，投身中国新兴版画运动，成为第一代版画家代表人物。1939 年赴重庆，先后任育才中学绘画组组长、《新华日报》美术科主任。中华人民共和国成立后，历任华东军政委员会文化部美术科科长、中国美术家协会上海分会秘书长、广西艺术学院副院长、中国美术家协会广西分会主席等。其版画以黑白木刻为主，多表现普通劳动者的生活和劳动，手法写实，画风质朴。代表作品有木刻《建设中的佛子岭》《鲁迅和他的伙伴们》《黄浦江上》等。著有《鲁迅与木刻》《新中国木刻》《烟桥木刻集》等。

含泪描绘鲁迅先生遗容

20 世纪 30 年代，针对当时其他画种创作脱离实际，不能反映社会现实和民众要求的状况，鲁迅推出了成本低、创作时间短的新兴版画品种——木刻。1929 年，爱好美术的陈烟桥如愿考进了广州市美术专科学校学习西洋画。这时，一本由鲁迅先生编撰的《近代木刻选集》从上海传到了广东。

一种“清新刚健”的画风迎面扑来，陈烟桥思路顿开，开始转向木刻学习，继而想到应该到其发源地——上海寻找“中国木刻之父”鲁迅。于是，在转入上海新华艺术专科学校学习的同时，他将自己的创作寄给鲁迅，并得到鲁迅的迅速回复。1930 年 10 月，鲁迅与内山完造合办的外国版画展览会在北四川路举行。陈烟桥前去参观，受到鲁迅的热情接待。陈烟桥自此直接受鲁迅教诲，投入到中国新兴版画创作中。从 1932 年至鲁迅逝世，陈烟桥共收到鲁迅先生的书信二十多封。

1934 年 3 月 28 日，鲁迅在致陈烟桥的信中写道：“我看先生的木刻，黑白对比的力量，已经很能运用的了……”

1934 年，中国在法国和苏联举办画展，鲁迅把征集作品之事交给陈烟桥、陈铁耕。在征集到的作品中，鲁迅和宋庆龄选了 78 幅，以“革命的中国之新艺术”为题送巴黎和莫斯科展出。陈烟桥的《某女工》《天灾》《受伤者的呐喊》和《投宿》等入选参展。鲁迅于 6 月 20 日写信给陈烟桥：“我们的绘画及木刻，在巴黎展览，很成功……在莫斯科展览，评论很好。”

为“鼓吹木刻”，1934 年 10 月，鲁迅自费出版了《木刻纪程》，收录了 8 位作者的 24 幅黑白木刻作品。其中陈烟桥的《窗》和《风景》两幅作品受到鲁迅的特别称赞。

1936 年 10 月，“第二回全国木刻流动展览”在上海西藏路八仙桥青年会举行。8 日，鲁迅抱病出席参观，并与在场的陈烟桥、黄新波、林夫等青年版画家和《木刻创作法》一书的编译者白危等座谈。青年摄影家沙飞用镜头记录了这难忘的一刻。

11 天后，1936 年 10 月 19 日，鲁迅先生因积劳成疾而谢世。当天，陈烟桥闻讯，急忙赶到山阴路大陆新村 9 号鲁迅寓所，怀着对导师的尊敬和悲痛之情，含泪画下了鲁迅先生的遗容……

建筑简介：五原路281弄6号

陈烟桥旧居位于五原路281弄6号，为花园住宅。房屋为假三层砖木结构，一层设有架空层，建筑平面近似呈矩形。房屋外立面为淡黄色水泥拉毛墙面，方形钢窗，窗上方有菱形装饰图样。南立面设有梁板式阳台，雕花镂空铁栏杆。红瓦坡屋面，木结构挑檐。一层入口位于房屋东侧，拱券门洞，一层窗内钢格栅设有精美雕花图样。木结构双跑楼梯，木踏步，木扶手。三层西侧有阁楼。房前有小花园。

CHEN Yanqiao

CHEN Yanqiao (1911–1970), native of Dongguan in Guangdong Province and known as printmaker, has such pen names as LI Wucheng. He graduated from Shanghai Xinhua Art College and later joined China Left-Wing Artists Union. After 1933, with the encouragement and support of Mr. LU Xun, he joined China new printmaking movement and became a representative of printmakers of the first generation. In 1939 he went to Chongqing, successively serving as painting group leader in Yucai High School and director of the Art Division of *Xinhua Daily*. After the founding of the People's Republic of China, he served as chief of the Art Division of the Culture Department of the East China Military and Political Committee, secretary-general of the Shanghai Branch of China Artists Association, vice president of Guangxi Arts Institute and chairman of the Guangxi Branch of China Artists Association. His printmaking is dominated by black and white woodcut, primarily representing the life and labor of ordinary workers with realistic techniques and simple style. His representative works include woodcut works such as *Foziling in Construction, LU Xun and his Fellows, On Huangpu River* and so on. He also authors works including *LU Xun and Woodcut, Woodcut in the New China, A Woodcut Collection by CHEN Yanqiao* and so on.

Depicting with Tears a Portrait of a Deceased, Mr. LU Xun

In the 1930s, LU Xun introduced a new style of printmaking—woodcut, with low cost and shorter time of creation in view of the fact that other paintings were deviated from reality and could not reflect the social life and the requirements of the people. In 1929, CHEN Yanqiao, who loved arts, was admitted into Guangzhou Academy of Fine Arts to learn western painting as he wished. At this time, a copy of *An Anthology of Modern Woodcut* compiled by Mr. LU Xun was distributed from Shanghai to Guangdong.

A kind of "fresh and vigorous" style rushed against his face, which found CHEN Yanqiao enlightened all of a sudden. Therefore, he began to turn to woodcut learning and then an idea crossed his mind that he should resort to its birthplace—Shanghai to find LU Xun, "the father of Chinese woodcut". Consequently, when he transferred himself to Shanghai Xinhua Art College, he sent his own creative works to LU Xun and got a rapid response from the latter. In October 1930, the Foreign Printmaking Exhibition jointly sponsored by LU Xun and Kanza Uchiyama was held on North Sichuan Road. CHEN Yanqiao went to pay a visit, where he

陈烟桥（右一）等与鲁迅（左一）在一起
CHEN Yanqiao (first from right) and others were together with LU Xun (first from left).

enjoyed a warm reception from LU Xun. Since then he got direct instructions from the latter and indulged himself into the creation of the new style printmaking in China. From 1932 to the time when LU Xun passed away, he received a total of more than twenty letters from Mr. LU Xun.

On March 28, 1934, Lu Xun wrote in a letter to him, "In my understanding of your woodcut, the tension of the contrast between black and white has been well used..."

In 1934, China held painting exhibitions in France and the Soviet Union. LU Xun gave the assignment of collecting works to CHEN Yanqiao and CHEN Tiegeng. Among the works collected, LU Xun and SONG Qingling selected 78 works, which were sent to Paris and Moscow for exhibition with the theme of "New Style of Art in Revolutionary China". The works including *A Woman Worker, Natural Disasters, The Screams of the Injured* and *To Stay for a Night* by CHEN Yanqiao were selected to join the exhibitions. On June 20, LU Xun wrote to him, saying, "Our paintings and wood carvings have enjoyed great success at the exhibition in Paris... and received nice review at the exhibition in Moscow."

To "advocate woodcut", LU Xun published *The History of Woodcut* in October 1934 at his own expense, including 24 works of black and white woodcut from 8 creators. Among them the two works *Window* and *Landscape* by CHEN Yanqiao received special praise from LU Xun.

In October 1936, the "Second National Woodcut Mobile Exhibition" was held at the Youth Club at Eight Immortals Bridge on Tibet Road in Shanghai. On October 8, LU Xun attended it against his sickness and had a talk with some young printmakers present, including CHEN Yanqiao, HUANG Xinbo, LIN Fu and others as well BAI Wei, compiler and translator of the book *Methods of Woodcut Creation*. The young photographer SHA Fei recorded this unforgettable moment with his camera.

After 11 days, Mr. LU Xun passed away of disease on October 19, 1936 due to fatigue. On the same day, CHEN Yanqiao heard the news and rushed to the apartment of LU Xun at No. 9 in Dalu New Village on Shanyin Road. With respect and grief for his teacher, he painted with tears in his eyes a portrait of Mr. LU Xun...

The former residence of CHEN Yanqiao is located at No. 6 in Alley 281 on Wuyuan Road. As a garden residence, the apartment is of a nominally three-storied structure of brick and wood. The first floor is built on stilts and the building plane is approximately rectangular. The outside facade of the building enjoys cement napped walls of light yellow with square steel windows, above which there are diamond-shaped decorative patterns. The facade at the south side has balconies with beams and plates, as well as carved and hollow iron railings. The building has a roof of slopes covered with red tiles and wooden structure eaves. The entrance at the first floor lies at the east side of the house, which has an arched door. The steel grilles of windows at the first floor are equipped with exquisite carved patterns. The building has double staircases of wooden structure with wooden steps and handrails. There are lofts at the west side of the third floor. There is a small garden in front of the house.

陈烟桥 （邬海佳画） CHEN Yanqiao （By WU Haijia）

陈鲤庭
（1910—2013）

出生于上海，曾用名陈思白，笔名麒麟等，电影导演、电影艺术理论家。1930 年毕业于大夏大学高等师范系。1931 年在南汇大团镇小学任教期间，创作短剧《放下你的鞭子》，后经改编，广为流传。1934 年初，任《民报》副刊“影坛”特约撰稿人，为当时新兴的左翼戏剧、电影呐喊，并作了必要的理论准备，同年在上海任《晨报》影坛专栏特约撰稿人，翻译介绍了苏联 V.I. 普多夫金等人的电影理论。1940 年编著了中国电影第一部较为系统的理论著作《电影轨范》。1941 年至 1942 年，导演了话剧《钦差大臣》《岁寒图》《屈原》等。1947 年，编剧并导演了第一部影片《遥远的爱》。此后又先后导演了《幸福狂想曲》《丽人行》等。1950 年以后，导演了《人民的巨掌》和《劳动花开》等影片。历任中国文学艺术界联合会委员，中国戏剧家协会理事，全国政协第三、四届委员。

在实践中创新

对艺术创新的追求，贯穿了陈鲤庭的话剧、电影创作以及文艺理论研究。

早在构思戏剧处女作《放下你的鞭子》之探索阶段，他便开始尝试新颖的形式：将“舞台”设于观众之中，在观众中设一个合唱队，形成与台上演员对答唱和的开放式表演，大大增加短剧的真实感，使观众身临其境，更深切地认识到帝国主义、地主豪绅、贪官污吏对人民的残酷剥削。成为话剧导演后，他更不断追求创新突破，以多种舞台效果丰富话剧的艺术表现力。

他以红蓝色脚光的强烈对比与变化，强化了《结婚进行曲》的控诉力量；运用壁灯的明暗闪烁和不同音乐的交替出现，渲染衬托《复活》主角的内心冲突。

当讽刺腐败当局的喜剧《钦差大臣》被搬上舞台时，布景极为简约，仅有舞台中央的若干景片，隔断与传统写实主义布景的关联，使演员和观众与喜剧剧情保持一定疏离感，增强夸张的戏剧效果。周恩来与邓颖超曾特意询问他：“为什么舞台上四面空空，就在当中搭一些布景？”他回答说，话剧同行把这称为“空间舞台”。

执导郭沫若编剧的话剧《屈原》，他采用了空前的创新——将台前几排座位拆除，安置一支庞大的交响乐队，现场演奏气势恢宏的原创音乐，与剧中核心“雷电颂”交相辉映。

为拍摄影片精益求精，他还翻译研究国外的电影理论书籍，如英国的史波提斯乌德的《电影文法》等，并形成了自己的见解，创作了中国第一本较为系统的电影蒙太奇理论著作《电影轨范》。

直到去世前，他依然保持着手不释卷、勤于思考的习惯，他常谦虚地说“没拍几部电影”，但他早已成为中国电影、话剧史上不可磨灭的华彩。

建筑简介：复兴西路34号

陈鲤庭旧居位于复兴西路34号卫乐公寓，原名卫乐精舍，建于1934年，赉安洋行设计，占地面积1720平方米，建筑面积3797平方米，汽车间附屋802平方米，属现代点式建筑风格的公寓住宅。建筑为十三层钢筋混凝土结构，两翼跌落一层，立面对称，竖三段布置，中间凸出，设一串挑出的半圆阳台为构图中心，两边为卧入式阳台形成竖向线条；水泥砂浆外墙，立面中部竖线条及突出的半圆阳台为暗红色粉刷，其余部分为浅黄色粉刷，山墙顶部及南侧有重复线条装饰，楼前有小花园。解放后，吕蒙与黄准夫妇、吴强、赖少其、峻青、王西彦等一批文化人在此居住。1994年2月15日上海市人民政府公布其为市优秀历史建筑。

CHEN Liting

CHEN Liting (1910–2013) was born in Shanghai with a former name of CHEN Sibai and pen names like Qilin. He is known as a Chinese film director and film art theorist. In 1930, he graduated from the department of teachers of Daxia University. In 1931, when working as a primary school teacher in the town of Datuan in Nanhui district, he finished the creation of a short play *Put Down Your Whip*, which was adapted and widely circulated. At the beginning of 1934, he served as a special writer of "Filmdom", the supplement of *Minbao Monthly*, publicizing for the newly emerging left-wing drama and film and also making necessary theoretical preparations for them. In the same year he served as a special contributor of film column of *Morning Newspaper* in Shanghai, translating and introducing the film theories of the Soviet Union such as those by V. I. Pudovkin. In 1940, he edited *The Grammar of the Film*, the first comparatively systematic theoretical work of the Chinese film. From 1941 to 1942, he directed dramas including *Imperial Commissioner, Drawing of Cold Season*, and *QU Yuan*. In 1947, he wrote and directed the first film *Remote Love*. Since then he directed in succession such films as *Happiness Rhapsody, Three Women* and others. After 1950, he directed films including *The Might of the People* and *Fruits of Labour*. Successively he served as member of China Federation of Literary and Art Circles, director of Chinese Dramatists Association and member of the Third and Fourth Committees of the CPPCC.

Innovation Based on Practice

The pursuit of artistic innovation by CHEN Liting ran through his dramas, films and literary theories.

As early as the exploration stage of the planning of his maiden drama *Put Down Your Whip*, he began experimenting with a novel form—putting the "stage" among the audience and setting a chorus among them with the result of the formation of open performance with the audience and the actors on the stage answering each other and singing together in a chorus. This greatly

陈鲤庭在家中书房
CHEN Liting in his study at home.

increased a sense of reality of short drama and created an immersive experience for the audience, who secured a deeper understanding of the brutal exploitation of imperialism, landlord gentry and corrupt officials against the people. Having become a drama director, he continued to pursue innovative breakthroughs to enhance the artistic expressive power of drama with a variety of stage effects.

He made use of strong contrast and changes of red and blue footlight to strengthen the accusing power in *The Wedding March* and made use of the bright and dark flickering of wall lights and the alternating appearance of different music, exaggerating and foiling the inner conflict of the protagonist in the film *Resurrection*.

When the comedy *Imperial Commissioner* which satirized corrupt authorities was put on stage, the setting was very simple with only some pieces of stage scenery on the central stage to separate the association with traditional realist scenery, to maintain a sense of alienation among actors, actresses, the audience and the comedy plot, and to enhance the exaggerated dramatic effect. ZHOU Enlai and DENG Yingchao had specifically asked him, "Why the stage is empty, on which only some pieces of scenery are set up on the center of the stage?" He replied that people in the field of drama called this "space stage".

In directing the drama *QU Yuan* by GUO Moruo, he adopted an unprecedented innovation— removal of seats in the front rows and placement of a large symphony orchestra, making live performance of magnificent original music which added radiance and beauty to the dramatic core "Ode to Thunder and Lightning".

In order to constantly strive for perfection in the production of film, he also translated and studied books on foreign film theories, such as *A Grammar of the Film: An Analysis of Film Technique* by the British scholar Raymond J Spottiswoode, and formed his own views and created China's first theoretical work *A Grammar of the Film*, which was a relatively systematic study on film montage.

Until his death, he still kept the habit of reading books and thinking diligently. He used to say modestly, "I did not produce quite a few films", but he had become an indelible glory in the history of Chinese cinema and drama.

The former residence of CHEN Liting is located in Willow Apartment at No. 34 on West Fuxing Road, formerly known as Willow Court. Designed by Leonard-Veysseyre-Kruze Architects and built in 1934, it covers an area of 1,720 square meters with a construction area of 3,797 square meters and attached rooms of 802 square meters for garage. It is an apartment house of point construction and modern architectural style. The building has thirteen floors with a reinforced concrete structure. Its facade is symmetrical with three sections with the middle standing out and the two wings being one floor lower than the middle. A series of projected semi-circular balconies form the center of the composition. At both sides the receding balconies form vertical lines; exterior walls are coated with cement mortar; the vertical lines and prominent semi-circular balconies in the middle section have color of dark red, and the remaining parts are of light yellow. At the top and south side of the gable repeated lines are used for decoration. In addition, a small garden is in front of the building. After the liberation, a number of intellectuals once lived here. On February 15, 1994, it became a Heritage Architecture issued by the Shanghai Municipal People's Government.

陈鲤庭 （刘为民画） CHEN Liting （By LIU Weimin）

周璇
（1920—1957）

江苏常熟人，乳名小红，又名啸红。12岁入明月歌舞团，学习演唱。嗓音别具一格，音色甜润，曾被评为上海十大歌星之一，有“金嗓子”之誉。1935年开始电影演员生涯。1937年在影片《马路天使》中扮演女主角卖唱歌女小红，一举成名。1938年进国华影业公司。1946年去香港。1950年回上海，不久参加电影《和平鸽》拍摄，期间因突发精神疾病而被送入上海虹桥疗养院。1957年9月22日因并发脑炎症去世。主演的影片除《马路天使》外，还有《天涯歌女》《忆江南》《夜店》等，歌曲有《四季歌》《民族之光》等。

永远的“金嗓子”

1931年，周小红加入由音乐家黎锦晖创办的明月歌舞剧社习艺。一次她演唱抗日歌曲《民族之光》，唱到“与敌人周旋于沙场之上”一句时，黎锦晖称赞说：“小红，这是你进剧社以来唱得最好的一句。你姓周，以后就改名叫周旋吧！”后有人建议给“旋”字加上“王”字旁，成了“璇”（美玉之意）。从此，演艺圈里的人亲热地称她为“璇子”。

1934年，周璇转入新华歌剧社。这年，年仅14岁的周璇在上海“播音歌星竞选”中脱颖而出，与老歌星白虹只差50多票，名列第二。她演唱的代表曲《五月的风》令人陶醉。有记者撰文赞美周璇的嗓音“如金笛鸣沁入人心”，于是，“金嗓子”的美誉，伴随“五月的风”，吹遍上海滩。

1937年，上海艺华公司拍摄歌舞片《三星伴月》，周璇主演并演唱主题歌《何日君再来》。这首歌随电影和唱片广为传播，成为当时最流行的歌曲，后又成为舞厅里最热门的伴舞曲。不久，周璇出演电影《马路天使》，其中两首插曲《四季歌》和《天涯歌女》，又使周璇名声大振，成为上海滩首屈一指的歌影两栖明星。

1945年3月，周璇在金都大戏院举行首场独唱音乐会。演唱会座无虚席，舞台上摆满花篮，最引人注目的是《凤凰于飞》的导演方沛霖送的大花篮，上面用鲜花扎成“金嗓子”三个字。

自1935年周璇拍摄了她的第一部电影《风云儿女》后，两年间已拍了9部电影。1937年周璇主演《马路天使》，她一进片场就进入了角色，令大明星赵丹、魏鹤龄等人惊叹不已。编导袁牧之认为，周璇的表演自然、质朴，把戏里的人物歌女小红演活了。

“金嗓子”周璇一生出演了43部电影，演唱电影插曲达100多首。她在中国电影和音乐史的地位几乎无人可替代。1995年，在纪念电影诞生100周年、中国电影90周年颁发“世纪奖”的庆典上，她参演的电影《马路天使》被列为20世纪中国10部经典作品之一。周璇与阮玲玉、胡蝶等一同被授予中国电影世纪奖。

建筑简介：武康路391弄1号

周璇旧居位于武康路391弄1号，建于1916年，占地面积125平方米，砖木结构假四层，每层两户，自带煤卫。建筑主入口上方有混凝土浇筑的宽檐拱形雨厦，拱券型门洞向外呈喇叭形，墙面则以红砖与仿石间隔排列来装饰，较有特色。上海抗战孤岛时期，周璇曾住在临街的一号楼第三层。房屋内部保存较好，建筑结构及其风貌依旧。局部有扩建，部分厨卫设施仍在保留使用，南侧花园则完全被扩建物侵占。目前由八户居民合用。

ZHOU Xuan

ZHOU Xuan (1920–1957) has her ancestral family from Changshu in Jiangsu Province with her pet name as Xiaohong. At the age of 12, she joined the Bright Moon Song and Dance Troupe to learn the singing skills. Due to her unique, sweet and mellow voice, she was ranked as one of the top ten singers in Shanghai and enjoyed the reputation of a "golden voice". She started her film career in 1935, and in 1937 she rose to fame when she played the leading role of Xiaohong, a girl singing for a living, in the film named *Street Angel*. Later she was admitted to the Guohua Film Company in 1938. She went to Hong Kong in 1946 and returned to Shanghai in 1950. Shortly after that, she resumed to perform in the film called *Peace Dove*. During that time, she was sent to the Shanghai Hongqiao Sanatorium as a result of her paroxysmal psychosis. On September 22, 1957, she died from concurrent cerebral inflammation. In addition to the film *Street Angel*, she starred in many other films, including *The Wandering Alma, Memory of Jiangnan* and *Nightclub*, and the songs she sang include *Song of Four Seasons, National Glory* and so on.

"Golden Voice" Forever

In 1931, ZHOU Xiaohong joined the Bright Moon Song and Dance Troupe founded by the musician LI Jinhui. Once she sang *National Glory*, a song against Japanese Invasion. When she reached the line "dealing with the enemy on the battlefield," LI Jinhui praised her, "It is your best line you have sung since you joined the troupe. Your surname is ZHOU and we will call you ZHOU Xuan (meaning 'deal with')." Later it was suggested adding the Chinese radical "Wang" to the former character "Xuan" to become "Xuan" (meaning "beautiful jade"). Since then, people in the circle of entertainment business affectionately addressed her as "Xuanzi."

周璇（右）出演《马路天使》
ZHOU Xuan (right) performed in *Street Angel*.

In 1934, she was transferred to the New China Opera Club. In this year she was only 14 years old and stood out and ranked the second in the "Broadcast Singers Campaign", only 50 votes behind the experienced singer BAI Hong. The song *Breeze in May* she performed was enchanting and intoxicating. A reporter extolled her voice as "the sound of golden flute making us refresh." In this case, the fame of "golden voice" blew all over the Shanghai beach with the *Breeze in May*.

In 1937, she starred in and sang the theme song *See You Again* of the musical *The More, The Merrier*, which was produced by the Shanghai Yihua Film Company. The song spread far and wide and became the most popular together with the film and recording and later became the most popular dance music in dance halls. Soon she starred in the film *Street Angel*, and two episodes in the film, *Song of Four Seasons* and *The Wondering Alma*, greatly boosted her reputation as a top singer and film actress.

In March 1945, she held her first solo concert in Golden Castle Theatre and had a full house. The concert stage was filled with flower baskets and the most striking was the big basket with flowers decorated as "Golden Voice" sent by FANG Peilin, director of *The Pair Fly Together*.

Since she performed in her first film *Children of the Storm*, she had taken part in another nine films in two years. In 1937, she starred in *Street Angel*. She was able to enter the role the moment she was on the spot so that superstars ZHAO Dan and WEI Heling marveled. The playwright and director YUAN Mu held the opinion that her performance was natural and unvarnished, which produced a girl singer Little Red as vivid as alive.

The "Golden Voice" starred in 43 films and sang over 100 episodes in films in her lifetime. Her position in the history of Chinese film and music is almost irreplaceable. In 1995, at the 90th anniversary ceremony of Chinese film to issue "Century Award" in commemoration of the 100th anniversary of the birth of film, the film *Street Angel* she starred was listed as one of the 10 classic works in the 20th century. Together with RUAN Lingyu and HU Die, she was awarded China Film Century Award.

The former residence of ZHOU Xuan is located at No. 1 in Alley 391 on Wukang Road. It was originally built in 1916, covering an area of 125 square meters. The building is of a nominally four-story structure of brick and wood with two households on each floor with gas and toilet. Above the main entrance of the building, there is a broad arch canopy of concrete and the arched door has the shape of a horn. The walls are characteristically decorated with red bricks and imitation stones at intervals. During the War of Resistance against Japan in Shanghai, ZHOU Xuan lived on the third floor in Building No. 1 which faces the street. The interior of the house is of better preservation and its structure and style remain the same. The architecture has been partially expanded and some bath and kitchen facilities are still in use. The garden at the south side is completely occupied by the expansion. It is now shared by eight households.

周璇 （刘为民画）

ZHOU Xuan （By Liu Weimin）

周小燕
（1917—2016）

出生于武汉。花腔女高音歌唱家及美声声乐教育家，上海音乐学院终身教授，中国音乐家协会第八届顾问。1935 年考入上海国立音乐专科学校。1938 年赴巴黎学习声乐。1945 年 10 月，经七年磨砺登上巴黎国家大剧院的舞台，获得了极大成功。1988 年 5 月，周小燕在上海音乐学院成立了周小燕歌剧中心。因为在声乐艺术和声乐教学上的杰出贡献，先后荣获中国音乐家协会颁发的中国音乐艺术最高荣誉奖——金钟奖，法国政府授予的法国国家军官勋章，上海市政府授予的 2002 年文学艺术特殊贡献奖和 2003 年市教育功臣奖。代表作品有《长城谣》《最后的胜利是我们的》《蚌壳》等，被赞誉为“中国之莺”。

桃李燕教

曼妙的音乐从玫瑰别墅二楼的那扇窗口飘向远方，周小燕正在家中教授学生声乐课程。每次授课她都精神矍铄、神采飞扬，但等学生离开家门，她常常累得躺在沙发上不愿动弹。家中的保姆心疼周小燕，想帮她婉拒一些上门请教的学生，于是在接听请求拜访的来电时小声称周老师不在家，可是十有八九被听力敏锐的周小燕听到，她急得大声喊：“我在！我在！”帮助有学习声乐潜质的晚辈被周小燕视为自己义不容辞的职责。

一只黄色的大皮球在周小燕家中的钢琴下格外醒目。这是 20 世纪末，周小燕歌剧中心大师班的一位专家送给周小燕强身健体的。周小燕看着这只体积庞大、弹性十足的皮球，思索能否通过大皮球的作用让学生感受到原本虚无缥缈的音乐支点？男高音歌唱家汪任酩在高中时就曾经在周小燕家坐在大皮球上练唱。

起初，汪任酩坐在一颠一跳的大皮球上手忙脚乱、不知所措。周小燕让汪任酩先站起来，自己坐在皮球上做示范。她像顽皮的孩子般一边弹跳一边歌唱，轻松愉悦的氛围驱散了汪任酩忐忑不安的情绪。汪任酩模仿老师将上胸微抬，在皮球上保持身体的平衡，和着老师打的节拍，尝试带动皮球产生律动并保持气息平稳。刚开始，他顾此失彼，气息和节奏比较混乱，但在周小燕的耐心指导与热切鼓励下，经过一段时间的刻苦训练，他能有效地掌控气息，捕捉到微妙的音乐支点，声音也越发富有弹性和穿透力了。

一批又一批学子，走进周小燕的家，在这只黄色大皮球上练唱。在他们心目中，跳动的不仅仅是这只坚韧的大皮球，更是老师全身心耕耘声乐教育园地的赤子之心。

建筑简介：复兴西路44弄7号

周小燕旧居位于复兴西路44弄（玫瑰别墅）7号。玫瑰别墅建于1940年，由七幢造型典雅的住宅式公寓组成。因建造时在弄口地面上砌有“玫瑰”两字，老上海人称之为“玫瑰别墅”。占地面积4393平方米，建筑总面积3175平方米。原主人是蓝妮（孙科二夫人），后收归国有并作为地方民房。建筑为三层砖木结构，每层都有厨房间、备餐间、卫生间、客厅、卧室等。七幢建筑均为平屋顶、水泥砂浆外墙，形体简洁，体现现代建筑风格。屋前有花园。

ZHOU Xiaoyan

ZHOU Xiaoyan (1917–2016), born in Wuhan, is singer and vocal music educator, a full professor of Shanghai Conservatory of Music and also a consultant of the Eighth National Congress of Chinese Musicians Association. In 1935, she was admitted to Shanghai National Academy of Music. In 1938, she went to Paris to learn vocal music. In October 1945, she stepped onto the stage at the National Grand Theatre in Paris after seven years of practice and won great success. In May 1988, she founded the ZHOU Xiaoyan Opera Center at Shanghai Conservatory of Music. Because of her outstanding contribution to the art of vocal music and its teaching, she won in succession the Golden Bell Award—the highest honor in the art of music in China awarded by Chinese Musicians Association, the French National Officer Medal awarded by the French government, Special Contribution Award in Literature and Art in 2002 and Meritorious Service Award in Education in 2003 issued by the Shanghai Municipal Government. Her representative works include *The Great Wall Ballad, The Final Victory is Ours* and *Shell,* and she was praised as “China’s warbler”.

Teaching Students Singing

The graceful music drifted into the distance from the window on the second floor of the Rose Villa. That’s because ZHOU was teaching students a class of vocal music at home. Every time when she was teaching a class she was in high spirit. But when students left her house, she often lay down on the sofa too tired to move. Her nurse at home felt sorry for her and wanted to help her turn down some students who came to ask for instruction. So in answering the call to request for a visit, her nurse would quietly say that she was not at home. But in all likelihood she would be able to hear the call because of her keen hearing and she would anxiously

周小燕
ZHOU Xiaoyan.

shouted loudly, "I am in! I am in!" She considered it her responsibility to help those kids with the potential to learn vocal music.

A big yellow ball under the piano in her house was particularly eye-catching. It was from an expert in the class of masters in the Opera Center at the end of 20th century for her to do physical exercise. Looking at the big and resilient ball, she was thinking whether it was possible to use it to enable students to feel the illusory music supporting point. The tenor WANG Renming, who was in high school at that time, once sat on the ball to practice singing in her house.

At first, WANG sat on the bouncing ball feeling at a loss. ZHOU told him to stand up first and she herself sat on the ball to set an example. Like a naughty child, she jumped with the ball while she continued singing. The easy and cheerful atmosphere calmed his nerves. He imitated the teacher to keep balance on the ball and, to the accompaniment of the beat from the teacher, tried to drive the ball to produce rhythmical movement and keep his breath smooth. At the beginning, he gained for this and lost for that so that his breath and rhythm were chaotic. But with the patient instruction and encouragement of the teacher and also after a period of hard training, he could effectively control breath and capture the subtle music supporting point. In accordance, his voice was more resilient and penetrating.

One group of students after another went into the house of this teacher, doing practice of singing on this big yellow ball. In their minds, what was beating was not only the tough big ball, but also the heart of the teacher who cultivated the garden of vocal music education heart and soul.

The former residence of ZHOU Xiaoyan is located in Rose Villa at No. 7 in Alley 44 on Fuxing Road. The villa was built in 1940, composed of seven residential apartments of elegant style. Since the word "rose" was on the ground at the mouth of the lane during the time of construction, the Shanghai natives called it "Rose Villa" in the old days. The building covers an area of 4,393 square meters with a total construction area of 3,175 square meters. Its original owner was Lanny (second wife of SUN Ke) and later it was taken over by the government and used as local people's house. It is of three-storied structure of brick and wood. On each floor there are kitchen, dining room, bathroom, living room and bedroom. All the seven buildings have flat roofs and exterior walls of cement mortar. The residence has a concise form, reflecting the modern style of architecture. In front of the house is a garden.

周小燕 （戴晓明画）

ZHOU Xiaoyan （By DAI Xiaoming）

周作民
（1884—1955）

江苏淮安人，名维新。1906年赴日本留学，入京都第三高等学校，两年半后回国。1917年5月，金城银行在天津法租界成立，任总经理兼上海分行总经理。1935年任金城银行总董兼总经理，次年总行迁至上海。1937年后任农产调整委员会委员，仍在上海租界指挥各地金城银行分支银行的营业。1948年国民政府发行金圆券，被蒋经国勒令交出黄金外汇，并禁止离开上海，后经美国陈纳德航空公司庇护去香港。1951年返回北京，受到周恩来总理的接见，并被特邀为中国人民政治协商会议全国委员会委员。1951年9月，任公私合营的“北五行”董事长，1952年12月，任统一的公私合营银行副董事长。

电文从这里发出

1941年12月，香港沦陷，身处香港的周作民遭日军拘捕，4个月后被遣返上海。他早年在日本留学后曾担任中日贸易协会会长，与日本政要有过来往，且与陈公博等人颇为熟悉，日伪欲利用他在金融界的地位，希望他出任伪职。

1943年3月，陈公博、周佛海等人邀周作民出任成立于上海的“全国商业统制总会”主席，他婉言谢绝，却私下里悄悄与日伪方面往来，原来他肩负着蒋介石委托的与日本人周旋的秘密任务。他的举动消除了日伪的戒心，从而使金城银行在沦陷区从日伪“中储”银行那里得到金融上的帮助和便利，掩护、协助了国民党不少抗日工作。军统曾在周作民位于福开森路（今武康路）的住宅内设有一个与重庆通电的秘密电台，蒋介石致电冈村宁次令其赴芷江何应钦处投降及条款内容，以及冈村回复蒋介石的电报等，都是通过周作民住宅这个电台收发的。周作民在日记中写道：“此乃历史上之事件，两电均在余宅收发，亦幸事也。”

1945年10月，周作民被戴笠派来的两名特务押至海格路一个秘密机关中拘留。他的家人只得致电杜月笙和张嘉璈之妹张嘉蕊以联系戴笠从而营救，经努力，周作民终于被释放回家。过了一周，周作民又面临被汤恩伯军队上门逮捕之险境，幸而到别处躲避未被逮捕。事后周作民不无遗憾地说：“数年来在沦陷区仅得比较重要事件托张岳军转陈，未能随同为国家有显著之贡献，抱歉万分，且为掩护工作计，不免有些沾染之处……”

建筑简介：武康路117弄

周作民旧居位于武康路117弄，共两幢楼。1号楼建于1943年，范能力设计，占地面积1620平方米，建筑面积667平方米，独立汽车间38平方米，花园1051平方米。建筑为三层砖木结构，底层连续半圆拱券门洞，两侧为螺旋纹柱敞廊。开放窗或券形窗，窗套作连续尖券，有花饰。平缓四坡瓦顶，挑檐较深。底层水泥砂浆仿石墙面。二、三层贴黄色面砖。室内用中国传统的彩画平顶和广漆地板。楼梯为半圆形式，另有小楼梯。2号楼建于20世纪30年代，占地面积722平方米，建筑面积342平方米。建筑为砖混结构，主体为二层，局部三层，立面采用重檐大屋顶，西班牙筒瓦屋面。底层拱券敞廊，西部外墙前凸，入口以上面凸出的阳台作雨篷，设铸铁栏杆。缓坡顶，檐口有券齿带饰。小圆窗，白色水泥外墙。室内装饰多为中国传统木装修、彩画平顶和广漆地板，楼梯为半圆式，另设有小楼梯。室内底层客厅外是大平台，平台两侧卧石狮一对，南部庭园仿中国式园林布局。1999年9月23日上海市人民政府公布其为市优秀历史建筑。

ZHOU Zuomin

ZHOU Zuomin (1884–1955) has his ancestral family from Huai'an in Jiangsu province and has another name of Weixin. In 1906, he went to study in the Third Advanced School in Kyoto in Japan. After two and a half years he returned to China. In May 1917, Jincheng Bank was established in the French Settlement in Tianjin and he served as its general manager as well as general manager of its Shanghai branch. In 1935, he served as general chairman and general manager of Jincheng Bank and its head office was moved to Shanghai the following year. After 1937, he served as member of the Agricultural Product Adjustment Committee, and he was still in Shanghai Settlement to command the business of the branches of Jincheng Bank at various places. In 1948, the National Government released the "Gold Yuan Notes", so he was forced by JIANG Jingguo to surrender his gold and foreign exchanges and not allowed to leave Shanghai. Later he went to Hong Kong under the help of the American Chennault Airline. In 1951, he returned to Beijing and was received by Premier ZHOU Enlai. He was specially invited as member of the National Committee of the CPPCC. In September 1951, he served as chairman of the five banks in the North which were composed of the public and private ones; in December 1952, he served as deputy chairman of the Unified Bank.

Cabled Orders Sent from Here

In December 1941, Hong Kong was occupied. ZHOU was in Hong Kong and was arrested by the Japanese invaders who sent him back to Shanghai after four months. After his study in Japan, ZHOU had once served as chairman of the Sino-Japanese Trade Association in his early days. Therefore he had contacts with some Japanese politicians. In addition he was quite acquainted with such traitors as CHEN Gongbo. Consequently the puppet government wanted to make use of his position in the financial sector and

周作民
ZHOU Zuomin.

hoped he would take up a post in the puppet government.

In March 1943, he was invited to serve as chairman of the "National Commercial Control Association" which was established in Shanghai. He declined, but privately got into contact with the Japanese puppet government. This was because he was shouldering secret tasks to deal with the Japanese invaders which were commissioned by JIANG Jieshi. His actions eliminated the vigilance of the Japanese puppet so that Jincheng Bank in the enemy-occupied area was able to get financial assistance and convenience from the puppet "Central Reserve" bank in order to screen and assist the KMT in its resistance against the Japanese invasion. The Military Statistics Bureau once had a secret radio transmitter in his residence on Ferguson Road (now Wukang Road) to get connected with Chongqing. The telegraphs from JIANG Jieshi to Okamura Yasuji to order him to surrender to HE Yingqing at Zhijiang County, in addition to the contents of provision and the replies, were all sent and received by means of the radio transmitter. He wrote in his diary, "This is the factual event in history. Telegraphs were sent and received in my residence. It is also a blessing."

In October 1945, he was sent by two secret agents from DAI Li to a secret place for detention on Haige Road. His family members had to send telegraphs to the younger sister of Zhang Jia'ao and DU Yuesheng to further contact DAI Li in order to rescue him. After various efforts, he was finally released and sent home. After a week, he was in another danger of being arrested by the military forces of TANG Enbo. Fortunately, he escaped elsewhere and was not arrested. ZHOU said with a pity, "Over the years I was in the enemy-occupied areas, only able to transfer important information to you instead of making obvious contributions to the country. For that I feel extremely sorry. For the sake of screening underground work, I was inevitably contaminated in one way or another..."

The former residence of ZHOU Zuomin is located in Alley 117 on Wukang Road. There are two buildings in total. Building No. 1 was built in 1943 and designed by FAN Nengli, which covers an area of 1,620 square meters with a construction area of 667 square meters. There are an independent garage of 38 square meters and a garden of 1,051 square meters. The building is of a three-storied structure of brick and wood. The ground floor has continuous semi-circular arch doors and at both sides are open corridors with columns of swirl marks. Open or arch windows have frames with continuous pointed arches and decorations of patterns. The building has four gentle slopes and a roof covered with tiles and deep eaves. The bottom floor has imitated stone wall surface of cement mortar. The second and third floors are coated with yellow face bricks. Inside the building are used a flat ceiling of Chinese traditional color paintings and a painted floor. The stairs are of a semi-circle in addition to a small staircase. Building No. 2 was built in 1930s, which covers an area of 722 square meters with a construction area of 342 square meters. It is of a structure of brick and concrete. The body part has two floors and other local parts have three floors. The front adopts a large roof of double eaves with Spanish tiles on it. The ground floor has arched open corridor and the exterior wall in the west projects forward. At the entrance the projected balcony in the above serves as canopy with cast iron railings. The roof has gentle slopes with toothed belts of arched ornaments. Round windows are small and exterior walls are of white cement. The interior is mostly of Chinese traditional wooden decoration with a ceiling of color paintings and a painted floor. The stairs are of a semi circle type with a small staircase. Outside the living room on the ground floor is a large platform, on both sides of which lie a pair of stone lions. The garden in the south imitates the layout of Chinese garden style. On September 23, 1999, it became a Heritage Architecture issued by the Shanghai Municipal People's Government.

周作民 （齐亚明画） ZHOU Zuomin （By QI Yaming）

周谷城
（1898—1996）

湖南益阳人。早年就读于北京高等师范学院，毕业后在湖南第一师范执教。大革命时期参加农民运动，接受毛泽东的委托，任全国农民协会宣传干事。1927年后执教于上海暨南大学附中、中国公学，先后任中山大学教授兼社会学系主任，暨南大学教授兼史社系主任，复旦大学历史系主任、教务长、教授、博士生导师。中华人民共和国成立后，任中国农工民主党中央主席、全国人大常委会副委员长兼科教文卫委员会主任委员。长期从事学术研究的组织领导工作，教学和研究涉及史学、哲学、美学、逻辑学、政治学、社会学、教育学等学科。60多年来，著述数百万字，出版专著十余部，发表论文两百余篇。编著的《中国通史》《世界通史》在海内外产生了很大影响。

史海丹心周谷城

20世纪初，在梁启超、章太炎等以进化史观为指导重新撰写中国历史的倡导下，不少中国史著作问世。而周谷城以其独创的通史编纂理论和严密的体系撰写的《中国通史》，成为这一时期的代表作之一。这本《中国通史》1939年由上海开明书店出版后，至1957年再版了13次，1957年修订后，又多次重印。

1942年春，周谷城受聘于迁址重庆北碚的复旦大学，任历史系教授，并在陈望道任系主任的新闻系开设英文报纸分析课。

结合教学，周谷城开始致力于对世界历史的研究。他发现当时流行的世界史著作，都是以欧洲为中心，置亚洲、非洲和拉丁美洲的古老文明于不顾。于是，他决定编写一本格局一新的《世界通史》，力求将人类社会发展的全局综合为统一整体，蔚成一幅波澜壮阔的世界历史画面。

1949年，周谷城的三卷本《世界通史》正式面世。在这部通史中，以埃及、巴比伦、波斯、印度、中国和墨西哥六大文化中心的相互关联、日趋融合为主旨，描绘了世界文化彼此交流和互为因果的内在联系。

中华人民共和国成立近30年后，周谷城迎来了人生和学术道路上的第二个春天。1978年后，他先后发表了诸多史学论文，出版了《史学与美学》一书，与此同时，重新修订出版了《中国通史》。1982年，他的两本重要著作《中国通史》和《世界通史》被列为全国高等院校文科教材。

令人惊叹的是，周谷城先生还以八十高龄登上教坛，讲授世界史，为培养新时期第一批史学硕士和博士研究生再作贡献。创言立论，老而弥坚。1984年，他主持创办《中国文化研究集丛》；1986年，担任“世界文化史丛书”主编；1988年，主持编纂大型“民国丛书”。

建筑简介：淮海中路1202号

周谷城旧居位于淮海中路1202号淮海公寓，原名盖司康公寓，又名万国储蓄会大楼，建于1935年，万国储蓄会出资建造，赉安公司设计，中法营造厂承建，以万国储蓄会大班盖司康名字命名。公寓分前后两排，主楼在后排，十三层钢筋混凝土结构。前排为二号楼，为五层公寓大楼。占地面积4533平方米，主楼建筑面积9062平方米，辅楼建筑面积3318平方米，属现代派建筑风格的公寓住宅。主楼建筑立面为中轴对称，形体上由中部向两侧逐步跌落，中央有三条凸出的白色垂直带饰，入口挑出雨篷，卧入式阳台。一层青灰色大理石，以上外墙全部贴以米黄色面砖，仅各层阳台板为白色。二号楼底层为出租商号，二层以上为居住层，二间一套，每层六套，共二十四套。1994年2月15日上海市人民政府公布主楼为市优秀历史建筑。1999年9月23日上海市人民政府公布二号楼为市优秀历史建筑。

ZHOU Gucheng

ZHOU Gucheng (1898–1996) has his ancestral family from Yiyang in Hunan province. In his early years, he studied in the Beijing Higher Normal College and served as a teacher in Hunan First Normal School after graduation. During the Great Revolution in China, he participated in the farmers' movement and received a commission from MAO Zedong to assume the post of publicity officer of the National Farmers Association. After 1927, he taught at the High School affiliated to Jinan University in Shanghai and the National High School. Successively he served as professor and head of the Department of Sociology in Sun Yat-sen University, professor and head of the Department of History in Jinan University, and provost, professor, doctoral tutor and head of the Department of History in Fudan University. After the founding of the People's Republic of China, he served as chairman of the Central Committee of Chinese Farmers and Workers Democratic Party, vice chairman of the National People's Congress as well as chairman of its Branch Committee of Science, Education, Culture and Health. He was engaged in organizing and leading academic research for a long period of time. His teaching and researches cover such fields as history, philosophy, aesthetics, logic, politics, sociology, pedagogy and others. During his career of over 60 years, he had written millions of words and published more than ten books and over two hundred papers. The *General History of China* and *General History of the World* compiled by him had a significant influence both at home and abroad.

His Devotion and Loyalty to the Study of History

At the beginning of the 20th century, many works on Chinese history were published due to the promotion to rewrite Chinese history with the guidance of the evolutionary outlook by LIANG Qichao, ZHANG Taiyan and others. The *General History of China* written by ZHOU Gucheng was one of the masterworks during this period with his original general history compilation theory and strict system. After the *General History of China* was published by Kaiming Book Company in Shanghai, it went through 13 editions until

周谷城（中）与苏步青、吴斐丹
ZHOU Gucheng (middle), SU Buqing and WU Feidan.

1957. After its revision in 1957, it has been reprinted many times.

In the spring of 1942, he was employed by Fudan University which was relocated at Beibei in Chongqing. He served as professor of history and offered courses on analyzing English newspapers in the Department of Journalism, whose head was CHEN Wangdao.

Combining teaching, he devoted himself to the study of world history. He found that popular works on world history at that time all centered on Europe and disregarded the ancient civilizations of Asia, Africa and Latin America. So he decided to write a *General History of the World* which broke the old pattern in order to synthesize the overall development of human society to a unified whole and paint a magnificent historical panorama of the world.

In 1949, his three-volume work *General History of the World* was officially available. It depicted the inner links of the world's cultures which exchanged and interacted with each other, centering on the interrelationships and integration of six major cultural centers—Egypt, Babylon, Persia, India, China and Mexico.

Nearly 30 years after the founding of the People's Republic of China, he ushered in a second spring in his life and academic career. After 1978, he published a number of historical papers successively and his book *History and Aesthetics* also came out at that time. Meanwhile, he revised and published the *General History of China*. In 1982, his two important works, i.e. *General History of China* and *General History of the World*, were listed as textbooks of liberal arts for national colleges and universities.

Amazingly, he still came to the classroom at the age of 80 to teach the knowledge of world history, which made further contribution to cultivate the first masters and doctors of history in the new era. He established his own theory and became ever more resolute with his growing age. In 1984, he presided over the founding of *Collections of Studies on Chinese Culture*; in 1986, he acted as chief editor of "Series of History of World Cultures"; in 1988, he headed the compilation of the large-scale "Series of the Republic of China".

The former residence of ZHOU Gucheng lies in Huaihai Apartment at No. 1202 on Middle Huaihai Road, which was formerly called Gascogne Apartment and also known as the International Savings Society Building. Built in 1935 by Sino-French Construction Company, it was invested by the International Savings Society and was designed by Leonard-Veysseyre-Kruze Architects. It was named after Gascogne, the manager of the International Savings Society. The apartments are divided into two rows—the front and back rows. The main building which has thirteen floors with a reinforced concrete structure is the back row. The front row is Building No.2, a five-story apartment. The building covers an area of 4,533 square meters, the main building has a construction area of 9,062 square meters and the auxiliary building has a construction area of 3,318 square meters. It is of modern architectural style. The facade of the main building is symmetrical, the two wings being one floor lower than the middle gradually, and the centre of the building has three white vertical belt decorations that stand out. The entrance has projected canopy and balconies are receded. The first floor has cinereous marbles for walls while the exterior walls above the first floor are coated with beige tiles. Only the balcony plates at all floors are white. The ground floor of Building No. 2 has shops for lease and rooms above the first floor are for residence. There are two rooms in one suite and six suites on each floor and twenty four suites in total. Both the main building and Building No. 2 became a Heritage Architecture issued by the Shanghai Municipal People's Government on February 15, 1994 and September 23, 1999 respectively.

周谷城 （桑麟康画）　　ZHOU Gucheng （By SANG Linkang）

周碧珍
（1921—2013）

原籍广东中山县，生于上海，曾用名周韵芳，女高音歌唱家。16岁离家参加抗日宣传一队，活跃在粤、桂、湘、鄂、赣等地，积极参加抗日歌咏活动。1949年毕业于上海国立音乐专科学校。中华人民共和国成立后，加入上海音乐工作团（上海乐团前身）、上海合唱团等任演员。曾参加赴朝慰问团到前线演出。随中国文化代表团出访缅甸、印度、印度尼西亚等国演出。其音色圆润明亮，歌声轻盈灵活，富有抒情性，给人以热情奔放、真挚生动之感。善于演唱花腔技巧较高的作品，并能塑造多种不同性格的人物。其歌剧代表作有《苏武牧羊》，歌曲代表作有《我美丽的故乡延边》《梭罗河》《姑娘生来爱唱歌》《布谷鸟叫迟了》等。曾为电影《山间铃响马帮来》配唱片头曲《秋收对歌》（与刘明义合唱）和插曲《清清河水流不完》等。

歌唱家“站台”合唱

从16岁参加抗日宣传一队演唱抗日救亡歌曲开始，周碧珍的歌唱生涯长达七十年。

1940年，在广西柳州，周碧珍以一曲独唱《黄河怨》，震撼了观众的心灵。1943年，在重庆歌剧学校主演歌剧《苏武牧羊》，再次显现了她的歌唱艺术才华。1954年，她随中国文化代表团访问印度尼西亚，一曲《梭罗河》名震千岛之国，被总统苏加诺称为银嗓子。周碧珍那夜莺般的花腔女高音歌声，在20世纪五六十年代全国各地的音乐会上，赢得连连掌声。

20世纪60年代的一天，上海合唱团举行音乐会，周碧珍身着高雅而朴素的深蓝偏紫色中式旗袍，微露笑意走上舞台。那天她演唱的是聂耳为电影《风云儿女》创作的插曲《铁蹄下的歌女》：明亮圆润而有弹性的音色，宽广而舒展的音域，加之稳定的气息控制，把聂耳笔下“到处哀歌”“永远漂流”的歌女字字血、声声泪的辛酸表现得淋漓尽致，尤其是在最后感人肺腑的呐喊声中唱出了“铁蹄下歌女”的悲剧力量，给观众留下极深刻的印象。

周碧珍是团里的独唱演员，按规定完全可以不参加团里的合唱排演，但她却主动加入。她积极参加各种合唱，不只是室内合唱、无伴奏合唱，就连《长征组歌》这样带表演、造型的合唱，她也上台配唱。1965年秋，词作者肖华将军特来上海观看演出。周碧珍毫无架子，与全团演员一起排练。

当时的乐团指挥是刚出校门的赵家圭，他清楚地记得当时的周碧珍老师：她不但每次准时参加排练，而且几乎每次排练后都主动留下，在艺术处理和声音要求等方面，与指挥坦诚地用商量的口吻说：“这样处理是否会更好些……”作为一位享誉全国的歌唱家，她对歌唱艺术的执着追求让大家深深感动，传为佳话。

建筑简介：五原路212弄5号

周碧珍旧居位于五原路212弄5号。五原路212弄大华新村，为新式里弄，1947年建造，共有17幢，占地面积5420平方米，总建筑面积7226平方米。建筑略具现代派风貌，三层砖混结构。平屋顶四周设置女儿墙，立面简洁，极少装饰。南部二层设有悬挑的阳台，下部为底层门廊。素色水泥砂浆外墙面均布钢窗，窗裙板仅以网格细槽略作装饰。楼内布局紧凑，功能齐备，原用锅炉水汀供暖。大华新村居住过许多社会各界名人，有国民党将领张发奎、大新公司创始人蔡昌、画家汪观清、大中华橡胶厂经理洪念祖、指挥家陈传熙等。

ZHOU Bizhen

ZHOU Bizhen (1921–2013) has her ancestral family from Zhongshan County in Guangdong province and was born in Shanghai. With a former name of ZHOU Yunfang, she is known as a soprano singer. At the age of 16, she left home to participate in the First Publicity Team against Japanese invasion and actively involved herself in singing activities against Japanese in provinces like Guangdong, Guangxi, Hunan, Hubei, Jiangxi and some other places. In 1949, she graduated from the Shanghai National Academy of Music. After the founding of the People's Republic of China, she joined the Shanghai Music Troupe (predecessor of Shanghai Philharmonic) and Shanghai Chorus Troupe to work as an actress. Once she joined the relief team to the DPRK to give performance to the front line. Also she visited Myanmar, India, Indonesia and other countries as a member of the Chinese Cultural Delegation. Her voice is rich, melodious and resonant, and her singing is light and flexible with lyricism to give people a passionate and sincere feel. She was adept in the singing of works demanding higher coloratura skills and was able to create a variety of characters with different personalities. Her opera representatives include *Shepherd SU Wu* and her representative songs embrace *Yanbian, My Beautiful Home*, *Solo River*, *Girls Born to Sing*, *Cuckoo Sings Too Late* and so on. She had dubbed the opening theme *Autumn Harvest Song* for the film *Caravans with Ring* (with LIU Mingyi) and the episode song *Clear River Flows Endlessly* and so on.

A Singer in Chorus on the Platform

From the age of 16, ZHOU Bizhen participated in the First Publicity Team to sing national salvation songs against Japanese invasion and her singing career lasted for seventy years.

In 1940, she sang a solo *Yellow River Resentment* in Liuzhou in Guangxi province, which shocked the audience. In 1943, she starred in the opera *Shepherd SU Wu* in Chongqing Opera School, which once again demonstrated her singing and artistic talent. In 1954, she visited Indonesia with the Chinese Cultural Delegation. Her song *Solo River* resounded throughout the Thousand Island

周碧珍（右一）、周小燕（右二）、曹鹏（右三）等指导上海乐团•好小囡合唱团汇报演出

ZHOU Bizhen (first from right), ZHOU Xiaoyan (second from right), CAO Peng (third from right) and others directing a reporting performance by Good Children Chorus of Shanghai Orchestra.

Country, so President Sukarno called her the Silver Throat. Her coloratura soprano was like that of a nightingale, which won her continuous applause at concerts all over the country in the 1950s and 1960s.

One day in the 1960s, the Shanghai Chorus Troupe held a concert. She walked onto the stage with a smile on her face, dressed in an elegant and simple Chinese-style cheong-sam in a color of dark blue close to purple. That day she sang an episode *The Girl Singer under the Iron Heels* created by NIE Er for the film *Children of the Storm*. Her singing was bright, round and elastic with a broad and stretched range of sound in addition to a stable atmosphere control, which demonstrated incisively and vividly the girl-singer's hardship of blood and tears in each word and each sound under NIE Er's pen who "lamented everywhere" and "drifted forever". In particular, she sang out the tragic power of *The Girl Singer under the Iron Heels* in the last moving cry, which left a deep impression on the audience.

She is a soloist in the troupe. According to the regulations, she had absolute excuse not to participate in the chorus rehearsal, but she took the initiative to join in it. She actively participated in a variety of chorus, including both indoor chorus or cappella and even the *Long March Chorus* with performances and postures, where she also came onto the stage to join the singing. In the autumn of 1965, the lyricist General XIAO Hua specially came to Shanghai to watch the performance. Amiable and approachable as she was, she rehearsed together with the other players of the troupe.

The conductor at that time was ZHAO Jiagui, who was just out of the school. He clearly remembered that she not only always participated in rehearsals on time but also offered to stay behind almost every rehearsal to consult modestly with the conductor about the artistic processing and voice requirements, saying, "This treatment may be better or not ..." As a nationally renowned singer, her persistent pursuit of the art of singing moved everybody deeply, which has become a favorite tale.

The former residence of ZHOU Bizhen is located at No. 5 in Alley 212 on Wuyuan Road, which was also called New Dahua Village, a new-style alley. Built in 1947, it has a total of 17 buildings, covering an area of 5,420 square meters with a total construction area of 7,226 square meters. With a touch of modern style, it has three stories of mixed structure of brick and concrete. Around the flat roof are constructed parapets with a concise facade of very little decoration. On the second floor of the south, there are cantilevered balconies and under them is the ground floor porch. The outside walls coated with plain cement mortar are evenly covered by steel windows and window skirts are only slightly decorated with grids of thin grooves. The layout in the building is compact with all functions available, which was originally heated with steam from water boiler. The New Dahua Village once accommodated celebrities from various circles of the society, including the KMT general ZHANG Fakui; CAI Chang, founder of Daxin Company; painter WANG Guanqing; HONG Nianzu, manager of Greater China Rubber Factory and conductor CHEN Chuanxi.

周碧珍 （何祖明画）

ZHOU Bizhen （By HE Zuming）

孟波
（1916—2015）

江苏常州人，作曲家、文化活动家。抗日战争爆发后，结识吕骥、冼星海等人，成为上海歌曲协会主要成员。1936年任《大众歌声》编辑。后任新四军抗敌剧团团长，延安鲁艺教员、戏剧音乐资料室主任，延安中央管弦乐团指导员。中华人民共和国成立后，历任中国音协天津分会主席，广州市文化局局长，中国音协党组书记兼秘书长，上海音乐学院党委书记兼副院长，上海市文化局、电影局局长，中共上海市委宣传部副部长，上海市文联副主席，上海市人大教科文卫副主任，上海对外友好协会会长。创作歌曲有《牺牲已到最后关头》《高举革命大旗》等数百首。参与创作电影文学剧本《聂耳》，著有传记文学《冼星海传》《麦新传》。

严金萱
（1924—2014）

贵州贵阳人，作曲家、教育家。1939年赴延安，先后在抗日军政大学、鲁迅艺术学院、华北联合大学学习。在冲锋剧社、中央管弦乐团等任作曲、独唱、歌剧演员、小提琴手和研究员等职。1952年自中央音乐学院毕业后，先后担任中国福利会儿童艺术剧院、上海越剧院和上海市舞蹈学校的领导工作。离休后被聘为上海艺术教育委员会等单位顾问、上海儿童音乐学会会长。为芭蕾舞剧《白毛女》、歌剧《双双和姥姥》等36部歌剧、舞剧、电影、电视剧作曲配乐。著有《歌声里的故事》《彩色的梦——严金萱歌曲集》《献给孩子们的歌》等。

音乐舞蹈史诗《东方红》的由来

1964年6月，时任上海文化界主要领导的孟波，正忙于第五届“上海之春”音乐会的工作，以及有3000人参演的大型歌舞《在毛泽东的旗帜下高歌猛进》的组织演出工作。6月10日下午，国务院副总理兼外交部长陈毅陪同坦桑尼亚第二副总统卡瓦瓦访问上海。陈毅问孟波：“你们有什么新节目可招待国宾？”孟波介绍起这个大型歌舞。陈毅说：“那好嘛，就拿这个节目招待。”

第二天，陈毅对孟波说：“卡瓦瓦副总统看完演出后非常激动，节目很好。今年10月1日是建国15周年，许多国家的贵宾都要来北京。我一直在想，用什么节目来招待他们。今天看了大歌舞，形象地反映了中国人民的革命斗争史。当然，是否可以作为国庆招待会的演出，必须请周总理来决定。”

7月中旬，周恩来总理和陈毅副总理出访东南亚回京途中路过上海。于是，孟波马上召集相关人员，紧急动员，确保演出成功。在文化广场，周恩来总理和陈毅副总理仔细地观看演出。演出结束，孟波等马上赶到文化俱乐部，倾听领导的意见和指示。周总理说：“我来之前已听陈老总介绍了，今天特地来上海看一看。”周总理肯定了这台节目，但直言它的不足之处：“这台节目反映了中国革命斗争历史，气势宏伟。你们选择了不少群众喜爱的革命历史歌曲，听起来很亲切。有些场次如‘飞夺泸定桥’等的舞蹈设计得不错。可是你们没有写遵义会议，这是很大的缺陷。另外，历史的跨度太长，是否写到中华人民共和国成立就可以了。建国以后如何写，那又是一篇大文章，得好好研究。”

经商量后决定，《在毛泽东的旗帜下高歌猛进》的主要编导、演员、指挥等人员调往北京，加上北京和各方面的力量，进行再创作，并且将其定名为音乐舞蹈史诗《东方红》。三个月后，1964 年 10 月 2 日，《东方红》首演式在人民大会堂隆重举行。自此，《东方红》作为歌舞史诗巨作，成为艺术的经典。

建筑简介：湖南路8号

孟波、严金萱旧居位于湖南路 8 号，为现代风格的花园住宅，建于 1930 年。建筑为三层砖混结构，建筑面积 290 平方米，占地面积 460 平方米。东面入口门洞饰叠涩线脚，上有雨篷，南面二、三层设水平悬挑阳台，弧形转角，大面积方形钢窗。院内植草坪和杉树。1962 至 1979 年，电影表演艺术家赵丹曾在此居住。当时赵丹住在三楼，有三个房间，两间朝南，一间朝北，北面还有一个较大的顶层平台。

MENG Bo and YAN Jinxuan

MENG Bo (1916–2015) has his ancestral family from the city of Changzhou in Jiangsu province. He is a music composer and cultural activist. After the outbreak of the War against Japanese Invasion, he got to know some friends like LÜ Ji, XIAN Xinghai and others,and became a major member of Shanghai Song Association. In 1936, he served as editor of *Public Song*. Later he served as head of the resisting-enemy troupe of the New Fourth Army, teacher of LU Xun Art Academy at Yan'an, director of drama music library of the school and instructor of Yan'an Central Orchestra. After the founding of the New China, he served successively as chairman of the Tianjin Branch of Chinese Musicians Association, director of Guangzhou Culture Bureau, secretary of the Party Committee and secretary-general of Chinese Musicians Association, secretary of the Party Committee and vice president of Shanghai Conservatory of Music, director of Shanghai Municipal Culture Bureau and Shanghai Municipal Film Bureau, deputy director of the publicity department of Shanghai Municipal Committee of the CPC, vice chairman of Shanghai Municipal Federation of Literary and Art Circles, vice director of education, science, culture and health of Shanghai Municipal People's Congress, and president of Shanghai International Friendship Association. The songs he composed amount to hundreds including *Sacrifice Has Been to the Last Moment, Holding High the Banner of the Revolution* and so on. He also involved himself in the creation of the film literature script *NIE Er* and created biographical literary works such as *A Biography of XIAN Xinghai* and *A Biography of Maixin.*

YAN Jinxuan (1924–2014) has her ancestral family from the city of Guiyang in Guizhou province. She is a music composer and educator. In 1939, she went to Yan'an and studied in succession at Resisting-Japanese Military and Political University, LU Xun Art Academy and North China Union University. At that time she served as music composer, soloist, opera actor, violinist and researcher in Charge Theater and Central Philharmonic Orchestra. After graduating from Central Conservatory of Music in 1952, she successively served as leader in the Children's Art Theater of China Welfare Institute, Shanghai Yue Opera Theater and Shanghai Dance School. After retirement, she was hired as consultant of such organizations as Shanghai Art Education Committee and president of Shanghai Children's Music Society. She composed music for 36 operas, dance operas, movies and TV plays such as the ballet *White-Haired Girl* and opera *Shuangshuang and Grandma.* Also she is the author of such books as *Stories in Songs, Dream in Colors—Collection of Songs by YAN Jinxuan* and *Songs for Children.*

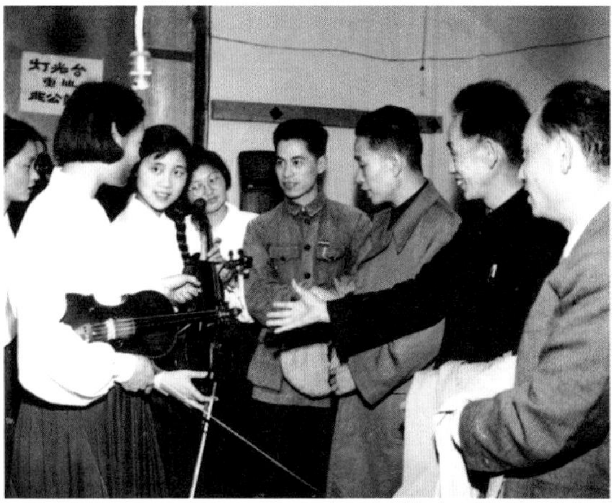

孟波（右三，时任上海音乐学院党委书记）等领导看望该院民族化“实验小组”

MENG Bo (third from right, then party secretary of Shanghai Conservatory of Music) and other leaders paid a visit to "the experiment team" for nationalization.

The Origin of *The East Is Red*—An Epic of Music and Dance

In June 1964 when MENG Bo was one of the main leaders of Shanghai cultural circle, he was busy with the Fifth Shanghai Spring and *Advancing Triumphantly under the Banner of MAO Zedong*, a large-scale singing and dancing program with some 3,000 participants. On the afternoon of June 10, CHEN Yi, then the second vice premier and foreign minister of China, accompanied Kawawa, then vice president of Tanzania, to come to visit Shanghai. The vice premier asked MENG Bo: "What new programs do you have to entertain our state guests?" The latter introduced this large-scale program. The vice premier said: "Well, take this program for entertainment."

The next day, the vice premier said to MENG: "Vice president Kawawa was very excited after watching your performance. The program is very good. October 1 this year is the 15th anniversary of the founding of the People's Republic of China and very important state guests from many countries will come to Beijing. I've been thinking what programs we will perform to entertain them. Yesterday I watched the large-scale program of singing and dancing, which vividly reflects the history of the revolutionary struggle of the Chinese people. Of course, whether it could be a performance at the National Day reception should be decided by Premier ZHOU."

In mid-July, Premier ZHOU Enlai and vice premier CHEN Yi paid a visit to Southeast Asia and they passed by Shanghai on their way back to Beijing. For this, MENG Bo immediately called together people concerned and made an urgent mobilization to ensure the success of the performance. At the Cultural Square, Premier ZHOU Enlai and vice premier CHEN Yi watched the performance attentively. When it was over, MENG Bo and others rushed to the cultural club to hear the comments and instructions of leaders. Premier Zhou said: "Before I came, I heard Mayor CHEN introduce your program. Today I came specifically to Shanghai to take a look." The premier affirmed this program, but pointed out its shortcomings directly. "This program reflects the history of the Chinese revolutionary struggle and has its magnificent vigor. You have chosen a lot of songs of the revolutionary history which people like and sound very amiable. The dances of some scenes are well designed, such as those in the scene of 'Dashing to Seize Luding Bridge'. But you do not have anything about Zunyi Conference, which is a very big flaw. In addition, the historical span is too long. You may as well have put an end to the program when the People's Republic of China is established. How to describe the period of time after the founding of the New China is a big article and you must make detailed studies."

Later, after the discussion, it was decided that the main writers, directors, actors, actresses, instructors and others of the large-scale singing and dancing program *Advancing Triumphantly under the Banner of MAO Zedong* would be transferred to Beijing. They pooled efforts together with those in Beijing to make re-creation and the title of newly created works was decided as *The East is Red*—An Epic of Music and Dance. Three months later on October 2, 1964, the premiere of *The East is Red* was held grandly in the Great Hall of the People. Since then, it got to become a classic of art as a masterpiece epic of song and dance.

The former residence of MENG Bo and YAN Jinxuan is located at No. 8 on Hunan Road and is a garden house of modern style. Built in 1930, it is of a three-storied brick and concrete structure, which covers an area of 460 square meters with a construction area of 290 square meters. The door at the east entrance is decorated with corbel architrave and a canopy above. On the second and third floors at the south are constructed horizontal cantilevered balconies, curved corners and large square steel windows. In the garden are planted lawns and cedars. From 1962 to 1979, ZHAO Dan, film artist, once lived here. At that time, ZHAO Dan lived on the third floor, where there were three rooms, two facing south and one facing north. At the north side there is a large top platform.

孟波、严金萱 （邬海佳画）

MENG Bo and YAN Jinxuan （By WU Haijia）

罗伯昭
（1899—1976）

四川巴县人，名文炯，号沐园，钱币收藏家，钱币学术研究专家。1921年毕业于上海圣约翰大学。1924年开始搜集古钱币，是中国钱币收藏界“三大收藏家”之一，世人誉为“南张（张叔驯）、北陈（陈仁涛）、巴蜀罗（罗伯昭）”。1940年当选为中国钱币学社副社长。曾任上海市第二、三、四、五届人民代表，黄浦区政协副主席，黄浦区副区长，编著有《泉友录》《沐园四十泉拓》《沐园泉拓》等。

博收日月 涌“泉”相报

1938年，日军大举侵华，时局紧张，罗伯昭所在的生利洋行被迫停业。当时，生利洋行的美商范格夫妇居住在上海，劝说罗伯昭举家由汉口移居上海。1940年春，罗伯昭辗转抵沪。范格夫妇已为他代买了一幢花园洋房，即安福路7号。

工作之余，罗伯昭最大的癖好就是搜集古代钱币。他集币不仅求品种、数量，更重珍品。每当搜集到自己没有的品种，罗伯昭都要翻阅古籍考证，他的书房里有二十四史和很多线装书，有时罗伯昭还去书摊搜集相关书籍加以研究。若仍心存疑惑，罗伯昭会向泉友虚心求教，千方百计提升自己鉴赏古泉的水平。

来上海定居后，罗伯昭每周必去广东路上海古玩市场与古泉爱好者茶叙。在古泉界诸公的倡议下，1940年初春，在安福路7号罗氏宅邸，罗伯昭与丁福保、张絅伯、蒋伯埙等8人发起筹建“中国泉币学社”，罗伯昭任副社长，他把安福路7号的寓所作为学社活动场所。该社是中华人民共和国成立前历时最长、影响最大、名人最多、办得最好的民间钱币组织，以“研究古今泉币，沟通中外学界，交换知识，联络同志”为宗旨。自1940年8月31日至1946年3月16日，该社有案可查的例会多达178次。每次例会召开前，必先确定研究课题，各社员分头充分准备，围绕议题，各抒己见。罗伯昭负责将每次例会内容做好记录，以备查看，并将例会上展示的作品认真制成拓本妥善保存。抗战胜利后，物价飞涨，中国泉币学社编的杂志《泉币》经费出现亏空，罗伯昭出资40万元弥补。他还为《泉币》双月刊撰写《所谓天监五铢之疑问》等考据文章20余篇，积极推动中国的钱币研究。

罗伯昭热爱祖国，1957年将珍藏的“新币十一铢”等全部古泉捐赠给中国历史博物馆，受到文化部褒奖。1962年，罗伯昭撷取1957年后陆续搜集的古泉精品捐赠给上海博物馆，受到上海市人民政府褒奖。当罗伯昭看到古钱商人手中有一枚“壮泉四十”，正是上海博物馆缺品，他不惜以重金购买，无偿地捐献，令人钦佩。1976年，罗伯昭因病在沪与世长辞。子女遵照父亲遗嘱，将遗存的古泉币分赠给上海博物馆和家乡的四川博物馆，圆了罗伯昭先生毕生奉献祖国文博事业的心愿。

建筑简介：安福路7号

罗伯昭旧居位于安福路7号，建于1922年，建筑面积400多平方米，花园面积500多平方米。建筑为假三层砖混结构，带半地下室，入口上方有拱顶雨厦，以雀替形支架承托。方形门窗，灰瓦四坡屋顶。罗伯昭1940年入住，直至去世。该旧居现为民居。

LUO Bozhao

LUO Bozhao (1899–1976), coin collector and academic researcher of coins, has his ancestral family from Baxian County in Sichuan. His name is Wenjiong, alias Muyuan, and he is known for Bozhao, his courtesy name. In 1921, he graduated from St. John's University in Shanghai. In 1924, he started collecting ancient coins and became one of the "three collectors" in coin collection in China, who were known as "South ZHANG, North CHEN and Sichuan LUO (for LUO Bozhao)". In 1940, he was elected vice president of the China Numismatic Society. He once served as representative for several times of Shanghai People's Congress, vice chairman of CPPCC and deputy head of Huangpu District. Under his name were published such books as *Records of Ancient Coin Collectors*, *Rubbings of Forty Ancient Coins by Muyuan*, and *Rubbings of Ancient Coins by Muyuan*.

Erudite and Grateful

In 1938, the Japanese invaders intruded into China in a large scale and the situation became pressing. Mckesson & Robbins Bridgeport Connecticut U.S.A where LUO Bozhao worked was forced to put up the shutters. At that time, Mr. and Mrs. Fanger, an American couple who lived in Shanghai, advised LUO to move his family from Wuhan to Shanghai. In the spring of 1940, he floundered a lot before he finally arrived in Shanghai. The Fangers had bought on his behalf a garden villa at No. 7 on Anfu Road.

In his spare time, his biggest hobby was to collect ancient coins. In coin collection, he not only sought for variety and quantity, but also laid more focus on curiosities. Whenever he found a variety he did not possess, LUO read through ancient books to do textual research. In his study he had the Twenty-Four History Books and many thread-bound books. Sometimes he also went to visit bookstalls to look for related books for his research. If he still had doubts, he would turn to coin friends with an open mind to ask for advice in order to improve the level of appreciation of ancient coins.

Having settled down in Shanghai, he would definitely visit the antique market on Guangdong Road in Shanghai every week to drink tea and talk with hobbyists of ancient coins. Under the initiative of friends in the circle of ancient coins, the China Numismatic Society was initiated by 8 persons in the residence of LUO at No. 7 on Anfu Road in the spring of 1940, with LUO serving as vice president and his residence as the site for activities of the society. The society was a non-government organization which lasted for

罗伯昭在家中鉴赏古钱币
LUO Bozhao is appreciating ancient coins at home.

the longest, remained the most influential, included the most celebrities and continued to be the best organized one of its kind before the founding of the New China. It aimed at "the study of ancient and modern coins, the communication between academic circles both in China and in foreign countries, the exchange of knowledge and the connection of people with the same interests". From August 31, 1940 to March 16, 1946, the society had recorded regular meetings for up to 178 times. Before each meeting, research topics must be first determined and each member separately prepared to the full. At meetings each member aired his own views around the topic. LUO took the responsibility to keep a record of the content of each meeting for future reference, and he also made rubbings of the works displayed at the meetings and preserved them properly. After the victory of the War against Japanese Invasion, prices soared so that the *Ancient Coins*, a journal edited by the Society, was faced with the difficulty of budget deficit. LUO invested 400 thousand yuan for it. He also wrote over 20 textual research papers for the bi-monthly journal, such as "Questions on the so-called five-zhu coin cast during the reign of Emperor Wu of Liang Dynasty", actively promoting coin research in China.

LUO loved his motherland. In 1957, he donated all his collection of ancient coins he treasured up, including "eleven zhu coin cast in Xin Dynasty", to the Museum of Chinese History in Beijing, for which he was praised by the Central Ministry of Culture. In 1962, he donated to Shanghai Museum the elaborate ancient coins he salvaged since 1957 and was honored by Shanghai Municipal People's Government. When he saw a merchant of ancient coins possessed a coin of "zhuangquan forty cast in Xin Dynasty" and it was the coin Shanghai Museum was short of, he did not hesitate to spend lots of money to get one and gratuitously donated it. This really deserved admiration. In 1976, he passed away of illness in Shanghai. His children followed their father's wills and donated all the remaining ancient coins respectively to Shanghai Museum and Sichuan Museum in his hometown, thus realizing his aspiration to dedicate all his life to the cause of national prosperity of culture.

The former residence of LUO Bozhao is located at No. 7 on Anfu Road. Built in 1922, it has a building area of 400 square meters and a garden area of over 500 square meters. It is of a nominally three-storied brick structure with a semi basement. Above the entrance is a vaulted canopy supported by a QT-shaped bearing. The building has square doors and windows, grey tiles and a four-sloped roof. LUO began to live here in 1940 until his departure. It is now a residential house.

罗伯昭 （叶雄画） LUO Bozhao （By YE Xiong）

郁华
（1884—1939）

浙江富阳人，原名庆云，字曼陀，郁达夫之兄。1900年，在杭州考取光绪乙亥科府道试第一名。1906年到日本，先后在早稻田大学和政法大学学习。1910年回国，应清政府留学生考试合格，获法科举人衔，以七品京官分发外务部工作，任天津交涉公署翻译2年。1912年考取法官资格，曾任京师高等审判厅推事、大理院推事，并兼任朝阳大学、东吴大学等校教授。1929年到沈阳，曾任最高法院东北分院刑庭庭长。“九一八事变”后回到北平。1932年到上海任江苏高等法院第二分院刑庭庭长，曾尽力帮助被捕的革命人士。1939年11月23日在上海被日伪特务暗杀。1947年4月，富阳地方人士在鹳山修筑郁华血衣冢，由郭沫若撰写《郁曼陀先生血衣冢志铭》，马叙伦书写。1952年经中央人民政府批准，追认郁华为革命烈士。著有《曼陀诗钞》《静远诗集》《静远画集》《窃电集》《刑法总则》《判例》等。

威武不能屈

清末，郁华以官费生资格留学日本，先后攻读师范科和法科，1910年学成回国。1912年郁华考取法官资格，曾任大理院推事，1929年调任大理院东北分院推事，后任最高法院东北分院刑庭庭长。“九一八事变”后，郁华不愿委身事敌，化装潜回北平。1932年，他奉调至上海，供职于江苏省高等法院第二分院，担任刑庭庭长。辛亥革命以后，上海租界当局曾经霸占中国政府设在租界里的会审公廨，江苏省高等法院第二分院就是由收回的公共租界会审公廨改组而成。它地处租界之中，当时人都称之为新衙门。

身为法官，郁华一身正气。他还兼擅诗画，参加过以文学创作弘扬民族气节的文学社团南社。南社创始人之一的柳亚子说郁华的诗如“鹏举冲冠之作（岳飞字鹏举，《满江红》词有‘怒发冲冠’句），文山正气之歌（文天祥字文山，有《正气歌》诗）”。

“八一三”淞沪抗战之后，上海华界沦于日寇之手，租界则成为孤岛。表面上看，这里市廛繁华，实际上多种力量交织在一起，斗争形势错综复杂，同样是中华民族与日本侵略者殊死斗争的战场。郁华坚持司法尊严和民族大义，站在爱国主义的立场上维持正义。上海沪江大学校长刘湛恩在上海沦陷后积极从事抗日救国活动，惨遭日伪暗杀，凶手顾某当场被周围民众捕获。郁华不顾环境险恶，在法庭上痛斥这个民族败类，并判以极刑。

郁华坚守中国法官的原则，必然遭到敌对势力的忌恨。他曾经收到过装有子弹的信件。朋友们为他担心，劝他暂时外出避祸。他回答，国家民族正在危急之时，我怎能抛弃职守，我当做我应做的事，生死就不去计较了。1939年11月23日早晨，郁华像往常一样跨上等候他的黄包车的一刹那，罪恶的枪声响起。郁华成为中国司法界牺牲于日伪暗杀之手的第一人，时年55岁。

建筑简介：常熟路188弄2号

郁华旧居位于常熟路188弄2号，英式花园住宅，建于1932年，占地面积370平方米。住宅为砖木结构假四层，主体淡黄色水泥拉毛墙面。二层房间东西外墙各建有人字坡顶的长方形凸窗，南侧中部两间前出，二层原为开敞式内阳台，三面皆有尖拱窗洞，西侧有圆弧楼梯通往花园。三层为三面开窗的阳光厅。底层为基座层，采用清水红砖外墙，内设厨房及服务用房。北侧原主入口已封闭。原先通往二层的单独楼梯间已整体改为房间。标准层室内局部多处有改建，装饰基本都已更新。郁家后代曾长期在此居住，现由多户居民合用。

YU Hua

YU Hua (1884–1939) has his ancestral family from Fuyang in Zhejiang province. With a former name of Qingyun and a courtesy name of Mantuo, he is an elder brother of YU Dafu. In 1900, he won the first place in the Provincial Imperial Examination during the reign of Guangxu. In 1906, he successively studied in Waseda University and University of Political Science in Japan. After returning to China in 1910, since he passed the examination for students studying abroad which was organized by the Qing Government, he was entitled a successful candidate in the law subject of the imperial examination. Then he was assigned to work at the Ministry of Foreign Affairs as a high-rank officer and also served as a translator for two years in the Bureau of Foreign Affairs in Tianjin. In 1912, he achieved the qualifications of judges and once served as judge of the Super Court in capital and Central Judicial Office, and as professor in Chaoyang University, Soochow University and other universities. In 1929, he was appointed as chief judge of Criminal Division in Northeast Branch of Supreme Court. After the "September 18 Incident", he returned to Beijing. In 1932, he served as chief of the Criminal Division of the Second Branch Court of the Jiangsu High Court in Shanghai and tried his best to help the revolutionaries under arrest to escape from the prisons. On November 23, 1939 he was assassinated by the spy of the Japanese and puppet government in Shanghai. In April of 1947, local people in Fuyang built the blood clothes tomb for him in Guanshan Mountain. GUO Moruo wrote the tomb inscription entitled "the Inscription of YU Hua" with the calligraphy by MA Xulun. In 1952, the Central Government of the PRC ratified him as a revolutionary martyr. His works include *Poems by YU Hua, Collection of Poetry by YU Hua, Album of Paintings by YU Hua*, *Collection of Stealing Electricity*, *General Provisions of Criminal Law*, *Legal Cases* and so on.

Never be Subdued by Force

In the late Qing Dynasty, YU Hua studied aboard in Japan as a government scholarship student, and successively studied education and law. In 1910, he returned home. In 1912, he obtained the qualifications of judges. Once serving as judge at the Super Court, he was transferred to the judge at its northeast branch in 1929 and later served as chief judge of Criminal Division in the northeast branch of the Supreme Court. After the "September 18 Incident", he was unwilling to be submitted to the enemy and disguised himself to return to Beijing. In 1932, he went to Shanghai as requested and served as president of the Criminal Division of the Second Branch

郁氏三兄弟（左起）：郁达夫、郁华、郁养吾
The three brothers of the YU family (from left): YU Dafu, YU Hua and YU Yangwu.

Court of the Jiangsu High Court in Shanghai. After the 1911 Revolution, the authority of Shanghai settlement once usurped the Shanghai Mixed Court which was set by the Chinese government, from which the Second Branch Court of the Jiangsu High Court was made on the basis of its reorganization. Since it was in the settlement, people regarded it as a new Yamen at that time.

As a judge, YU Hua kept awe-inspiring righteousness all the time. Also he was adroit at poetry and painting and participated in the literary community, the South Society, which was celebrated for its national integrity. LIU Yazi, one of the founders of the society, once evaluated his poetry as "works with rage bristling under the cap (a line '*rage bristling under the cap*' in the *ci* poem with the tune *The River All Red* by YUE Fei) and a song with Wenshan's justice (WEN Tianxiang has the courtesy name of Wenshan and a poem *The Song of Justice*)."

After the "August 13" Battle of Shanghai against Japanese invasion, the Chinese territory in Shanghai was occupied by the Japanese invaders and the settlement became an isolated island. On the surface, the markets here were booming, but the fact was that a variety of forces intertwined with each other and the situation of struggle was complicated, so it was the same as the battlefield with fierce fighting between the Chinese people and Japanese invaders. YU Hua insisted on judicial justice and national rights and stuck up for justice at the standpoint of patriotism. LIU Zhan'en, president of University of Shanghai, took an active part in the movement to resist Japanese aggression and to save the country after the fall of Shanghai. Thus he was assassinated by the spy of the Japanese and puppet government. At the same time the murderer was captured by the surrounding people on the spot. Regardless of the perilous situation, YU Hua denounced the national scum in court and sentenced him to the capital punishment.

He adhered to the principles of the Chinese judges and must attracted hatred from hostile forces. Once he received letters with bullets enclosed. His friends worried about him and advised him to temporarily go out to avoid disaster. He replied that, when the nation was in crisis, how I could abandon my duty and I must do what I should do without caring about life and death. On the morning of November 23, 1939, he stepped on the rickshaw waiting for him as usual when the evil gunfire sounded. He became the first in China's judicial circle who encountered the assassination of the Japanese and puppet government. He was at the age of 55 that year.

The former residence of YU Hua is located at No. 2 in Alley 188 on Changshu Road, which is a garden house typical of a British style. Built in 1932, it covers an area of 370 square meters. The residence has a nominally four-storied structure of brick and wood. Its main body is composed of light yellow stuccoed walls. Rooms on the second story have rectangular projected windows with gable roofs at the east and west sides, and two rooms at the middle part of the south side protrude forward. At the second floor was formerly an open balcony, the three sides of which have pointed arch windows. At the west side there is an arc staircase which leads to the garden. The third floor has a sunshine hall with open windows on three sides. The bottom floor is the base with water red bricks for outer wall surfaces, in which there are kitchen and service rooms. The former main entrance at the north side has been closed. The separate staircase which led to the second floor has now been totally changed into rooms. Many interior parts have been reconstructed and decorations have been updated. His descendants had lived here for a long period of time. It is now shared by many households.

郁华 （忻秉勇画）　　YU Hua （By XIN Bingyong）

郁达夫
（1896—1945）

浙江富阳人，现代小说家、散文家。1913年赴日本留学。1919年考入东京帝国大学。1921年与郭沫若等在东京成立创造社。1922年回国后，曾任北京大学讲师，武昌师范大学、中山大学教授，并先后主编《创造月刊》《大众文艺》等刊物。1930年与鲁迅、宋庆龄等发起中国自由运动大同盟，同年参加中国左翼作家联盟。1936年任福建省政府参议。1938年前往南洋，利用各种宣传阵地号召爱国侨胞支援抗战。曾任新加坡华侨抗敌动员委员会执行委员兼文化界抗日联合会主席。1945年9月被日本宪兵秘密杀害于苏门答腊。1952年被追认为烈士。有《郁达夫文集》行世。

“以笔代戈”真勇士

郁达夫从来不觉得自己是个书生，1913年在日本留学的时候，他就在日记中写道：“……余有一大爱焉，曰爱国……国即余命也，国亡则余命亦绝矣！”

面对神州大地遭受日寇侵略，郁达夫没有“躲进小楼”，而是以笔代戈，投身于抗日救亡运动之中。

1937年，郁达夫被推为福州文化界救亡协会理事长，并担任《救亡文艺》主编。在47天内，他发表的作品就有20篇。他在为一个文学青年题词中写道：“我们这一代，应该为抗战而牺牲。”

这年冬天，正是郁达夫废寝忘食执笔为文最紧张的时候，老家富阳沦陷的消息传来，郁达夫70多岁的母亲因不愿伺候日寇吃喝而躲进后山，在风雨交加中饿死在山洞。听闻噩耗，郁达夫几近昏厥。丧服尚未脱下，郁达夫就接到国民政府军委会政治部第三厅厅长郭沫若的来电，邀他出任设计委员。郁达夫二话没说，马上赶往武汉，开始“笔尖上的抗战”。

1938年4月，台儿庄战役打响，郁达夫奔赴前线慰问抗日将士。在硝烟弥漫的战场上，郁达夫目睹官兵们浴血奋战、顽强拼杀，被他们的报国精神所震撼。短短15天，他一口气写下了20多篇战地通讯和战地评论。

1938年年底，应《星洲日报》邀请，郁达夫来到新加坡。在担任《星洲日报》主笔期间，他还同时编辑四五种刊物，发表了400多篇支援抗日和分析国内外政治、军事形势的政论、杂文、文艺杂论等，积极宣传抗日。

1942年2月，新加坡沦陷后，郁达夫和胡愈之、王任叔等人被迫撤离，流亡至印度尼西亚苏门答腊的巴亚公务镇。为隐蔽身份和解决生计，郁达夫开起了“赵豫记酒厂”。郁达夫巧于周旋，这里成了抗日人士的活动中心。郁达夫还建立了秘密组织“同仁社”，搜集情报，开展抗日宣传。

一天，有个日本兵发现郁达夫能讲一口流利的日语，即报告上司，于是郁达夫被迫给日本宪兵队当“翻译”。郁达夫“将计就计”，利用各种机会掩护和支持华侨及印尼民众的抗日活动。

1944年，因汉奸告密，郁达夫的真实身份被暴露。对于这位曾目睹日本宪兵种种暴行的重要抗日分子，日本宪兵下了毒手。1945年8月，郁达夫被秘密逮捕，后殉难于苏门答腊的丛林中。

建筑简介：常熟路188弄2号

郁达夫曾居住于常熟路188弄2号。建筑为英式花园住宅，建于1932年，占地面积370平方米。住宅为砖木结构假四层，主体淡黄色水泥拉毛墙面。二层房间东西外墙各建有人字坡顶的长方形凸窗，南侧中部两间前出，二层原为开敞式内阳台，三面皆有尖拱窗洞，西侧有圆弧楼梯通往花园。三层为三面开窗的阳光厅。底层为基座层，采用清水红砖外墙，内设厨房及服务用房。北侧原主入口现已封闭，原先通往二层的单独楼梯间已整体改为房间。标准层室内局部多处有改建，装饰基本都已更新。此处是郁达夫胞兄、爱国法学家郁华的住所，郁家后代曾长期在此居住，现由多户居民合用。

YU Dafu

YU Dafu (1896–1945), modern novelist and essayist, has his ancestral family from Fuyang in Zhejiang province. In 1913, he went to Japan for education. In 1919, he was admitted to the Imperial University in Tokyo. In 1921, together with GUO Moruo and others, he set up the Creation Society in Tokyo. After returning home in 1922, he once served as lecturer at Beijing University as well as professor at Wuchang Normal University and SUN Yat-sen University. Also he successively edited the magazines including *Creation Monthly* and *Popular Literature*. In 1930, along with LU Xun and SONG Qingling, he initiated China Freedom Movement Alliance. In the same year, he joined China Left-Wing Writers Union. In 1936, he was appointed as counselor of Fujian provincial government. In 1938, he went to Southeast Asia, making use of various means of publicity to call from the patriotic compatriots for support for the War against Japan. Once he severed as member of the Executive Committee of the Singapore Overseas Chinese Resisting-enemy Committee and chairman of the Resisting-Japanese Federation in the field of culture. In September 1945, he was secretly killed in Sumatra by the Japanese military policemen. In 1952, he was conferred posthumously as a martyr. The book *A Collection of Works by YU Dafu* was published.

A Real Warrior with "Pen as Weapon"

YU Dafu never feels that he is a scholar. When he was studying in Japan in 1913, he wrote in his diary, "... I have a great love—love for my country... my country is my life; if my country were conquered, my life would be taken away!"

In the face of the invasion of China by the Japanese, he did not "hide himself in the small studio", but used pen as weapon to join in the national salvation movement against Japanese invasion.

In 1937, he was promoted to chairman of the Salvation Association of the cultural community in Fuzhou and also served as editor of *Salvation Literature and Art*. Within forty-seven days, he published as many as 20 papers. In an inscription for a literary youth, he wrote, "Our generation should sacrifice ourselves for the War against Japanese Invasion."

The winter that year was just the most intense time when he experienced sleepless nights to fight with his pen. The news came

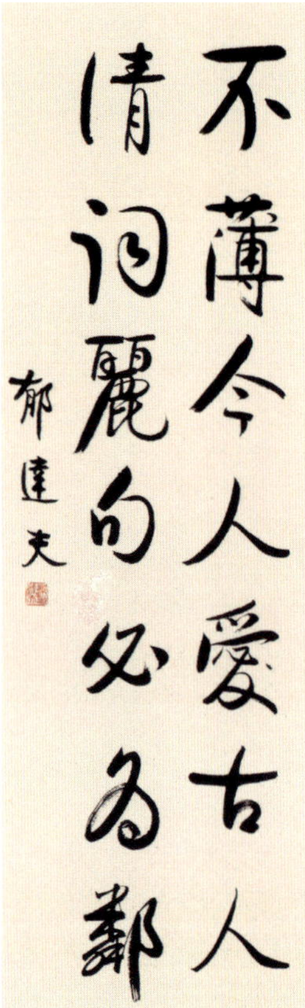

郁达夫手书：不薄今人爱古人，清词丽句必为邻

A complete written by YU Dafu in person: I love modern poets, but I love the ancient all the more. Those with elegant poetic lines, I will learn from them all.

of the fall of Fuyang his hometown, when his 70-year-old mother, who did not want to attend on the Japanese and hid herself in the mountains, starved to death in a cave in the storms. Hearing the sad news, he almost fainted. No sooner had he put an end to the mourning service than he received a telegram from GUO Moruo, head of the Third Division of the Political Department of the National Government Military Commission, inviting him to serve as member of the Design Committee. He said nothing and immediately hurried to Wuhan to begin his "war with the tip of pen".

In April 1938, the Battle of Taierzhuang started when he went to the front line to express sympathy and solicitude for officers and soldiers resisting Japanese invaders. In the smoke of gunpowder at the battlefield, he witnessed them in fierce and bloody battles, fighting tenaciously against the enemy. He was shocked by their patriotic spirit. During the 15 days, he finished writing over 20 battlefield communications and battlefield reviews.

At the end of 1938, he came to Singapore at the invitation of *Sin Chew Daily*. During the time when he served as its editor in chief, he also edited four or five magazines and published more than 400 political reviews, essays, and literary and artistic criticism to support resistance against Japanese invasion and analyze domestic and foreign political and military situations, actively publicizing resistance against Japanese invaders.

In February 1942, after the fall of Singapore, YU Dafu, HU Yuezhi, WANG Renshu and others were forced to withdraw, exiled to a town on Sumatra of Indonesia. For the concealment of identity and for livelihood, he originated a winery. For his cleverness in dealing with people around, this plant became the center of activities for resisting Japanese invasion. Also he established a secret organization "Tongren Society" to collect intelligence and carry out resisting-Japanese publicity.

One day, a Japanese soldier found that he could speak Japanese fluently and reported it to the officer. So he was forced to become a "translator" for the Japanese military policemen. To play the Japanese invaders at their own game, he made use of various opportunities to cover and support the resisting-Japanese activities of overseas Chinese and Indonesian people.

In 1944, his true identity was exposed because the traitors blew the gab. Since he was an important person witnessing the atrocities of Japanese military policemen, they laid murderous hands on him. In August 1945, he was secretly arrested and murdered in the jungles on Sumatra.

YU Dafu once lived at No. 2 in Alley 188 on Changshu Road, which is a garden house typical of a British style. Built in 1932, it covers an area of 370 square meters. The residence has a nominally four-storied structure of brick and wood. Its main body is composed of light yellow stuccoed walls. Rooms on the second floor have rectangular projected windows with gable roofs at the east and west sides and two rooms at the middle part of the south side protrude forward. On the second floor was formerly an open balcony, the three sides of which have pointed arch windows. At the west side there is an arc staircase which leads to the garden. The third floor has a sunshine hall with open windows at three sides. The bottom floor is the base with water red bricks for outer wall surfaces, in which there are kitchen and service rooms. The former main entrance at the north side has been closed. The separate staircase which led to the second floor has now been totally changed into rooms. Many interior parts have been reconstructed and decorations have been updated. Here is the residence of YU Hua, brother of YU Dafu and a patriotic jurist. The descendants of the YU family had lived here for a long period of time. It is now shared by many households.

郁达夫 （钱定华画） YU Dafu （By QIAN Dinghua）

郑君里
（1911—1969）

原籍广东中山，生于上海，原名重，又名千里。1927年考入南国艺术学院戏剧科学习。1931年参加左翼戏剧家联盟。1932年进联华影业公司当演员，从此开始电影艺术生涯。1943年导演了《戏剧春秋》等话剧。1947年与蔡楚生合作导演故事片《一江春水向东流》。1948年执导故事片《乌鸦与麻雀》，该片在1957年获文化部颁发的1949—1955年优秀影片一等奖。1959年导演故事片《聂耳》，同年加入中国共产党。曾任上海电影制片厂导演，上海市第一、二、三届人民代表大会代表。主要著作有《论抗战戏剧运动》《画外音》《角色的诞生》等。

大导演的“画外音”

郑君里家中有一间很大的书房，安放着一张大写字台和一只大沙发。他经常半躺在沙发上全神贯注地阅读。写字台旁的书架上摆放着他需要使用的资料，书架旁及靠近门的地方列满了一排排书柜，书和资料可谓汗牛充栋。郑君里将几乎所有的时间和精力投入对电影艺术的探索中，每次获得薪酬后，他做的第一件事就是列出书目，大批量地买书，然后废寝忘食地认真阅读、思索，却舍不得为自己添置衣物，上下班也仅以破旧的自行车代步。

郑君里下班回家后及休息日仍伏案思考、笔耕不辍。他对电影艺术创作精益求精，非常注重归纳总结、汲取经验教训。每一部影片完成后他都会一丝不苟地整理汇集资料，把导演阐述、分镜头剧本、工作笔记、与合作者交流的信件、镜头剪辑、工作总结乃至上映后的观众反响等，都一一记载，精心装订成册。在郑君里家中，至今仍保存着他当年留下的一套套电影分镜头的图，那全是郑君里亲自一笔一画绘制而成的。

如此殚精竭虑、细致入微的总结和思考，成就了我国重要的电影导演艺术理论专著《画外音》。郑君里在这部自己多年从事导演工作后的呕心沥血之作中逐一介绍了《一江春水向东流》《乌鸦与麻雀》等6部影片的创作背景和导演意图，深刻总结了创作中的得失，并对电影与时代的关系、人物、情节、表演、分镜头、场面调度、歌曲处理等作了理论探讨，在最后一篇《漫谈导演在摄制组的组织工作》中详细分享了组织摄制组工作的经验，体现了作为一位出色的电影艺术家的厚积薄发的才情、渊博的理论修养和严谨的治学精神。

建筑简介：淮海中路1842—1858号武康大楼

郑君里旧居位于淮海中路1842—1858号武康大楼，旧称东美特公寓，又称诺曼底公寓，建于1924年，万国储蓄会投资建造，克利洋行邬达克设计，高30米，占地面积1580平方米，建筑面积9755平方米，属法国文艺复兴式建筑风格的公寓住宅，是上海最早的外廊式公寓建筑。建筑为八层钢筋混凝土结构，平面依楔状地形布置，楼身狭长似船。其前部为骑楼，骑楼形式为连续券廊。立面作横三段划分，第一、二层处理成基座，连续半圆券廊，水泥仿石墙面。三层挑出长阳台，四至七层挑出小阳台。一、二层水泥墙面，三至七层为清水红墙外砖。顶层由连续的挑出阳台和女儿墙构成双重檐部水平线脚。1930年，又在该楼东侧再建五层混合结构新武康大楼，建筑面积1700平方米。底层为商店，二至五层为住宅。1945年抗战结束后多为国民政府官员居住。1953年改名为武康大楼，许多文艺界名人在此安家。1994年2月15日上海市人民政府公布其为市优秀历史建筑。

ZHENG Junli

ZHENG Junli (1911–1969) has his ancestral family from Zhongshan in Guangdong province. Born in Shanghai, he had former names of Zhong and Qianli. In 1927, he was admitted to the department of drama of South China Institute of Arts. In 1931, he joined the China Left-Wing Dramatists Union. In 1932, he entered into Lianhua Film Company to work as an actor, starting his film art career from then on. In 1943, he directed dramas including *Drama's Spring and Autumn*. In 1947, he co-directed with CAI Chusheng the feature film *A Spring River Flows East*. In 1948, he directed the feature film *Crow and Sparrow* and won first prize of excellent films from 1949 to 1955 awarded by the Ministry of Culture in 1957. In 1959, he directed the feature film *NIE Er* and in the same year joined the CPC. Once he served as director of Shanghai Film Studio and representative of the first, second and third sessions of the Shanghai Municipal People's Congress. His major works include *On the Drama Movement against Japanese Invasion*, *Voice-over* and *The Birth of the Role* and so on.

The "Voice-over" of a Famous Director

ZHENG Junli had a spacious study in his house, where he placed a sizeable desk and a large sofa. Often he lay on the sofa and concentrated on his reading. On the bookshelves next to the desk he placed the documents he needed. Next to the bookshelves and near the door were rows of bookcases filled with an immense number of books and other documents. He almost contributed all of the time and energy to the exploration of film art. Each time he got the pay, the first thing he did was to make a book list and buy large quantities of books. Then he spent sleepless nights doing serious reading and thinking, but he was reluctant to buy clothes for himself. In addition, he went to work and came back home by an old bike.

After he came back home from work and even on holidays, he still bent over the desk thinking and continued working. In the

在《聂耳》拍摄现场，郑君里（中）给赵丹（左）说戏
On the spot shooting of *NIE Er*, ZHENG Junli (middle) was explaining the acting to ZHAO Dan (left).

artistic creation of films, he constantly strived for excellence, attaching great importance to induction and summarization, and drawing lessons and experience. After the production of each film, he would fastidiously clear up and collect materials and also record director's elaboration, continuity, work notes, correspondences with collaborators, film editing, work summary and even audience responses after the release and finally bind them together with care. At his home, collections of pictures are still preserved of film shots which he left in the past years and were drawn stroke by stroke by himself.

He racked his brains in the painstaking summarization and thinking, which led to the birth of the important theoretical works on film direction *Voice-over*. In this book which was the result of his painstaking efforts in film direction for years, he introduced one by one the creation background and intentions of the director of six films including *A Spring River Flows East* and *Crow and Sparrow*. Here he also made a profound summary of the gains and losses in the process of the creation and made theoretical discussions about the relationship between films and the times, characters, plot, performance, shots, mise-en-scène and song processing. In the last paper with the title "On the organization of director in the film crew", he discussed in detail the work experience of organizing the crew, embodying his well-grounded knowledge, profound theoretical cultivation and rigorous academic spirit as an excellent film artist.

The former residence of ZHENG Junli is located in Wukang Building at No. 1842-1858 on Middle Huaihai Road, formerly known as East Meite Apartment and also known as Normandy Apartments. Founded in 1924 by the International Savings Society and designed by Ladislaus Edward Hudec from R. A. Curry Company, the building is 30 meters in height and covers an area of 1,580 square meters with a construction area of 9,755 square meters. It is an apartment of French Renaissance style and is the earliest apartment building with outside corridor in Shanghai. With eight stories of reinforced concrete structure, it has a wedge-shaped layout and its body part once long and narrow like a boat. Its front is of an arcade, which takes on the form of continuous arched corridors. The facade adopts the horizontal division of three sections with the first and second floors as the foundation, which have continuous semicircular arched corridors and wall surface of cement imitation stone. At the third floor long balconies are projected and from fourth to seventh floors small balconies are protruded. Wall surfaces from the first to the second floor are of cement and those from the third to seventh floors are of exposed red brickwork. At the top floor continuous projected balconies and parapets constitute the horizontal architrave of double eaves. In 1930, a new Wukang Building of a five-story mixed structure was constructed to its east side with a construction area of 1,700 square meters. The bottom floor is for stores and floors from the second to the fifth are for residence. After the end of the War in 1945, it was mostly occupied by national government officials. In 1953 it was renamed as Wukang Building and many literary celebrities once lived here. On February 15, 1994, it became a Heritage Architecture issued by the Shanghai Municipal People's Government.

郑君里 （陆小弟、陆旻画） ZHENG Junli （By LU Xiaodi and LU Min）

郑振铎
（1898—1958）

原籍福建长乐，生于浙江永嘉，笔名西谛、CT、郭源新。1917年入北京铁路管理学校学习。后任商务印书馆编辑。五四时期在北京参加学生运动，与瞿秋白合编《新社会》旬刊。1921年与茅盾、叶圣陶、王统照等组织文学研究会。1923年主编《小说月报》。1931年后，相继任燕京大学、清华大学、复旦大学、暨南大学教授，致力学术研究，并编辑文学刊物。抗日战争期间留居上海，坚持进步文化工作。解放战争时期积极参加民主运动。中华人民共和国成立后，任中国科学院考古研究所所长、文化部文物局长和副部长、对外文化联络委员会委员、中国作家协会理事、中国民间文艺研究理事会副主席、全国政协委员。1958年10月17日在出国访问途中因飞机失事遇难。著有插图本《中国文学史》《中国俗文学史》，另有《郑振铎文集》等。

“蛰居”斗室　心忧文化

抗日战争时期，很多知识分子、著名学者为了避难及开展敌后文化工作，纷纷离开上海，迁移至大后方。但是郑振铎一直没有走，他在中华民族危急存亡之际，以上海租界作掩护，为抢救沦陷区的中国古代文化珍籍默默奔走。

1942年，郑振铎搬迁至僻静的高邮路5弄，“蛰居”于25号二楼的两间小房间内。为了不使邻居们生疑，郑振铎每天夹着皮包装作去上班，其实是去书店里搜寻有珍藏价值的历史文献。妻子和母亲未能与他同住照顾他的日常起居，以前从来不碰锅碗瓢盆的郑振铎在清苦的生活中学会了生煤球炉、烧简单的饭菜。

“蛰居”期间，敌占区人民水深火热的生活，硝烟弥漫下中华历史文献的去向，凡此种种，都牵动着郑振铎的心。虽然不能在上海公开发表文章，但他仍笔耕不辍。1944年3月6日，他在斗室中写下了诗篇《野狼》。其中“野狼在嚎，黑暗把天与地涂成一片，倦了的旅客独自踯躅在莽原。天边远远的有一颗黄星，是黑漆一片的天地间仅有的光明。仅这一星星的光亮啊，已足够使旅人慰安了”的诗句，含蓄地表达了他彷徨苦闷，但仍以乐观主义情怀坚定自己作为一名知识分子维系中华民族的文化精神、保存文化重建之根的信念。

他“陆续地整理了不少的古书，写了好些跋尾”，并把每天寻访搜集历史古籍的具体情况、内容评价、版本鉴定等一一记载于日记中，后单独列入《求书日录》，成为极具学术研究价值的著作。1944年夏，经济已十分拮据的郑振铎仍自费编印了《长乐郑氏汇印传奇第一集》，共两大函十二册，收录明代传奇六种，并以“幼秋山馆主人”的化名印行了《明季史料丛书》十二册，在战火纷飞中延续中华文脉。

抗战胜利后，郑振铎怀着庄严的历史责任感，将“蛰居”时期自己的经历、见闻和感悟写入《蛰居散记》，连载于抗战胜利后上海乃至全国新创办的第一份综合性周刊《周报》。

建筑简介：高邮路5弄25号

郑振铎旧居位于高邮路5弄25号，是他在上海现存的唯一旧居，建于1935年，是一座二层混合建筑，坐西朝东，白色糙面水泥墙，双坡顶。1942年，郑振铎在友人的帮助下，搬至这幢小洋房二楼东部的两间小房间内，一间做卧室，另一间做书房，至1945年，他在此共"蛰居"四年。现为普通民居。

ZHENG Zhenduo

ZHENG Zhenduo (1898–1958), born in Yongjia county in Zhejiang province, has his ancestral family from Changle County in Fujian province. He had pen names such as Xidi, CT and GUO Yuanxin. In 1917, he studied in Beijing Railway Management School. Later he served as editor of the Commercial Press. During the May Fourth Movement he participated in the student movement in Beijing and co-edited the magazine *The New Society* together with others. In 1921, he and others organized the Literary Research Society. In 1923, he was the editor-in-chief of *Fiction Monthly*. After 1931, he successively worked as professor in Yenching University, Tsinghua University, Fudan University and Jinan University, and committed himself to academic research and editing of literary magazines. During the War against Japanese Invasion, he stayed in Shanghai, adhering to progressive cultural work. During the War of Liberation, he actively participated in democratic movement. After the founding of the New China, he served as director of the Archaeological Research Institute of the Chinese Academy of Sciences, director of Cultural Relics Bureau of Ministry of Culture and its vice minister, member of Foreign Cultural Liaison Committee, director of China Writers Association, vice chairman of the China Folk Literature and Art Research Council and member of the CPPCC National Committee. On October 17, 1958, he passed away in an air crash on the way to go abroad for a visit. He is the author of the illustrated version of *History of Chinese Literature*, *History of Chinese Folk Literature*, and *An Anthology of ZHENG Zhenduo*.

Living in Seclusion and Worrying about Culture

During the War against Japanese Invasion, many intellectuals and famous scholars left Shanghai for the rear in order to seek shelter and do cultural work. But ZHENG did not leave all the time. At the critical moment of national crisis, he worked silently for the rescue of Chinese ancient culture works in the enemy-occupied areas under the shadow of the Shanghai Settlements.

In 1942, he moved to the quiet Lane 5 on Gaoyou Road and "lived in seclusion" in two small rooms on the second floor at

1948 年，郑振铎五十寿辰时在书斋中的留影
A photo of ZHENG Zhenduo in his study at the age of 50 in 1948.

No. 25. In order to avoid the suspicion of neighbors, he pretended to go to work every day with a leather bag under his arm, but in fact he went to bookshops in search of valuable historical documents. His mother and wife were unable to come to live together with him to take care of his daily life. Though he never touched cooking utensils before, he learned a lot in the plain and poor life, including cooking simple meals.

During this period of time, people in the enemy-occupied areas lived in misery and sufferings, and the Chinese historical documents under the smoke of war—all these tugged at his heartstring. Although he was not able to get papers published publicly in Shanghai, he still kept on writing. On March 6, 1944, he wrote a poem *Wild Wolf* in his small room. In this poem, there were such lines as—"The wild wolf howls,/Dark integrates the sky and the earth,/ And the tired traveler walked lonely in the wilderness./ At the far horizon is a yellow star,/ The only brightness in the darkness./ This only brightness is enough to console the traveler." These poetic lines implicitly expressed his optimistic feelings even in anxiety and depression to have the faith as an intellectual to maintain the cultural spirit of the Chinese nation and preserve the root for cultural reconstruction.

He successively sorted out many ancient books and wrote quite a few postscripts. In addition, he made daily records of the specific circumstances, content evaluation and version identification of the ancient historical documents he found and collected. Later he separately listed all of the information in the book *A Daily Record of Searching for Books*, which was of great academic research value. In the summer of 1944, in spite of his difficult economic situation, he edited and printed at his own expenses *A Collected Printing of Legends by Mr. ZHENG* (I), which was composed of totally 12 volumes, including the six types of legends of the Ming Dynasty. Moreover, he also printed 12 volumes of *Series of Ming Dynasty Historical Documents* in a pseudonym. In this way he was extending the Chinese system of culture in the flames of war.

After the victory of the War, he cherished a solemn sense of historical responsibility and included in *Random Notes of Seclusion* his own experience, knowledge and understanding during this period. The book was serialized in *Weekly*, the first comprehensive magazine newly founded in Shanghai and even the whole country after the war.

The former residence of ZHENG Zhenduo is situated at No. 25 in Alley 5 on Gaoyou Road. It is his only former residence now extant in Shanghai. Built in 1935, it is a two-storied mixed construction facing east. It has stuccoed walls and a gable roof. In 1942, with the help of friends he moved to the two rooms in the east of the second floor of this small villa; one room was for bedroom and the other for the study. He lived here "in seclusion" for four years till 1945. Now it is an ordinary house.

郑振铎 （吴耀明画） ZHENG Zhenduo （By WU Yaoming）

金焰
（1910—1983）

原籍朝鲜平壤市郊，生于首尔，原名德麟。1912 年随父亲举家迁至中国东北。曾就读于南开中学。1927 年到上海，入民新影片公司做场记工作。1928 年加入南国艺术剧社。1929 年因主演《风流剑客》而成名。1933 年加入中国左翼戏剧家联盟。抗日战争期间流寓香港和大后方。抗战胜利后回上海。1949 年入上海电影制片厂，担任演员剧团团长多年。后历任上海电影制片厂艺委会副主任、中国影协理事、上海影协副主席等职。主演过几十部影片，曾有“电影皇帝”之誉。

秦怡
（1922—　）

祖籍江苏高邮，电影表演艺术家。1938 年进入中国电影制片厂担任话剧演员，1941 年成为中华剧艺社演员。1946 年凭借在影片《遥远的爱》中的演出成名。中华人民共和国成立后成为上海电影制片厂演员、演员剧团副团长。50 年代因主演《马兰花开》被观众所熟知。1983 凭借电视剧《上海屋檐下》获得第 1 届大众电视金鹰奖优秀女演员奖。1995 年获评中国电影世纪奖。2004 年被授予上海市慈善之星称号。2005 年被授予国家有突出贡献电影艺术家称号。2008 年获选第 7 届中国十大女杰。2009 年获得上海文艺家终身荣誉奖及第 18 届金鸡百花电影节终身成就奖。

从爱情到亲情

抗战胜利后，金焰从重庆返回上海，居住于好友刘琼家中。秦怡常到刘琼家做客聊家常，由他热心引见，与金焰相识。金焰是秦怡从小就崇拜的偶像，进入演艺圈后，她也听说过不少关于金焰这位“电影皇帝”的传说，更增加了对他的崇拜之情。随着交往的深入，金焰政治上爱憎分明和强烈的民族感、爱国心，深深地打动了秦怡。1947 年冬天，秦怡应香港建华影业公司邀请，赴香港拍摄《海茫茫》。金焰正好有空，便和秦怡一同去了香港。在朋友的撮合下，12 月 15 日，两人在香港举行了婚礼。

完婚、蜜月、生子、聚少离多……各自忙于事业的他们，彼此个性与观念差异造成的矛盾也暴露出来，时有“冷战”。只有不断演绎角色，沉浸于艺术创作才使她暂时忘却现实的苦恼；而他频繁借酒消愁，对酒精的依赖严重损害了健康，多次胃出血后便缠绵病榻了。从此，她尽力悉心照料他，忙于工作之外，还要抚养呵护年幼的儿子。

当她参演的影片《雷雨》还在紧张拍摄时，他病危的噩耗传来，她心急如焚从片场赶到医院，眼前的他衰弱得奄奄一息，悲伤、自责、不舍……五味杂陈，涌上心头，她喃喃重复说着“我来晚了！我来晚了！对不起！真对不起！”握着他冰凉的手，守到他的最后一刻。

当爱情已成往事，亲情与责任是她的牵挂，他们唯一的儿子，是她照顾了一生。

建筑简介：复兴西路44弄2号

金焰与秦怡曾居住于复兴西路44弄（玫瑰别墅）2号。玫瑰别墅建于1940年，由七幢造型典雅的住宅式公寓组成。因建造时在弄口地面上砌有"玫瑰"两字，老上海人称之为"玫瑰别墅"。占地面积4393平方米，建筑总面积3175平方米。为三层砖木结构，建筑平面每层都有厨房间、备餐间、卫生间、客厅、卧室等。七幢建筑均为平屋顶、水泥砂浆外墙，建筑形体简洁，体现现代建筑风格。屋前有花园。原主人是蓝妮（孙科二夫人），后收归国有并作为地方民房。

JIN Yan and QIN Yi

JIN Yan (1910–1983), born in Seoul, has his ancestral family from Pyongyang in North Korea and has a former name of JIN Delin. In 1912, he fled with his father and the whole family to northeast China and once studied at Nankai High School. In 1927, he went to Shanghai and entered Minxin Film Company to serve as log keeper. In 1928, he joined the Southland Art Theater Club. In 1929, he made a name for himself for starring in the film *Rose and Beauty*. In 1933, he joined China Left-Wing Dramatists Union. During the War of Resistance against Japanese Invasion he stayed in Hong Kong and the rear area. After the victory, he returned to Shanghai. In 1949, he entered into Shanghai Film Studio and served as director of actor troupe for many years. Later he served in succession as deputy director of the Art Committee of Shanghai Film Studio, director of China Film Association, and vice chairman of Shanghai Film Association. Once he starred in dozens of films and was reputed as King of Movie.

QIN Yi (1922–), film performing artist, has her ancestral family from the city of Gaoyou in Jiangsu province. In 1938, she entered China Film Studio to work as a drama actress. In 1941, she became actress of Chinese Drama Society. In 1946, she established her fame by virtue of her performance in the film *Remote Love*. After the founding of the New China, she became actress of Shanghai Film Studio and deputy director of its actor troupe. In the 1950s, she was well known among the audience for her starring in the film *Orchid Flowers Bloom*. In 1983, she won the First Public TV Golden Eagle Award for Outstanding Actress by virtue of the TV series *Under the Roofs of Shanghai*. In 1995, she won China Film Century Award. In 2004, she was awarded the title of Shanghai Charity Star. In 2005, she was awarded the honorary title of National Film Artist with Outstanding Contribution. In 2008, she was elected into the Seventh Session of China's Top Ten Women. In 2009, he won the Lifetime Honor Award of Shanghai Artists and the Lifelong Achievement Award at the Eighteenth Golden Rooster & Hundred Flowers Film Festival.

From Love to Family Affection

After the victory of the War against Japanese Invasion, JIN Yan returned from Chongqing to Shanghai, living in the home of

金焰、秦怡和金捷
JIN Yan, QIN Yi and JIN Jie.

a friend, which QIN Yi frequented for a visit and chat. With the introduction of the friend, JIN got acquainted with QIN. Jin had been an idol she adored since her childhood. After entering into the field of entertainment, she heard a lot about the legend of JIN Yan, "a movie king", for which her admiration for him intensified all the more. With the increase of communication, she was deeply moved by his clear political distinction between love and hatred as well as his strong sense of nationality and love for his motherland. In the winter of 1947, she went to Hong Kong to participate in the film *In the Sea of Life Enisled* at the invitation of Hong Kong Jianhua Film Company. It happened that he was not occupied. In this case he went to Hong Kong in her company. With the promotion and encouragement of their friends they held their wedding ceremony in Hong Kong on December 15.

Marriage, honeymoon, giving birth to son, less gathering and more separation...both were so busy with their own work that they experienced the seven-year itch. Differences in personality and idea resulted in exposed contradictions, which led further to "cold war". Only the constant interpretation of roles and immersion in artistic creation made it possible that she temporarily forgot the reality of distress; he frequently drank to forget and his dependence on alcohol seriously damaged his health condition. After stomach bleeding for several times, he had to linger on sickbed. Since then, she tried her best to take good care of him. In addition to busy work, she must also care for their son in his young age.

When the film *Thunderstorm* in which she starred was still in the tight process of shooting, the bad news of his dying came. Torn with anxiety, she rushed from the shooting location to the hospital. He was weak at his last gossamer of gasp. Sadness, remorse, strong attachment... Mixed emotions rose in her heart. She murmured repeatedly, "I'm late! I'm late! I'm sorry! I'm sorry!" Holding his cold hands, she was with him to his last moment.

When love became the past, family affection and responsibility began to be her new concerns. She lived a life with their only son for the rest of her lifetime.

JIN Yan and QIN Yi once lived at No. 2 in Alley 44 (Rose Villa) on Fuxing Road. Rose Villa was built in 1940 and consists of seven elegantly styled residential apartments. It is called "Rose Villa" by former natives in Shanghai because of the word "Rose" made by bricks on the ground at the mouth of the alley when its construction was started. The building covers an area of 4,393 square meters with a total construction area of 3,175 square meters. It is of a three-storied structure of brick and wood. At each floor there are kitchen, dining room, bathroom, living room and bedroom. All of the seven buildings enjoy flat roofs and exterior walls with cement mortar. The building is concise in form and structure, reflecting the modern architectural style. There is a garden in front of the house. The original owner is LAN Ni (second wife of SUN Ke). Later it was nationalized and used for a local house.

金焰、秦怡 （刘为民画）

JIN Yan and QIN Yi （By LIU Weimin）

俞振飞
（1902—1993）

原籍江苏松江（今属上海市），生于苏州，名远威，号箴非，京剧、昆曲表演艺术家。6岁跟随父亲、昆曲名家俞粟庐习曲，14岁起向昆曲前辈沈锡卿、沈月泉学习。后在上海师从蒋砚香学习京剧小生。29岁经程砚秋介绍，拜京剧小生前辈程继光为师，成为专业演员。先后参加程砚秋、梅兰芳的剧团，长期与梅兰芳、程砚秋、周信芳、马连良、张君秋等合作演出。1923年秋与程砚秋合演昆曲《游园惊梦》，一炮打响，从此声名远扬。30年代，任上海暨南大学文学院讲师。1957年起，任上海市戏曲学校校长。历任中国文联副主席、中国剧协上海分会副主席、上海京剧院院长、上海昆剧团团长等职。代表剧目有：昆曲《太白醉写》《牡丹亭》《长生殿》等，京剧《群英会》《状元谱》等。著有《振飞曲谱》《念白要领》等。

君子之交淡如水

1945年8月，日本投降。俞振飞前去看望老朋友梅兰芳，蓄须罢演多年的梅兰芳已将胡须剃净，意欲重返舞台，无奈嗓子不听使唤，吊嗓唱不上去，表演京剧心有余而力不足。俞振飞见梅兰芳愁容满面，安慰他说："你蓄须明志，大家都很钦佩，八年不唱戏，一时唱不上去，决不能说'完了'。"第二天，俞振飞带上笛子来到梅家，鼓励梅兰芳"唱昆曲试试"。在俞振飞的伴奏下，梅兰芳唱《游园惊梦》后重拾信心。俞振飞考虑到梅兰芳没有唱昆曲的班底和场面，便主动请缨，热心地帮老朋友四处张罗联系。

11月28日，在俞振飞尽心尽力的奔走筹措下，梅兰芳在上海美琪大戏院挂牌演出《游园惊梦》《断桥》《奇双会》等6出京昆剧目。当时人们奔走相告梅兰芳复出的喜讯，欲重睹梅兰芳风采者人山人海，几乎挤破了售票处的门窗。原定演10场，应热情的观众之请，又加演3场。演出结束，收入相当可观，梅兰芳要多分钱给俞振飞，俞振飞却连连摇手，无论如何也不肯接受，微笑着说帮助朋友焉能收钱。梅兰芳过意不去，买了衣料等礼品送至俞振飞府宅，俞振飞笑言心领了这份好意，却仍坚持"君子之交淡如水"，亦推辞不受。梅兰芳当着梅剧团成员的面力邀俞振飞加入梅剧团，盛情难却，俞振飞欣然应允。但他表示自己在梅剧团的"包银"（薪酬）决不能高于同为头路小生的姜妙香，虽然姜妙香声名远不及他。

俞振飞自幼接受儒家传统道德教育，重情重义，淡泊名利，养成超凡脱俗的"书卷气"，秉承高尚的艺德，心无旁骛地钻研表演艺术。

建筑简介：五原路258号

俞振飞旧居位于五原路258号协发公寓，建于1933年，著名建筑师范文照设计，建筑面积2128平方米，占地面积441平方米，混合结构四层（现五层），平面长方形，为现代风格的成套公寓住宅。公寓三层楼东边的一组套房为俞振飞旧居。公寓南立面挑出阳台，北立面中间圆形凸出，底层方形门洞，有水泥雨厦。方形门窗，水泥拉毛墙面，平顶。公寓沿五原路北边布置，平面为一字型，由两个单元组合而成。每个单元标准层平面为一梯一户，每户为四室户型，居室大多为套间，并巧妙地在房间分隔处设置壁橱。起居室通向阳台，有六扇落地长窗，阳光充足，通风良好。厨房特别大，一间为洗切，另一间为烹烧。佣人房设在洗切间旁，且朝南，虽然面宽狭长，但面积不小，在上海公寓中仅此一例。楼梯间半平台悬挑，底层设汽车库、锅炉间，两边尽头各设两室户型。现为民居。

YU Zhenfei

YU Zhenfei (1902—1993) has his ancestral family from Songjiang (now in Shanghai) in Jiangsu province. Born in Suzhou, he had the former name Yuanwei with a style name of Zhenfei (literally "admonition against wrongs") and was known as a performing artist of Beijing opera and Kunqu opera. At the age of 6, he followed Yu Sulu, his father and a famous opera artist, to learn opera. At the age of 14, he learned from SHEN Xiqing and SHEN Yuequan, two predecessors of Kunqu opera. Later he learned to perform the young man's role of Beijing opera from JIANG Yanxiang in Shanghai. At the age of 29, he was introduced by CHENG Yanqiu to take as his teacher CHENG Jiguang, predecessor of Beijing opera, and became a professional actor. In succession he joined in the CHENG Yanqiu Troupe and MEI Lanfang Troupe. He cooperated in performance on a long-term basis with such well-known artists as MEI Lanfang, CHENG Yanqiu, ZHOU Xinfang, MA Lianliang and ZHANG Junqiu. In the autumn of 1923, he cooperated with CHENG Yanqiu in the performance of the Kunqu opera *Sweet Dream in the Garden*, and won an immediate success. He enjoyed a widespread reputation ever since. In the 1930s, he served as a lecturer in the College of Literature of Jinan University in Shanghai. Since 1957, he served as president of Shanghai Opera School. Successively he served as vice chairman of China Federation of Literary and Art Circles, vice chairman of Shanghai Branch of Chinese Dramatists Association, dean of Shanghai Beijing Opera Theater and head of Shanghai Kunqu Opera Troupe. The repertoire of his representative operas includes Kunqu operas such as *Taibai Writing in Drunkenness*, *Peony Pavilion* and *The Palace of Eternal Youth*, in addition to Beijing Operas including *The Meeting of Heroes* and *List of Number One Scholar*. He is the author of *Music by Zhenfei* and *Essentials for Spoken Parts in Opera*.

A Hedge between Keeps Friendship Green

In August 1945, the Japanese surrendered. YU Zhenfei went to visit his old friend MEI Lanfang. The latter, who had kept beards to stop performance for over eight years, had his beards shaved clean with the intention to return to the stage. But his helpless throat did not work. When he exercised his voice, he could not go up high in singing. He was willing but unable to perform Beijing opera any more. When the former saw that MEI looked worried, he consoled him, saying, "When you wore beards to make known your aspiration, admiration was expressed among your friends. Without performance for eight years, it is natural that you can not sing for a moment. But it does not mean complete failure." The next day, YU came to his home with a flute, encouraging him to have a try in Kunqu opera.

俞振飞（右）与梅兰芳合拍昆剧电影《游园惊梦》剧照
A photo of YU Zhenfei (right) and MEI Lanfang in the film *Sweet Dream in the Garden*.

In his accompaniment, MEI tried to sing *Sweet Dream in the Garden* and regained confidence afterwards. Taking it into account that MEI did not have troupe members and spectacles for the performance of the Kunqu opera, YU volunteered to get in touch with people around to help his old friend.

On November 28, with his active efforts and money-raising to his utmost, MEI had his bulletin board of performance put up in Shanghai Meggie Theatre to perform six Kunqu operas such as *Sweet Dream in the Garden*, *Broken Bridge*, *Meeting of Two Legends* and the others. At that time, people ran around to tell about the good news of Mei's comeback on the stage, and those who wanted to see with their own eyes his elegant demeanour amounted to mountains and seas and the crowd almost broke the doors and windows of the ticket office. The original schedule was that the performance would be done for ten times. But at the enthusiastic request of the audience three extra shows were added. At the end of the performance, the income was quite considerable. Therefore, MEI proposed to pay more money to YU, who shook his head again and again and refused to accept it in any case. He smiled and explained that how he could collect money when he intended to help his friend. MEI was thankful and bought gifts including cloth and other things and had them sent to YU's home. YU smiled as a token of appreciation of the good intentions, but he still adhered to the conception of "A hedge between keeps friendship green", and refused the gifts again. In the face of the members of the MEI Lanfang Troupe, MEI invited YU to join the troupe. Hard to turn down the warm-hearted offer, YU gladly assented. But he said that his "package silver" (pay) in the troupe must not be higher than that of JIANG Miaoxiang, also a first-class young man's role, whose fame was far lower than YU nonetheless.

YU Zhenfei accepted traditional moral education of Confucianism since childhood, valuing emotion and righteousness and being indifferent to fame and wealth. So he cultivated the extraordinary "bookishness", upheld the noble artistry and concentrated on delving into performing arts.

The former residence of YU Zhenfei is located in Yafa Apartment at No. 258 on Wuyuan Road. Built in 1933, it was designed by FAN Wenzhao, a famous architect. With a construction area of 2,128 square meters, it covers an area of 441 square meters. Enjoying a mixed structure of four floors (now five ones), it has a rectangular plane. The building is an apartment of modern style. One suite on the third floor at the east of the apartment was the residence for YU Zhenfei. At the south facade of the apartment balconies are projected and in the middle there are circular projections. The bottom floor has square doors with cement canopy. The building has square doors and windows, stuccoed walls and a flat roof. The apartment is arranged along the north side of Wuyuan Road and its plane is of a linear shape. It is composed of two units and each unit has one household at one floor with four rooms for each household. Most flats are of the type of suite and wardrobes are cleverly set at the separation between rooms. The living room leads to balcony, which enjoys a French window of six frames to allow in sufficient sunshine and fine ventilation. The kitchen is particularly large with one room for cleansing and cutting and the other for cooking. Maid rooms are located beside the one for cleansing and cutting and face south. Although these rooms are narrow, they are not small in area, which is the only one exception among the apartments in Shanghai. The staircase has semi-platform cantilevers and the ground floor has garages and boiler rooms. At both ends of each apartment are two-room suites. Now it is a residential house.

俞振飞 （陆小弟、陆旻画）

YU Zhenfei （By LU Xiaodi and LU Min）

柯灵
（1909—2000）

祖籍浙江绍兴，出生于广州，原名高季琳，作家、剧作家、文艺理论家。1926年开始发表作品。历任上海明星影片公司宣传主任、《万象》杂志主编、《周报》主编、《文汇报》副社长兼副总编辑、上海电影剧本创作所所长、上海电影艺术研究所所长、《大众电影》主编、上海作家协会副主席、上海电影家协会副主席、国际笔会上海中心会长等。著有散文、杂文集《文苑漫游录》《柯灵散文精编》《燕居闲话》《文心雕虫》《柯灵杂文集》《柯灵六十年文选》等约30种，儿童文学集《月亮姑娘》《蝴蝶的故事》，小说集《掠影集》《同伴》，评论集《电影文学丛谈》《剧场偶记》等，电影文学剧本《武则天》《腐蚀》《秋瑾传》《春满人间》《为了和平》《不夜城》等，戏剧剧本《飘》《夜店》《恨海》等。

柯灵慧眼识沈寂

1943年，柯灵接手主编《万象》杂志。经过两个月的筹划，《万象》7月号从内容到形式面目一新。一天，柯灵正为9月号杂志选稿，看到一篇小说《盗马贼》。小说一开始就有悬念，结尾又出人意料。以前，柯灵编发的大多是知名作家的作品，这篇来稿署名为沈寂，应该是一位新人。柯灵对作品很欣赏，但多了个心眼：这是否为作者的偶然之作？柯灵于是去信要沈寂再写几篇，并鼓励他可多做叙述方法的实验。于是沈寂试着用新方法讲故事，又将写京剧艺人遭遇的《被玩弄者的报复》和以盗尸为题材的《大草泽的犷悍》两部小说寄去。

柯灵读罢，大为叫好，当即决定在当年9月、10月、12月连续三期刊出，这在《万象》历史上绝无仅有。他在编后记中推荐道："这里想介绍的是《盗马贼》，细读之下，作者自有其清新的风致，沈寂先生是创作界的新人，这也是值得读者注意的。"沈寂在柯灵的提携下，由此踏进了文坛，从一个无名的新人成为有名的作家。后来，又成为写老上海的行家里手。

时光转到20世纪90年代，沈寂撰写的一部反映黄金荣在旧上海生涯的小说《上海大亨》在《新民晚报》上连载，引来很大反响。不久，上海召开文化系统的专题会议，柯灵和沈寂应邀参加。时任上海市市长汪道涵在会上谈到英国人写的《上海》一书翻译出版之事，说我们中国人为什么不能写老上海题材呢？

柯灵接着发言说，哈同是洋人在华从事房地产经营的成功人士，并推荐道，沈寂是写这方面内容的高手。沈寂没有辜负先生的期望，很快，长篇小说《上海大班》在《解放日报》上连载。沈寂的父亲当年与上海大世界创始人黄楚九认识，且是朋友。所以，沈寂又得心应手写起有关黄楚九的传记小说《上海大世界》。

这"三大"成为沈寂的代表作，当学林出版社为这"老上海文化系列"结集出版时，柯灵没有忘记给自己的学生、后来已成知己和老朋友的沈寂写序："不少作家回过头来，开始为已经消逝的十里洋场绣像……沈寂写了《上海大亨》《上海大班》《上海大世界》……改革开放的浪潮汹涌澎湃，上海正在经历新一轮的城市改造，抚今追昔，不是回光返照，也不是怀旧情结，而正是一种新的上海抒情。"

建筑简介：复兴西路147号

柯灵旧居位于复兴西路147号，为三层公寓住宅，建于1933年，占地面积1260平方米。建筑为西班牙风格，立面富有变化，室外楼梯到达二层。红瓦多坡顶，烟囱突出于屋面，檐下有齿形饰带。门和窗户的形式多样，窗间有绞绳状柱，黄色水泥拉毛外墙。此处还居住过董竹君、上官云珠、陈同生、刘连波、廖沫沙、白薇、陈子展、钟南夫等革命老干部和知名人士。2016年2月6日，柯灵旧居正式对外开放，展示了大量柯灵的书信、手稿和日常生活用品，并恢复了楼内原有的一座仅容一人通过的小型旋转楼梯，楼上复原了大书房、卧室、厨卫等。

KE Ling

KE Ling (1909–2000) has his ancestral family from Shaoxing in Zhejiang province. Born in Guangzhou, he had a former name of GAO Jilin and known as writer, playwright and literary theorist. In 1926 he began to have works published. In succession he served as publicity director of Shanghai Star Film Company, editor-in-chief of the magazine *Wanxiang*, editor-in-chief of *The Weekly*, vice president and deputy editor-in-chief of *Wenhui Newspaper*, director of Shanghai Film Art Institute, director of Shanghai Film Art Research Institute, editor-in-chief of *Popular Film*, vice president of Shanghai Writers Association, vice president of Shanghai Film Association, and chairman of International PEN Shanghai Center. He published some 30 kinds of prose and essay collections, including *Records of Literary Garden Stroll*, *Select Edition of Prose by KE Ling*, *Tattler about Daily Life*, *The Literary Mind and the Carving of Insects*, *Collection of Essays by KE Ling* and *Anthology of Essays for Sixty Years by KE Ling*; collections of children's literature including *Moon Girl* and *The Story of the Butterfly*; collections of stories such as *Collection of Sketches, Companion*; critical essay collections such as *Collected Writings of Movie Literature*, and *Radom Records at Theatre*; film literature scripts including *WU Zetian*, *Corrosion*, *Biography of Qiujin*, *Spring Reigns Everywhere*, *For Peace* and *City without Night*; and drama scripts including *Gone with the Wind*, *Nightclub* and *The Sea of Hatred*.

Discerning Eyes Finding Talents

In 1943, KE Ling took over the editor of the magazine *Wanxiang*. After two months of planning, it took on a new look from the content to form in the July issue. One day when he was soliciting contributions for the September issue, he came across a novel *The Horse Thief*. The novel started with suspense at the beginning and the ending was surprising. Previously, most of the works he edited and published were from well-known writers, but this one had a signature of SHEN Ji, who should be a new person. He appreciated it very much, but he made a second thought—whether this was the author's accidental work? Then he wrote to the author to ask for a few more and encouraged him to do more experiments with narrative methods. So the author tried to use new methods to tell stories and sent to him two novels including *Revenge of the Tampered* and *The Toughness and Intrepidity of the Marsh*. The former was about the encounters of the Beijing opera artists and the latter had the theme of stealing dead bodies.

柯灵（左）和钱锺书
KE Ling (left) and QIAN Zhongshu.

After reading, KE greatly applauded and immediately decided to publish them in three consecutive issues in September, October and December. This was unique in the history of the magazine, but he still made a recommendation in the postscript, "Here I would like to introduce *The Horse Thief*. A careful reading will help find the author has his own fresh style. Mr. SHEN Ji is a new writer in the field of creation, which also deserves the attention of readers." With his guide and support, SHEN entered the literary world and another nameless newcomer became a famous writer. Later, he became an expert in writing about the old Shanghai.

Time moved on to the 1990s when SHEN finished the writing of another novel *Shanghai Tycoon*, which was serialized in *Xinmin Evening News*. It reflected the life experience of HUANG Jinrong in the old time of Shanghai and attracted great responses. Soon Shanghai held a special session of the cultural system, and KE and SHEN attended it on invitation. At the meeting WANG Daohan, mayor of Shanghai at that time, talked about the translation and publication of the book *Shanghai* written by a British, and asked why we Chinese people couldn't write about the themes of the old time of Shanghai.

After that, KE said that Hardoon was a successful foreigner engaged in real estate business in China and recommended that SHEN was proficient in writing on this theme. Later SHEN lived up to his expectations and soon his novel *Foreign Managers General in Shanghai* was serialized in the *Liberation Daily*. His father was acquainted at that time with HUANG Chujiu, founder of the Great World in Shanghai, and was one of his friends. For that, he started the creation of a novel with high proficiency to write about the biography of HUANG Chujiu, i.e. *The Great World in Shanghai*.

These three novels became the representative works of SHEN Ji. When the Xuelin Press published this "old Shanghai culture series" in a collection, KE Ling did not forget to write for SHEN, his student and later his confidant and old friend, a preface, which reads, "Many writers turned around and began to create embroidered images for the past ten miles of luxury... SHEN Ji finished the *Shanghai Tycoon, Foreign Managers General in Shanghai* and *The Great World in Shanghai*... The waves of reform and opening up are surging, and Shanghai is experiencing a new round of urban transformation. Recalling the past in the light of the present does not mean the last radiance of the setting sun, nor does it mean a complex of nostalgia. It is a new style of lyrics about Shanghai."

The former residence of KE Ling is situated at No. 147 on West Fuxing Road. Built in 1933, it covers an area of 1,260 square meters. It is a three-storied apartment with the stylistic characteristics of Spanish architecture, whose facade is full of changes. Its outdoor stairs reach the second floor. It has a roof with multiple slopes covered with red tiles with chimney protruding from the roof and tooth-shaped ribbons under the eaves. Doors and windows are in various forms with rope-like columns between the windows. It has exterior walls napped with stucco veneer. During that period of time, the house had neighbors of quite a few elderly revolutionary leaders and well-known public figures, including DONG Zhujun, SHANGGUAN Yunzhu, CHEN Tongsheng, LIU Lianbo, LIAO Mosha, BAI Wei, CHEN Zizhan and ZHONG Nanfu. On February 6, 2016, the former residence of KE Ling was officially opened to the public. In it are shown a large number of his letters, manuscripts and daily necessities. In addition the original small rotating staircase accommodating only one person in the building was restored. Moreover, the big study, bedroom and kitchen were also restored upstairs.

柯灵 （忻秉勇画）　　KE Ling （By XIN Bingyong）

洪念祖
（1902—1990）

江苏江阴人，字博平，工商业人士。17 岁至上海学做生意，先后在义生昌、和昌盛、鸿裕等厂任职。鸿裕并入大中华橡胶厂后，他深得经理薛福基的器重和信任，被提为营业科长。1937 年，日军侵沪，薛福基遇难身故，洪念祖受命为副经理。1946 年以后，被推举为上海橡胶同业公会联合会理事长、全国橡胶同业公会联合会理事长、全国工业会理事、上海工业会常务理事、上海商会理事、上海机制国货工会联合会常务理事等职。中华人民共和国成立后，历任全国工商联执行委员、上海市工商联常务委员、民建上海市委员会执行委员和第六届副主任级顾问、上海市政协委员、上海市政协常委以及上海市人大代表等。

“双钱”力斗“邓禄普”

1926 年，中国第一家橡胶厂——大中华橡胶厂，在上海徐家汇诞生。

关于商标，厂创办人对有人提出的百吉、万年青等设想，都不甚满意。一天，创办人之一的吴哲生在苏州街上看到有人挑抬着箱橱盆桶等嫁妆，上面粘贴着用红纸剪成的“双钱”图形，不由灵机一动。他回来提出用“双钱”做商标，得到大家的赞同。1929 年，“双钱”牌商标注册成功，自此它随着中国橡胶工业经风雨，创辉煌。

这时，大中华橡胶厂来了位年轻人，他叫洪念祖。当大中华总经理薛福基得知洪念祖曾在原鸿裕边带厂当过营业科长和副经理时，把他请进了办公室。薛福基问：“来到我们厂，你有什么想法？”洪念祖直言道：“我认为，品牌宣传非常重要。大中华建立不久，‘双钱’牌刚刚创立，我们要动脑筋，让全国知道‘双钱’。”薛总微微点点头，继续问：“那你有什么建议？”“我们可以把大中华生产经营概况拍成影片到各地放映，让国人知道‘双钱’产品经久耐用，货真价实。另外，上海设立门市部的同时，在外埠要开办批零兼营的发行所。”薛总满意地说：“好，厂部已决定，提升你为大中华的营业科长。”

洪念祖走马上任。果然，宣传广告做向全国，同时，销售紧紧跟上，很快“双钱”橡胶制品走俏于各地城乡。

1934 年，大中华的“双钱”牌人力车胎一问世，就遭到英国邓禄普公司的强烈排挤和倾轧。面对一触即发的商战，洪念祖提出，要打败“邓禄普”，首先要提高我们产品的质量，所以，面料要精选，做到胎面厚、花纹深。针对“邓禄普”的保用期 8 个月，“双钱”延长至 10 个月。接着，洪念祖推出分期付款的方式，主动上门与同昌、得利、大兴、润大、泰昌等车行搞联销。与此同时，他拿出了自己的私房钱，购买了 10 辆人力车，装上“双钱”牌车胎，请车行以低价租给人力车夫，允许分期付款，还可赊账。这 10 辆车就此成了活广告，行驶在上海街头。

就这样，“双钱”日益深入人心，用今天的话说，它以自己的性价比的优势，击退了英商“邓禄普”的倾轧。

今天，当“双钱”作为中国的驰名商标继续散发出耀眼的光彩时，我们不应忘记曾为创立这个中国民族品牌付出毕生心血的前辈们。

建筑简介：五原路212弄10号

洪念祖旧居位于五原路212弄10号。五原路212弄大华新村，新式里弄，1947年建造，共有17幢，占地面积5420平方米，总建筑面积7226平方米。建筑略具现代派风貌，三层砖混结构。平屋顶四周设置女儿墙，立面简洁，极少装饰。南部二层设有悬挑的阳台，下部为底层门廊。素色水泥砂浆外墙面均布钢窗，窗裙板仅以网格细槽略作装饰。楼内布局紧凑，功能齐备，原用锅炉水汀供暖。在大华新村居住过的社会各界名人，有国民党将领张发奎、大新公司创始人蔡昌、画家汪观清、指挥家陈传熙、歌唱家周碧珍等。

HONG Nianzu

HONG Nianzu (1902–1990) has his ancestral family from Jiangyin in Jiangsu province. With a courtesy name of Boping, he is known as a businessman. At the age of 17, he went to Shanghai to learn how to do business and successively worked in plants such as Yishengchang, Hechangsheng, Hongyu and so on. After the merging of Hongyu Plant into the Greater China Rubber Factory, he was promoted to chief of the Business Section because he was highly regarded and trusted by his manager XUE Fuji. In 1937 when the Japanese army invaded Shanghai, he was appointed as deputy manager after the death of XUE Fuji because of disaster. After 1946, he was elected as president of Shanghai Rubber Industry Federation, president of National Rubber Industry Federation, director of National Industrial Associations, standing director of Shanghai Industrial Associations, director of Shanghai Chamber of Commerce, standing director of Shanghai Machinery Manufacturing National Product Union and some other positions. After the founding of the People's Republic of China, he successively held the posts of executive member of All-China Federation of Industry and Commerce, standing committee member of Shanghai Federation of Industry and Commerce, executive member of Shanghai Committee of China Democratic National Construction Association and its sixth deputy director consultant, member and standing committee member of Shanghai People's Political Consultative Committee, a deputy to Shanghai Municipal People's Congress and so on.

"Double Coins" against "Dunlop"

In 1926, China's first rubber factory called the Greater China Rubber Factory came into being in Xujiahui district in Shanghai.

As for its trademarks, some people proposed using Baiji or Evergreen, but the founders of the factory were not quite satisfied with them. One day, WU Zhesheng, one of the founders, saw some people carrying cases, pots and other dowry pasted with the "Double Coins" graphics cut from red paper on Suzhou Street. This aroused his inspiration. He came back with his proposal of "Double Coins" as their trademark and won the approval of all. In 1929, the trademark of "Double Coins" was registered. Since then, it had gone through thick and thin together with the development of the Rubber Industry in China and gained eye-catching achievements.

At this time, a young man called HONG Nianzu came to the Greater China Rubber Factory. When XUE Fuji, the general manager, got to know that he was once chief of the Business Section and deputy manager of Hongyu plant, he invited him into his

在徐家汇绿地保留的原大中华橡胶厂烟囱
The chimney of the Greater China Rubber Factory preserved on the grassland in Xujiahui district.

office and asked, "Do you have any idea of our plant?" HONG bluntly answered, "In my opinion, the publicity of brand is very important. Since both our factory of the Greater China, and our brand of 'Double Coins' were established for a short time, we should rack our brains to make the brand well-known nationwide." Manager XUE nodded slightly and continued his question, "Do you have some suggestions?" HONG replied, "We can produce a film of our production and operation and put it on across the country, and in this way people will know that 'Double Coins' products are durable in use, genuine in quality and low in price. In addition, we can set up sales outlets in Shanghai as well as in other provinces for both wholesale and retail business." The manger said with satisfaction, "Well, you are employed as chief of the Business Section of the Greater China by our factory authorities."

He took office. It was not surprising that advertisements were distributed across the whole nation and the sales grew up in the meantime. Before long "Double Coins" rubber products became popular in both urban and rural areas.

In 1934, immediately after the "Double Coins" tires for rickshaw came out from the Greater China Rubbery Plant, they were squeezed by the British Dunlop Tires Ltd. Facing the business war which might be triggered at any moment, HONG proposed that they must first improve the quality of their products in order to defeat their competitor "Dunlop", so they should select fabric materials carefully, and guarantee thick tread and deep pattern. For the 8-month warranty period of "Dunlop" tires, they extended the warranty period of "Double Coins" tires to 10 months. Then he carried out the way of installment and took the initiative to invite such rickshaw dealers as Tongchang, Deli, Daxing, Runda, Taichang and others to engage in joint sales. At the same time, he spent his private savings buying ten rickshaws and equipped them with their "Double Coins" tires. Moreover, he asked the dealers to rent their rickshaws to the rickshaw pullers at low prices. The rickshaw pullers were even allowed to pay by installment or on credit. These ten rickshaws thus became mobile advertisements in the streets of Shanghai.

In this way, the "Double Coins" tires were increasingly deeply rooted in the public. In today's buzzwords, the advantage of its performance-price ratio helped them defeat the British Dunlop Tires.

Today, as a well-known trademark in China, the "Double Coins" tires continue to yield unusually brilliant results. These pioneering businessmen who made life-time contributions to the national brand shall never be forgotten.

The former residence of HONG Nianzu is located at No.10 in Alley 212 on Wuyuan Road, which is New Dahua Village, a new-style alley. Built in 1947, it has a total of 17 buildings, covering an area of 5,420 square meters with a total construction area of 7,226 square meters. With a little bit of modern style, it has three stories of mixed structure of brick and cement. Around the flat roof are constructed parapets with a concise facade of few decorations. On the second floor of the south, there are cantilevered balconies under which is the ground floor porch. The exterior walls coated with plain cement mortar are evenly covered by steel windows and window skirts are only slightly decorated with grids of thin grooves. The layout in the building is compact with all functions available, which was originally heated with steam from water boiler. New Dahua Village once accommodated celebrities from various circles of the society, including the KMT general ZHANG Fakui; CAI Chang, founder of Daxin Company; painter WANG Guanqing; conductor CHEN Chuanxi and singer ZHOU Bizhen.

洪念祖 （钱定华画）

HONG Nianzu （By QIAN Dinghua）

胡蝶
（1908—1989）

祖籍广东鹤山，出生于上海，原名胡瑞华，中国早期女演员，有影后之称。幼年随父迁居天津、北平等地。16岁回到上海，参加中华电影学校演员训练班。结业后，先后进入大中华、天一、明星等影片公司，出演了《白云塔》《火烧红莲寺》《啼笑因缘》等影片。1931年主演中国第一部有声电影《歌女红牡丹》，轰动全国。1933年在《明星日报》发起的“电影皇后”评选中，以最高票数当选。曾主演《狂流》《脂粉市场》等左翼影片。在《姊妹花》中兼饰一对性格迥异的孪生姐妹，此片成为中国电影的经典之作。1959年，在香港、台湾等地主演《街童》《两个女性》《后门》等影片。1975年移居加拿大。1989年病逝于温哥华。曾获第七届亚洲电影节最佳女主角奖、中国电影世纪奖。著有《胡蝶回忆录》。

让中国电影“开口说话”

胡蝶在20世纪30年代的上海滩可谓红极一时，她脸上那对招牌式的酒窝成了美女的重要标志，而身上穿的旗袍、戴的首饰，都成为大众模仿的对象。胡蝶从影40余年，经历了中国电影从默片到有声片的时代，她为中国电影史写下了浓重的一笔。

1925年，胡蝶首次出演电影《战功》。很快，她就在电影《秋扇怨》中第一次担纲主演。她的素质和才华得到著名导演郑正秋、张石川等人的赏识。1928年，胡蝶正式加入明星电影公司。郑正秋、张石川不仅重用她主演公司着力推出的电影，甚至还请人专为她写剧本。在郑正秋编剧、张石川导演的影片《白云塔》里，胡蝶首次与阮玲玉合作，两人演得都很精彩，影片受到观众的一致称赞。接着，根据武侠小说《江湖奇侠传》改编而成的系列武侠片《火烧红莲寺》搬上银幕，胡蝶一改大家闺秀戏路，饰演侠女“红姑”，大获成功。从1928年到1931年，胡蝶一口气出演了《火烧红莲寺》18集中的17集。

这时，有声片诞生的时机成熟了。1931年，由洪深编剧、张石川导演的我国第一部蜡盘发音的故事片完成，它就是《歌女红牡丹》。胡蝶领衔主演，成为“中国电影首位发声者”。之所以选胡蝶主演，除了她当时具备极高的知名度与影响力，还与她具备旁人难比的语言优势有关。胡蝶幼年曾随父亲奔波于京奉线上，此外，她的“姥姥”是个北京旗人，多年来一直跟她同住。所以由默片进入有声片的时候，胡蝶有得天独厚的优势。因为当时电影演员以广东人居多，很多一线明星还不太会讲国语。

《歌女红牡丹》由“明星”公司和“百代”唱片公司合作摄制，耗资达12万元，费时6个月之久。在收音的试验过程中接连失败，第五次才成功，一共制成18张蜡盘。因胡蝶擅唱京剧，影片还穿插《穆柯寨》《玉堂春》《四郎探母》《拿高登》四个京剧片断，使观众第一次从银幕上听到戏曲的唱白。

1931年3月15日，《歌女红牡丹》在上海新光大戏院公映。明星公司专为该片制作了由周剑云编辑的《中国第一部有声影片——歌女红牡丹》特刊。该片公映后，不仅轰动全国，同时也吸引了南洋的侨胞。东南亚的影片公司以高价购买电影在南洋各地的上映权，一时传为美谈。自此，中国电影开始进入有声时代。

建筑简介：新乐路100弄29号

胡蝶旧居位于新乐路（原名亨利路）100 弄的永利村 29 号。建于 1938 年，单面行列式布置 44 幢，总建筑面积 8902 平方米，属新式里弄，砖木混合结构，三层，两幢连体，平面方形，立面对称，中间以一竖墙分隔，无阳台，相邻两个号码的主入口均设有方形雨厦。沿街住宅以褐色毛面砖贴墙，作竖直隔离装饰之用。弄堂主入口三层通高壁柱直达檐口。缓坡屋顶，挑檐较小，方窗，水泥砂浆外墙。永利村素有“影人村”之称，20 世纪二三十年代，张织云、高占非、高倩苹等众多著名影人云集于此。

HU Die

HU Die (1908–1989) has her ancestral family from Heshan in Guangdong province. Born in Shanghai, she has a former name of HU Ruihua. As an actress in the initial period of China's film industry, she enjoyed the reputation of the Queen of Movie. During her childhood she moved to Tianjin, Beijing and other places with her father. When she was 16 years old, she returned to Shanghai to participate in the actor training courses organized by the Chinese Film School. After graduation, she successively joined such film companies as Greater China, Tianyi, Star and so on. The films she starred in included *The White-Cloud Pagoda*, *The Burning of Red Lotus Temple*, and *Between Tears and Laughter* and so on. She caught nationwide attention for the first Chinese sound film named *Sing-song Girl Red Peony*, a film in which she starred in 1931. In 1933, she was elected as Queen of Movie by winning the most votes in the campaign launched by the newspaper *Star Daily*. She also starred in *Raging Waves*, *Powder Market* and other left-wing films. In the film *Twin Sisters*, she performed both roles of twin sisters with different personalities, which became a masterpiece in the film industry of China. In 1959, she starred in *Street Boys*, *My Daughter*, *Rear Entrance* and other films in Hong Kong, Taiwan and other places. In 1975, she migrated to Canada and passed away in Vancouver in 1989. She won the award of Best Actress in the Seventh Asian Film Festival and the Chinese Film Century Award. She authored a book *HU Die's Memoir*.

Making the Chinese Films Heard

HU Die was well-known for a time among the public in Shanghai in the 1930s. Her typical dimples had been a marker of beauty ever since and the cheong-sam and jewelry she wore had become popular among the public. Engaged in the film industry for over 40 years, she left a deep imprint in the history of Chinese film, experiencing the transformation of Chinese films from silent ones to sound ones.

In 1925, she made her debut in the film *Feats*. Before long in the film *Autumn Fan Complaints* she starred in, her talents and performance were appreciated by such famous directors as ZHENG Zhengqiu, ZHANG Shichuan and others. In 1928, HU Die officially joined the Star Film Company. Both directors not only invited her to star in the films her company prioritized, but also invited people

胡蝶和潘有声结婚照
A wedding photo of HU Die and PAN Yousheng.

to write scripts especially for her. In the film *The White-Cloud Pagoda*, in which ZHENG Zhengqiu was the scriptwriter and ZHANG Shichuan was the director, she cooperated with RUAN Lingyu for the first time. Both of them received unanimous praise from the audience for their excellent performance. Later, the TV series *The Burning of Red Lotus Temple*, adapted from the martial arts novel entitled *Strange Swordsmen*, were brought to the screen. In this film, she succeeded in playing the role of Honggu and transforming her usual film role of a lady. From 1928 to 1931, she performed in 17 of the total 18 episodes in the TV series of *The Burning of Red Lotus Temple*.

At that time, the opportunity for the birth of the sound films was mature. In 1931, the first wax disc pronunciation feature film *Sing-Song Girl Red Peony* was completed, whose scriptwriter and director were HONG Shen and ZHANG Shichuan respectively. She played a leading role in it and became "the first film vocalist in China". The reason why she was chosen to play the leading role was not just her fame and influence, but also her unrivalled command of language. In her infancy, she had to move along the Beijing-Shenyang Railway together with her father. Moreover, her grandmother, a Manchu living in Beijing, had lived with her for several years. Therefore, she got the opportunity easily when the silent films were on the way of transformation into the sound ones, since most of the film stars at that time were Cantonese and a large number of the leading stars were unable to speak Mandarin well.

The film *Sing-song Girl Red Peony* was shot by the Star Company in cooperation with EMI Record Company at the cost of 120 thousand yuan. The production of the film lasted for 6 months. In the experimental reception process, they failed several times before their fifth try. It consisted of 18 wax discs in total. Since HU Die did well in performing Beijing Opera, the film was also interspersed with four fragments of Beijing Opera, namely, *Muke Village*, *Yutangchun*, *YANG Silang's Visit to His Mother* and *Catching Gaodeng*, which enabled the audience to hear a rap of opera from the film for the first time.

On March 15, 1931, *Sing-song Girl Red Peony* had its premiere in Shanghai Xinguang Theater. The Star Company published a special issue named *Sing-song Girl Red Peony—China's First Sound Film*, which was edited by ZHOU Jianyun. After the release of this film, it not only had great influence nationwide, but also attracted the overseas Chinese in Southeast Asia. The film companies in Southeast Asia purchased its copyright at a high price to release this film there, which was spread as a nice tale at that time. Since then Chinese film started to enter its Sound Age.

The former residence of HU Die is located at No. 29 in Yongli Village in Alley 100 on Xinle Road (formerly Henry Road), which was built in 1938. As a new style alley, it has a one-sided layout of rows with 44 buildings with a total construction area of 8,902 square meters. The buildings have a mixed structure of brick and wood. Each having three stories, two buildings are connected. The horizontal plane is a square while the longitudinal one is symmetrical. The middle has a vertical wall to separate the two buildings, which have no balcony. The main entrances of two adjacent numbers are equipped with a square canopy. Residences along the street have walls with brown napped bricks for the purpose of decoration and vertical separation. The main entrance of the alley has high pilasters with a height of three stories reaching directly to cornices. The roof has gentle slopes with smaller eaves. Windows are square and exterior walls have cement mortar. The Yongli Village is known as the "Filmmakers Village". In the 1920s and 1930s, ZHANG Zhiyun, GAO Zhanfei, GAO Qianping and many other people of film performance gathered here.

胡蝶 （钱定华画）　　HU Die （By QIAN Dinghua）

草婴
（1923—2015）

浙江宁波人，原名盛峻峰，翻译家。1937 年随家人迁居上海。1941 年起，先后为《时代》《苏联文艺》《时代日报》译稿。中华人民共和国成立后，开始翻译俄国和苏联文艺作品。曾任中国翻译协会副会长、上海翻译家协会会长。主要译作有肖洛霍夫的小说《被开垦的处女地》《顿河故事》《一个人的遭遇》，莱蒙托夫的《当代英雄》，巴甫连柯的《幸福》等。经 20 年努力，于 1997 年翻译完成《托尔斯泰小说全集》12 卷，成为以一己之力，把托尔斯泰全部小说直接从俄文翻译成他国语言的第一人。1987 年获苏联"高尔基文学奖"。2006 年获俄罗斯"马克西姆·高尔基奖章"。2002 年被中国翻译协会授予"资深翻译家"荣誉称号。2014 年获上海文学艺术奖终身成就奖。

把托尔斯泰带给中国

1941 年，草婴开始为《时代》周刊译稿。1942 年，时代出版社出版《苏联文艺》月刊，第二期上刊出了草婴翻译文学作品的处女作——普拉东诺夫的短篇小说《老人》。草婴原名盛峻峰，当要发表这篇译作时，白居易的诗作"离离原上草，一岁一枯荣。野火烧不尽，春风吹又生……"涌上心头。他想，小草是渺小的，容易被人践踏，也容易被火烧掉，但是春风一吹，又重新恢复生命力。他觉得人应该有这样的精神，不屈服于任何压力。于是他用"草婴"作为自己的笔名。想不到，一用竟用了一生。

1977 年，上海筹办上海译文出版社。那天，市委宣传部的领导来到草婴家里，请他出任总编辑。他婉言谢绝了。原来草婴此刻已立下宏愿：要把托尔斯泰的全部小说翻译出来。他清醒地知道，此项工程浩大，翻译量多达 400 万字。草婴说，能当社长、总编辑的人肯定不少，但能搞翻译的，他就比较合适。于是，他把自己的想法与组织上说了，领导们最后答应了他的请求。就这样，草婴以一己之力，把托尔斯泰全部小说翻译成中文的重大工程开始了。

草婴每天早晨 6 点半起床，早饭后，进入书房开始工作。亲朋好友来访，他只是坐一会儿，就说："对不起，我要上班了。"他的长女不幸患上癌症，卧室与草婴的书房仅一步之遥。一边是女儿痛苦的呻吟声，一边是父亲笔头的沙沙声。老年丧女，草婴忍受了煎熬，但挺住了。他说，不能因为女儿影响工作，否则，就是"双重损失"，因为正在翻译中的《托尔斯泰小说全集》是他生命中的另一个孩子！

1997 年，历经整整 20 年，12 卷的《托尔斯泰小说全集》翻译完了。其中包括三部长篇小说：《战争与和平》《安娜·卡列尼娜》《复活》；四部中短篇小说：《一个地主的早晨》《哥萨克》《克鲁采奏鸣曲》《哈吉·穆拉特》；一部自传体小说《童年·少年·青年》。

2004 年，上海文艺出版社出版了这部全集的简体字版；2011 年，中国出版集团现代出版社出版了彩色插图本。

建筑简介：复兴西路34号

草婴旧居位于复兴西路 34 号卫乐公寓，原名卫乐精舍，建于 1934 年，赉安洋行设计，占地面积 1720 平方米，建筑面积 3797 平方米，汽车间附屋 802 平方米，属现代点式建筑风格的公寓住宅。建筑为十三层钢筋混凝土结构，两翼跌落一层，立面对称，竖三段布置，中间凸出，设一串挑出的半圆阳台为构图中心，两边为卧入式阳台形成竖向线条。水泥砂浆外墙，立面中部竖线条及突出的半圆阳台为暗红色粉刷，其余部分为浅黄色粉刷，山墙顶部及南侧有重复线条装饰，楼前有小花园。中华人民共和国成立后，吕蒙与黄准夫妇、陈鲤庭、吴强、赖少其、峻青、王西彦等一批文化人在此居住。1994 年 2 月 15 日上海市人民政府公布其为市优秀历史建筑。

CAO Ying

CAO Ying (1923–2015) has his ancestral family from Ningbo in Zhejiang province. He had a former name of SHENG Junfeng and was known as a translator. In 1937, he moved with his family to Shanghai. Since 1941, he translated successively for such journals as *Time*, *Soviet Literature and Arts* and *Time Daily*. After the founding of the New China, he began to translate Russian and Soviet literary and artistic works. Once he served as vice president of Translators Association of China and president of Translators Association of Shanghai. His main translations include such novels as *Virgin Soil Upturned*, *Tales from the Don* and *The Fate of a Man* by Mikhail Sholokhov, *A Hero of Our Time* by Mikhail Lermontov and *Happiness* by Pyotr Pavlenko. After efforts for 20 years, he completed the translation of *Complete Works of Tolstoy* (12 volumes) in 1997. In this case he became the first person to have translated all of Tolstoy's novels directly from Russian into another language only on the basis of his own efforts. In 1987, he won the Soviet "Gorky Literature Award". In 2006, he won Russian "Maxim Gorky Medal". In 2002, he won the honorary title of "senior translator" awarded by Translators Association of China. In 2014, he won Shanghai Literature and Art Award for Lifetime Achievement.

Bringing Tolstoy to China

In 1941, CAO Ying began his translation for the weekly *Time*. In 1942, the Time Press published the monthly magazine *Soviet Literature and Art*. The second issue published his first translation of literary works—Platonov's short story *An Old Man*. His original name was SHENG Junfeng, but when he was about to publish this translation, a poem of BAI Juyi came across his mind: "Luxuriant is the grass upon the plain, / That each year dies to flourish again. / Not even a prairie fire can destroy the grass,/ It grows again when the spring breeze blows…" He thought that the small grass was insignificant, easy to be trampled and also easy to be burned off. Once the spring breeze arrived, it regained its vitality again. He felt that one should be equipped with such a spirit of never yielding to

草婴在进行翻译工作
CAO Ying at his work of translation.

any pressure. So he used CAO Ying as his pen name. Unexpectedly, a first use should last for a lifetime.

In 1977, preparations were made in Shanghai in order to organize Shanghai Translation Publishing House. One day, a leader of the Municipal Publicity Department came to his home to invite him to serve as chief editor, he declined politely. It turned out to be the fact that at the moment he had made a magnificent decision to translate all of Tolstoy's novels. He was aware that the project was huge since the translation amounted up to 4 million words. He said that there should be a lot more persons who could be found for president and chief editor, but as far as translation was concerned, he was more appropriate. So he expressed his ideas to the leaders and they finally agreed to his request. In this way, he singlehandedly initiated the huge project to translate all the novels by Tolstoy into Chinese.

Every morning he got up at 6:30. After breakfast, he went into the study to begin his work. When friends came for a visit, he just sat for a while and then said: "Sorry, I want to go to work." His eldest daughter unfortunately suffered from cancer, and her bedroom was only one step away from his study. At one side were the painful groans of his daughter; at the other side was the rustling of the pen of the father. In his old age he lost his daughter and endured sufferings, but he held on. He said that he should not lose both daughter and work. Otherwise, he would suffer from "double losses", because translation of the *Complete Works of Tolstoy* was another child in his life!

In 1997, after full 20 years, the translation of 12 volumes of *Complete Works of Tolstoy* was finished. It included three novels: *War and Peace*, *Anna Karenina* and *Resurrection;* four medium-length novels and short stories: *A Landlord's Morning*, *The Cossacks* and *The Kreutzer Sonata* and *Haji Mulla*; and an autobiographical novel *Childhood, Boyhood, and Youth.*

In 2004, Shanghai Literature and Art Publishing House published one version of simplified Chinese characters of the complete works. In 2011, Modern Publishing House of China Publishing Group published a version of full-color illustrations.

The former residence of CAO Ying is located in Willow Apartment at No. 34 on Fuxing Road. Formerly known as Willow Court, it was designed by Leonard-Veysseyre-Kruze Architects and built in 1934, which covers an area of 1,720 square meters with a construction area of 3,797 square meters and attached rooms of 802 square meters for garage. It is an apartment of point construction and modern architectural style. The building has thirteen floors of a reinforced concrete structure with both sides one floor lower. Its front is symmetrical and has three vertical sections. The middle section protrudes with a series of semi-circular balconies for its center of composition. On both sides are receded balconies to form vertical lines. Exterior walls have cement mortar. In the middle, the vertical lines and protruded semi-circular balconies are painted dark red and the rest is painted light yellow. Both the gable top and the south side have parallel lines for decoration. There is a small garden in front of the building. After the liberation, quite a number of cultural people lived here. On February 15, 1994, it became a Heritage Architecture issued by the Shanghai Municipal People's Government.

草婴 （钱定华画）

CAO Ying （By QIAN Dinghua）

贺子珍
（1909—1984）

江西永新人，原名桂圆，又名自珍。1925年加入中国共产主义青年团，1926年加入中国共产党。曾任中共永新县委负责人之一、共青团永新县委书记、妇女协会组织部长。1927年参加组织永新农民武装暴动后上井冈山，参加创建井冈山革命根据地。1928年在中共湘赣边界特委和红四军前委机关工作。1934年随红一方面军参加长征。1937年冬去苏联治病和学习。1947年8月回国。中华人民共和国成立后曾在杭州市妇联工作，后调中共上海市委组织部工作。1979年当选全国政协委员。1984年4月19日在上海病逝。

当选全国政协委员

1979年6月，全国政协第五届二次会议在北京召开。会议上，贺子珍昔日的战友向党中央与全国政协提议：鉴于贺子珍为参加革命最早，并曾参加井冈山武装斗争的女红军战士，具有代表性与影响力，建议增补她为全国政协委员。提议得到采纳。

6月10日，上海市委书记王一平到医院看望贺子珍，向她传递喜讯。贺子珍眼含热泪，喜悦地说："我的心情太激动了，感谢党和国家，没想到组织上还记得我！"

市委招待处的人员向她献花，病床边花瓶里的艳丽芬芳，映衬着贺子珍微笑的脸庞。王一平对她说："贺大姐，一会儿上级就要派人来为你拍照了，照片要同这个消息一起刊登。"

之后，护士见她难得如此欣慰，便提议推着她到花园里看看。"好！好！"贺子珍连声说。她坐在轮椅上，沿医院南楼的小道至后花园绕行几圈，因为心境的豁然开朗，花园里绽放的鲜花在她眼里仿佛有了前所未有的色彩，一扫往日的阴霾。她对众人说："我们拍几张照片吧！"

她的信心与斗志被激发了，对医护人员说："我还要工作，要为四个现代化出力。你们要帮助我恢复健康，我也要同你们一起努力把身体搞好。"为使瘫痪的左腿复健，她每天中午、傍晚都在护士搀扶下进行艰难无比的行走，虽步履蹒跚、汗如雨下，但她咬牙坚持着，配合着每一次针灸与理疗，信念使她对此甘之如饴。

在刊登贺子珍当选政协委员消息的报纸上，附带了一张照片，照片里贺子珍平和慈祥地坐在轮椅上浏览画报，如沐春风。

贺子珍旧居位于湖南路262号湖南别墅。别墅建于1931年，为欧洲独立式花园住宅，原是英商锦隆洋行大股东的住宅，初名锦隆别墅。1943年周佛海居住后改名湖南别墅。占地面积4000平方米，建筑面积1167平方米，为假三层混合结构，南立面底层设通长的水平红瓦坡檐，二层为双柱敞廊，三层人字檐下有拱式石柱窗。山墙双坡檐在顶部折为四坡水平檐口，人字形山墙，歇山式屋顶。墙角、窗间壁柱等以不规则石块砌筑。平拱木门窗，白色水泥墙面。楼前有花园。上海解放后，陈毅、邓小平等领导先后在此短暂居住。自1954年起，贺子珍在这座花园住宅中一住就是30年，直到1984年去世。现为市政府机关使用。1999年9月23日上海市人民政府公布其为市优秀历史建筑。

HE Zizhen

HE Zizhen (1909–1984) has her ancestral family from Yongxin in Jiangxi province, with a former name of Guiyuan and another name Zizhen. In 1925, she joined the Communist Youth League of China, and joined Communist Party of China in the following year. She once served as one of the heads of Yongxin Committee of the Communist Party of China, secretary of the Yongxin Committee of the Communist Youth League as well as director of Organization Department of Yongxin County Women Association. The year 1927 witnessed her involvement in organizing the armed riot in Yongxin, after which she went to Jinggangshan where she participated in the establishment of the Jinggangshan Revolutionary Base. In 1928, she worked in the Hunan-Jiangxi Boundary Special Committee of the Communist Party of China and the Frontline Committee of the Fourth Branch of the Red Army. In 1934, she took part in the Long March with the First Branch of the Red Army. In the winter of 1937, she went to the Soviet Union for treatment and further study, and she returned to China in August, 1947. After the founding of the People's Republic of China, she worked in Hangzhou Municipal Women's Federation, and later transferred to work in the Organization Department of CPC Shanghai Committee. In 1979, she was elected as member of the CPPCC. On April 19, 1984, she departed of illness in Shanghai.

Her Election as Member of CPPCC

In June, 1979, the Second Session of the Fifth CPPCC National Committee was held in Beijing. At the meeting, the former comrade-in-arms of HE Zizhen put forward a proposal to the CPC Central Committee and the CPPCC National Committee that she should be added as member of the CPPCC National Committee, due to her representativeness and influence in view of the fact that she was one of the pioneer female Red Army soldiers participating in the revolution and also taking part in the armed struggle in Jinggangshan. Finally, the proposal was adopted.

井冈山雕塑园贺子珍塑像
The statue of HE Zizhen in the statue garden at Jinggangshan.

On June 10, WANG Yiping, secretary of Shanghai Municipal Committee, paid a visit to her in the hospital and shared the good news with her. Hearing that, she said with tears in her eyes, "I feel so excited and surprised that the Party still remembers me! Thanks to the Party and the State."

Some workers from Shanghai Municipal Party Committee presented flowers to her. The flowers in the vase were bright and fragrant against her smiling face. WANG Yiping told her, "Sister HE, the leader has already arranged for someone to take photos of you, which will be published together with the news."

Seeing that she was so pleased, which had seldom occurred, the nurses proposed to take her to the garden. "OK! Good idea!" said she repeatedly. Sitting in a wheelchair, she passed along the path of south building to the back garden for a few laps. She felt that the blooming flowers in the garden looked even brighter because the gloom of pessimism dispersed as her hope rekindled. She said to the people around, "Let's have some photos taken!"

With her confidence and morale inspired, she said to health care workers, "I want to work and to contribute to the four modernizations of our country. I hope to recover from illness with your help and I am bound to manage to make it." In order to rehab her paralyzed left leg, she walked with extreme difficulty, faltering and sweating with the support of nurses at every noon and evening. She persisted in the treatment of the acupuncture and physiotherapy and she endured it gladly with strong faith in her mind.

The news that she was elected as a CPPCC member was published in the newspaper. Attached to it was a photo, in which she was sitting in a wheelchair, browsing through pictorials peacefully and agreeably.

The former residence of HE Zizhen is located in Hunan Villa at No. 262 on Hunan Road. Built in 1931, it is an independent residential garden of European style. It was once the residence of the largest shareholder of the British Jinlong Foreign Company. Its original name was Jinlong Villa and was renamed as Hunan Villa after ZHOU Fohai lived here since 1943. A two-storied mixed structure with an interlayer, the building covers an area of 4,000 square meters with a construction area of 1,167 square meters. At the bottom floor of the south are full-length sloping eaves of red tiles; the second floor has a double-column open corridor; the third floor has arch windows with stone pillars under the eaves. The double-slope eaves of the gable fold into four-slope eaves on the top. It has inverted V-shaped cable and nine-ridge roof. The corners and window pillars are of irregular stones. It has arch wooden doors and windows as well as white cement walls. There is a garden in front of the building. After the liberation of Shanghai, CHEN Yi, DENG Xiaoping and other leaders have once lived here for a short time. Since 1954, it has been resided by HE Zizhen, who lived here for 30 years until 1984 when she passed away. The villa is now used by the Shanghai Municipal Government. On September 23, 1999, it became a Heritage Architecture issued by the Shanghai Municipal People's Government.

贺子珍 （杨宏富画） HE Zizhen （By YANG Hongfu）

贺绿汀
（1903—1999）

湖南省邵阳县（今邵东县）人，原名贺楷，作曲家、音乐教育家、音乐理论家，中华人民共和国高等专业音乐教育的奠基人之一。曾参加湖南农民运动和广州起义。1931年考入上海国立音乐专科学校，选修钢琴与和声学。1934年，作品《牧童短笛》和《摇篮曲》分别荣获苏联作曲家齐尔品先生举办的“征求中国风味钢琴曲”比赛一等奖和名誉二等奖。抗战时期创作的《游击队歌》获毛泽东赞誉。中华人民共和国成立后历任上海音乐学院院长，中国音乐家协会副主席、上海分会主席。他一生创作了260余首歌曲，代表作有《天涯歌女》《四季歌》《游击队歌》《嘉陵江上》《牧童短笛》《森吉德玛》《晚会》等，出版译著《和声学理论与实践》、专著《贺绿汀歌曲选》《贺绿汀音乐论文选集》等。1993年贺绿汀90岁寿辰时，江泽民亲笔为贺绿汀题词：“谱写生活的强音，讴歌人民的事业。”

传道授业　润物无声

1958年初，贺绿汀在上海音乐学院做关于群众歌曲创作的专题报告，学生们奔走相告，作曲系、声乐系、进修班的学生都争先恐后地带上纸笔前来聆听院长授课，教室里座无虚席。贺绿汀以略带乡音的语调与学生们交流自己在群众歌曲创作方面的经验与感悟：“创作不是拼盘，而是真情实感的流露。创作者应该有诗人般的热情，对政治、人民生活、自然界的各个方面，都要有敏锐的感受和丰富的幻想。”贺绿汀这堂课足足讲了三个小时，还进行了具体的艺术指导，给作曲系学生戴鹏海留下了深刻的印象。

四年后的一个冬日，已经毕业的戴鹏海和曾在上海音乐学院专修班进修、为《洪湖赤卫队》作曲而荣获首届电影百花奖最佳音乐奖的欧阳谦叔一起来到贺绿汀家中拜访他们崇敬的贺院长。

走进底楼南边的客厅，映入眼帘的首先是钢琴，贺绿汀把这儿辟作了琴房。“贺院长，您也收了学生？”看到摆放在钢琴上的小本子上列满了初级和声题，戴鹏海和欧阳谦叔异口同声地跟他们的老院长打趣。当时教师自带学生已经开禁，然而他们猜错了，贺绿汀淡淡地一笑，答道：“这些习题是我自己每天做练习用的。”这出人意料的回答深深震撼了两位年轻人，他们没想到音乐造诣已如此深厚的贺院长每天在家仍不断学习、磨炼自我。贺绿汀以实际行动诠释着四年前关于群众歌曲创作的专题报告中跟学生们谈到的：“这是一种艰苦的创造性的劳动，没有捷径，不能偷懒，来不得半点投机取巧。拳不离手，曲不离口，创作也是一样，要有很高的劳动强度，要不断地练笔，不停地写，做到不练笔就过不了日子。这要成为一种习惯。”他严于律己、以身作则，在练习、创作中提炼音乐教育理论的真谛，毫无保留地倾囊传授给学生们，培育了一批又一批杰出的音乐人才。

建筑简介：安福路191弄15号

贺绿汀旧居位于安福路191弄15号，为新式里弄住宅，建于1932年，占地面积52平方米，三层砖木结构，建筑面积171平方米。安福路191弄原名美华里，弄内前后三排房屋，屋面为红瓦人字坡顶，素色水泥砂浆外墙，墙面分布横向矩形木窗。室内底层客堂为落地长窗，后部为楼梯间、厨房；楼上为卧室、亭子间；北侧顶层有晒台。20世纪30年代，贺绿汀和妻子姜瑞芝在此居住。现为民居。

HE Luting

HE Luting (1903–1999), a former name of HE Kai, has his ancestral family from Shaoyang county (now Shaodong county) in Hunan province. He is a composer, music educator and theorist, and one of the founders of China's higher education of professional music. He once participated in the Hunan Farmer Movement and the Guangzhou Uprising. In 1931, he was admitted to Shanghai National Music Academy, studying piano and acoustics. In 1934, his works *Cowboy and Piccolo* and *Lullaby* were respectively awarded the first prize and honorary second prize in the competition "Collecting Chinese Style Piano Music" sponsored by the Soviet Union composer Alexander Tcherepnin. During the War against Japanese Invasion, his creation of *Guerrilla Song* won him the praise from MAO Zedong. After the founding of the New China he served in succession as president of Shanghai Conservatory of Music, vice chairman of Chinese Musicians Association, and chairman of its Shanghai Branch. In his life, he created more than 260 songs, the representatives including *Wandering Songstress*, *Song of Four Seasons*, *Guerrilla Song*, *On Jialing River*, *Cowboy and Piccolo*, *Senjidema* and *Evening Party*. He got published a translation of *Acoustics: Theory and Practice* and such books as *An Anthology of Songs by HE Luting* and *A Collection of Music Papers by HE Luting*. At his 90th birthday in 1993, JIANG Zemin wrote in person an inscription for him, which goes as "Composing the Strong Tone of Life and Eulogizing the Cause of the People".

Teaching to Nurture Silently

In the early 1958, HE Luting delivered a special speech about the creation of songs for the masses at Shanghai Conservatory of Music. Students excitedly rushed about to spread the news. Students from the departments of composition and vocal music as

贺绿汀在寓所弹奏钢琴
HE Luting was playing the piano at his apartment.

well as those for mid-career studies strived to be the first, bringing both pen and paper to come to attend the lecture by the president. The classroom was packed. With a slight tone of his hometown accent, he communicated with students about his experience and inspiration in the creation of songs for the masses. He said that "creation is not the assorting of cold dishes, but the outpouring of real feelings. The creator should be equipped with the passion of poets, having keen perception and rich imagination of politics, the people's life and all aspects of the natural world." The lecture lasted for three hours and he also made specific art instructions, leaving a deep impression on DAI Penghai, a student of composition department.

In a winter four years after that, two of the students came together to pay a visit to Mr. HE, the former president they revered—one was DAI Penghai who had graduated and the other was Ouyang Qianshu, who was a student for mid-career studies in Shanghai Conservatory of Music and won the Best Music Award in the First Hundred Flowers Awards for Films thanks to his music composition for the film of *Red Guards on Honghu Lake*.

Entering the living room in the south of the first floor, the first thing leaping to the eyes is the piano. After seeing the little notebook on the piano filled with exercise topics of primary harmony, the two former students bantered with one voice, "Mr. HE, you also have received pupils at home?" At that time the ban had been lifted for music teachers to have students at home. But they made a mistake in their guess. Smiling lightly, HE replied, "These exercise topics are what I use in my daily practice" The surprising answer deeply shocked the two young persons. They did not expect that Mr. HE, a musician with such musical achievements, still kept on practice every day at home. With his practical actions, HE was interpreting what he talked about with the students four years ago—the creation of songs for the masses is "a kind of hard creative work with no shortcut and allowing no laziness. Just as a Chinese saying goes that the boxer's fist must stick to its task and the singer's mouth no rest must ask, so is the case with creative production of music. Very high intensity of labor is needed to do constant practice and creative writing. One must form the habit to live a life with everyday practice." His self-discipline served to help set himself an example for others. By means of practice and creative production, he extracted the essence of music education theory and taught students with no reservation, having produced outstanding musical talents one group after another.

The former residence of HE Luting is situated at No. 15 in Alley 191 on Anfu Road. A new style alley residence, it was first built in 1932 and covers an area of 52 square meters. This three-storied structure of brick and wood has a construction area of 171 square meters. The former name of Alley 191 was Meihua Alley, in which there are three rows of houses. This building enjoys a gable roof of slopes covered with red tiles, exterior walls with plain cement mortar and horizontally rectangular wooden windows distributed on walls. Inside the building, the sitting room on the first floor has a long French window and in the rear are stairwell and kitchen; upstairs are the bedroom and garret; the top floor at the north side has a balcony. In 1930s, HE and his wife lived here. Now it is a residential house.

贺绿汀 （陆小弟、陆旻画） HE Luting （By LU Xiaodi and LU Min）

赵丹
（1915—1980）

山东肥城人，原名凤翱，电影表演艺术家。幼时全家迁居江苏南通。中学时曾与顾而已、朱今明、钱千里等人组织小小剧社。后入上海美术专科学校学国画，并参加学校话剧团和宋之的、郑君里等领导的新地剧社。1932年加入中国左翼戏剧家联盟，同年成为明星影片公司的基本演员，并加入上海业余剧人协会。1937年"七七事变"后，参加演出话剧《保卫卢沟桥》，后参加第三抗日救亡演剧队。中华人民共和国成立后，一直在上海电影制片厂任演员、导演。1957年加入中国共产党。曾当选为第一、二、三届全国人大代表，第五届全国政协委员，中国影协常务理事。1980年10月10日在北京病逝。曾主演《十字街头》《马路天使》《丽人行》《乌鸦与麻雀》《武训传》《李时珍》《林则徐》《聂耳》《在烈火中永生》等影片。

黄宗英
（1925—　）

原籍浙江瑞安，生于北京，电影演员、作家。1941年到上海参加话剧演出，先后在上海职业剧团、同华剧社、北平南北剧社任演员，因主演喜剧《甜姐儿》而知名。1947年开始从事电影表演。主演《追》《幸福狂想曲》《丽人行》等影片。1957年因在《乌鸦与麻雀》一片中的出色表演荣获文化部1949—1955年优秀影片一等奖。中华人民共和国成立后任上海电影制片厂演员，拍摄《家》《聂耳》等影片。1954年创作电影剧本《平凡的事业》。1965年后在中国作协上海分会专事创作，是中国作协第四届理事。所作《大雁情》《美丽的眼睛》《桔》分别获1979—1980年、1981—1982年、1983—1984年全国优秀报告文学奖。著有《星》《桔》《黄宗英报告文学选》等。

戏病

1973年春天，蒙冤入狱五年有余的赵丹终于回到了湖南路8号温馨的家。一个深夜，熟睡中的黄宗英被赵丹的自言自语、自问自答惊醒了。黄宗英不敢打岔，也不敢开灯，以为赵丹在说梦话。等赵丹安静下来，黄宗英轻轻地问赵丹："你睡着了吗？""我醒着。"赵丹睁开双眼迎上妻子关切的目光。"那……你想说话，就把我或孩子叫醒说吧，别自己跟自己说话，怪叫人害怕的。"赵丹叹了口气，缓缓地说道："大概是习惯自言自语了。这五年多我几乎不与别人交流。我担心失去说话能力，就不能再演戏了。戏，是我的命根子呀！"

黄宗英点点头，心疼地问道："阿丹，你是怎么挺过来的？"赵丹将目光投向了远方，那段艰辛的岁月历历在目，他喃喃低语："我想戏，想我拍过的每一个电影镜头。齐白石的电影剧本在我脑子里已经分好镜头了。山坡下，奔泉、溪流、短笛、牛群，牧牛的孩子们站在牛背上过河，小白石……当然，还想着演鲁迅、李白，还有阿Q、黄省三……"黄宗英有些惊讶，"我倒头一回知道你想演曹禺《日出》里的黄省三。"赵丹认真地答道："嗯，过去，人们多演他的可怜，我要演出他的自重。如果现在再让我演许云峰，我会比以前演得更好……"

赵丹阐述着他对人物形象的理解，黄宗英被深深地震撼了。从刚认识赵丹起，他对演戏精益求精、追求完美的态度就一直感染、鼓舞着同样身为演员的黄宗英。然而她没有料到，在那漫长而坎坷的五年中，丈夫不忧患自身安危，心中念念不忘的仍是表演事业。他憧憬着重返银幕，通过传神地塑造一个个艺术形象实现自己的人生价值。九十岁高龄的黄宗英在“纪念人民艺术家赵丹同志诞辰 100 周年座谈会”上深情地说：“我这辈子做得最对的一件事情就是嫁给了赵丹。赵丹确实是值得我爱的。”

建筑简介：湖南路8号

赵丹、黄宗英寓所位于湖南路 8 号，为现代风格的花园住宅，建于 1930 年，三层砖混结构，建筑面积 290 平方米，占地面积 460 平方米。东面入口门洞饰叠涩线脚，上有雨篷，南面二、三层设水平悬挑阳台，弧形转角，大面积方形钢窗。院内植草坪和杉树。赵丹 1962 至 1979 年在此居住。当时赵丹住在三楼，有三个房间，两间朝南，一间朝北，北面还有一个较大的顶层平台。

ZHAO Dan and HUANG Zongying

ZHAO Dan (1915–1980), a film performing artist, had a former name of Feng'ao with his ancestral family from the city of Feicheng in Shandong province. In his childhood, his family moved to the city of Nantong in Jiangsu province. When he was in high school, he and some other students organized a Little Opera Troupe. Later he entered the Shanghai Art School to learn painting and also joined the school opera troupe and the New Earth Troupe led by a would-be playwright, and a future well-known film actor and director. In 1932, he joined China Left-Wing Dramatists Union. In the same year, he became a regular actor in the Star Film Company and also joined the Shanghai Amateur Theatre Association. After the "July 7 Incident" in 1937, he participated in the performance of the opera *The Defense of Lugou Bridge* and later joined The Third Resisting-Japanese and Salvation Drama Team. After the founding of the New China, he had been working in Shanghai Film Studio as actor and director. In 1957, he joined the CPC. He was once elected as representative of the first, the second and third sessions of the National People's Congress, member of the fifth session of the CPPCC National Committee, as well as standing director of China Film Association. On October 10, 1980, he passed away of illness in Beijing. Films he starred include *Crossroads*, *Angels on the Road*, *Two for the Road, The Crow and the Sparrow*, *The Life of WU Xun*, *LI Shizhen*, *LIN Zexu*, *NIE Er* and *Living Forever in Burning Flames*.

HUANG Zongying (1925–), born in Beijing, film actress and writer, has her ancestral family from Rui'an in Zhejiang province. In 1941, she participated in opera performance in Shanghai and worked successively as actress in Shanghai Professional Troupe, Tonghua Opera Troupe and Beijing North and South Troupe. She was known for her starring in the comedy *Funny Face*. Since 1947, she engaged herself in film performance. Films she starred include *Pursuit*, *Happiness Rhapsody*, *Two for the Road* and others. In

赵丹与黄宗英新婚时光
ZHAO Dan and HUANG Zongying at their new wedding time.

1957, she won the first prize of excellent films between 1949 and 1955 issued by the Ministry of Culture for her outstanding performance in *The Crow and the Sparrow*. After the founding of the New China, she worked as actress in Shanghai Film Studio, performing in such films as *Family* and *NIE Er*. In 1954, she created the film script *The Ordinary Cause*. After 1965, she worked in Shanghai Branch of China Writers Association, specializing in creative writing. She was also director of the fourth conference of the association. Her works *The Wild Goose*, *Beautiful Eyes* and *Orange* were awarded national prizes for excellent report literature respectively in the years between 1979–1980, 1981–1982, and 1983–1984. She is the author of such works as *The Star*, *Orange*, and *Selected Report Literature by HUANG Zongying*.

Crazy for Performance

In the spring of 1973, ZHAO Dan finally returned home at No. 8 on Hunan Road after being wronged to be in prison for more than five years. At one night, his wife was awakened from deep sleep by his speaking to himself. She did not dare to interrupt or turn on the lights, thinking that he was talking in his dreams. When he was quiet, she asked, "Are you asleep?" "I'm awake." He opened his eyes to meet his wife's. "That... If you want to talk, wake me up and wake up any of the children. Don't speak with yourself. That would be scaring." He sighed a long sigh and said slowly, "Probably I've been used to talking to myself. For more than five years I almost did not talk with others. I was afraid of losing my ability to speak. Unable to speak, I couldn't perform any more. Performance is my lifeblood!"

She nodded and asked him with concern, "Darling, how did you make it?" He looked into the distance. The years of hardships leapt before his eyes. He whispered, "I was thinking of performance and of all the film scenes I have took. The film script of QI Baishi has been divided into scenes in my brain. At the foot of the hill, the running springs, streams, short flute, cattle, children on the back of cattle to cross the river, little white stones... Of course, I also thought about LU Xun and LI Bai in addition to Ah Q and HUANG Xingsan..." His wife was surprised, "This is the first time I've got to know you want to play the role of HUANG Xingsan in *Sunrise* by CAO Yu". He seriously replied, "Well, in the past, actors represented the pitiful aspect in this character, but I would like to depict his self-respect. If I were to play the role of XU Yunfeng again, I could do better than before..."

He explained his understanding of the characters and she was deeply shocked. Since the time she got to know him, his attitude to acting had been doing things still better in pursuit of perfection, which influenced and inspired her since she was also a player. But she did not expect that, in the long and bumpy five years, her husband was not afraid of his own safety and what he bore constantly in his mind was still the cause of performance. He hoped that he could return to the screen and realize the value of his life by shaping vivid artistic images. At the age of ninety, Huang said with emotion at a "Forum in Memory of the 100th Anniversary of the People's Artist ZHAO Dan" , "The most correct thing I have done in my life is to have married ZHAO Dan. He is really worthy of my love."

The apartment of ZHAO Dan and HUANG Zongying is situated at No. 8 on Hunan Road. A garden house of modern style, it was built in 1930 with three stories of mixed structure of brick and concrete. It covers an area of 460 square meters with a construction area of 290 square meters. The east entrance is decorated with corbel moldings and above it is also a canopy. In the south the second and third floors have overhanging balconies with arc angles and large square steel windows. In the courtyard there are pine trees and lawns. From 1962 to 1979 he lived here. At that time he lived on the third floor, where there were three rooms, two of which faced south and one faced north. In the north, there is a large platform on the top.

赵丹、黄宗英 （刘为民画）

ZHAO Dan and HUANG Zongying （By LIU Weimin）

赵宏本
（1915—2000）

祖籍江苏阜宁，生于上海，笔名张卿、张弓，现代连环画家。1932年入上海民众书局投师学绘连环画。1937年进日章夜校学习。1939年，创作了一批借古喻今，直接反映铁蹄下人民苦难生活的连环画，如《上海即景》《天堂与地狱》等。1947年加入中国共产党。先后创作出版《文天祥》《阿Q正传》等连环画一百二十余部。在20世纪40年代与朱润斋、周云舫、沈曼云有连环画界"四大名旦"之誉。1949年5月上海解放前后创办新声出版社，任社长。中华人民共和国成立后，历任新华书店华东总分店编辑部连环画组副组长、华东人民出版社连环画科副科长、新美术出版社编辑部副主任、上海人民美术出版社连环画创作室主任。为中国美术家协会会员、中国美协上海分会常务理事、中国连环画研究会副会长、中国出版工作者协会上海分会理事。毕生创作出版连环画三百五十余部。其中与钱笑呆合作的《孙悟空三打白骨精》获第一届全国连环画创作评奖绘画一等奖。另有代表作国画人物长卷《水浒一百零八将》等。

缘结"美猴王"

天下艺术文人可谓众矣，芸芸众生中能够相遇、相识，本身就有很大的偶然性。而相识后又能相知而成莫逆，则非机缘而莫属，六小龄童和赵宏本先生就是因"猴"而结缘。六小龄童在拍电视剧《西游记》时就曾多次去赵宏本先生家中拜访，两人一见如故，经常促膝长谈，两位"猴王"结下了不解之缘。

赵宏本先生给六小龄童讲述了《孙悟空三打白骨精》的创作过程，讲如何从戏曲、同辈和前辈的连环画作品中汲取养分，才塑造出造型独特、线条优美、性格突出的人物形象，尤其是每一页画面之间内在的故事和情感的联系，希望六小龄童吸取戏曲艺术的精华，根据自身的特点和优势塑造出独特的银屏美猴王形象。在讲到戏曲人物与连环画人物、影视剧人物艺术表现形式的区别时，先生说："戏曲中的猴戏注重动态，讲究身段，唱念做打，一板一眼的不能走样，而影视剧及连环画中更注重的是真实感，孙悟空既要有猴性，又要有人性，它就是人性与猴性的结合体。"先生说得兴起，当即起身，就地取材，将一把扫帚扛在肩上，双腿微屈，惟妙惟肖地学起了猴子走路。六小龄童见了，连忙起身，跟在先生身旁，亦步亦趋也学了起来。这一老一少，左摇右摆，耸肩缩背，蹒跚而行，之后两人相视，忍俊不禁，开怀大笑起来。电视剧播出后，先生还曾开玩笑说六小龄童饰演的孙悟空在《智激美猴王》中披的红斗篷及一些动作是脱胎于他的《孙悟空三打白骨精》连环画，应该付他稿费。

赵宏本先生的《孙悟空三打白骨精》取材于六龄童的绍剧，影响着一代又一代的美术爱好者，又影响了六小龄童而铸就新一代美猴王，更对现代《西游记》题材影视剧的创作产生了巨大的影响和推动作用。正可谓："画坛猴王，影坛猴王，承前启后，薪火相传。"

建筑简介：乌鲁木齐中路148弄4号

赵宏本旧居位于乌鲁木齐中路148弄4号，为花园里弄住宅。乌鲁木齐中路148弄原名琪美新村，建于1941年。房屋为三层砖木结构，一层设有架空层，建筑平面近似矩形。房屋外立面为涂料饰面，一层有水泥墙裙，钢门窗；南立面设有阳台，混凝土悬挑梁板结构；檐口、阳台等部位设有白色长条线脚；机制平瓦坡屋盖，木结构挑檐。一层入口位于房屋西侧，入口小门厅及一层走道地面均为水磨石饰面。房屋一至三层平面布局相似，沿西侧楼梯间分别分布有亭子间、卫生间和居住房间；室内走道及房间楼面基本为硬木长条地板。木结构双跑楼梯，木踏步、木扶手。

ZHAO Hongben

ZHAO Hongben (1915–2000) was born in Shanghai, with his ancestral family from Funing County in Jiangsu province. As a modern comic strips artist, he wrote under the pen names of ZHANG Qing and ZHANG Gong. In 1932, he was admitted into the Shanghai People's Bookstore to learn painting comic strips from masters and then he studied in Rizhang Night School in 1937. In 1939, he created a number of comic strips such as *Shanghai Scenery*, *Heaven and Hell* and so on, telling anecdotes of the past to allude to the present and reflecting the tragic life of the war-stricken people. In 1947, he joined the Communist Party of China. Later he successively created and published over 120 comic books such as *WEN Tianxiang* and *The True Story of Ah Q*. In the 1940s, together with ZHU Runzhai, ZHOU Yunfang and SHEN Manyun, he enjoyed the reputation of "Four Famous Creators" in the circle of comic strips creation. Before and after the liberation of Shanghai in May of 1949, he started up the New Voice Press and served as its president. After the founding of the People's Republic of China, he successively held the posts of deputy head of the Comic Division of the Editorial Department of East China Branch of Xinhua Bookstore, deputy chief of the Comic Strips Section of East China People's Publishing House, deputy director of the Editorial Department of New Fine Arts Publishing House and director of the Comic Strips Studio of Shanghai People's Fine Arts Publishing House. Also he was member of China Artists Association, executive director of Shanghai Branch of China Artists Association, vice chairman of China Comic Strips Research Society and director of Shanghai Branch of the Publishers Association of China. He spent all his life composing and publishing more than three hundred and fifty comic books. Among the works, *Monkey Subdues the White-Bone Demon*, which he created together with QIAN Xiaodai, won the first prize of the First National Comic Painting Award. He also has other masterpieces such as the traditional Chinese painting scroll *Outlaws of Marsh 108 Warriors* and so on.

Becoming Attached to "Monkey King"

Among so many literati all across the country, it is a slim chance for one to encounter and be acquainted with another. Therefore, it must be extremely lucky to become intimate friends after their encounter and acquaintance. In this sense, it is a great lucky

赵宏本（右）和六小龄童（左）
ZHAO Hongben (right) and Liuxiaolingtong (left).

chance for Liuxiaolingtong to get to know Mr. ZHAO Hongben and to form ties of friendship due to monkey. During the shooting of the TV series *The Pilgrimage to the West*, Liuxiaolingtong paid several visits to him. They were like old friends at their first meeting and always had long heart-to-heart talks, so a wonderful bond was built between both "Monkey Kings".

He told Liuxiaolingtong about the creation process of *Monkey Subdues the White-Bone Demon*, about how to draw lessons from the opera and the comic strips of peers and predecessors in order to create charming images characterized by unique styles, beautiful figures and distinctive personalities, especially the relationship between stories and emotions of each page. He expected Liuxiaolingtong to draw the essence from the Chinese operas and shape the distinctive image of Monkey King on the screen on the basis of his own features and advantages. When it came to the differences in artistic presentation of characters in opera, comic strips and movie & TV plays, he said, "In traditional Chinese operas, the performers acting as the monkeys should focus on their dynamic nature and postures and strictly adopt four traditional performing techniques, while in movie & TV plays as well as in comic strips, the character of Monkey King is actually a combination of human nature and monkey. So the lifelike performance is indispensable." When talking excitedly, he rose to his feet right away and put a broom on his shoulder to imitate the monkey's walks. With his legs bent, his imitation was quite vivid and lifelike. This scene encouraged Liuxiaolingtong to stand up and follow his behaviors. These two persons, old and young, waddled left and right with their shoulders hunched and backs bowed. They looked at each other then and burst into laughter. After the TV plays were put on, he said jokingly that the red cloak and some actions of the Monkey King in *Cleverly Stimulating the Monkey King* were derived from his comic strip *Monkey Subdues the White-Bone Demon*, so Liuxiaolingtong should pay him some royalties.

Monkey Subdues the White-Bone Demon, the comic strip created by ZHAO Hongben, was drawn from Shaoxing Opera performed by Liulingtong, and it inspired Liuxiaolingtong to complete the classic TV play and become a typical Monkey King. ZHAO's works also influenced generations of art lovers and even exerted a great impact on the creation of the modern TV play *The Pilgrimage to the West*. As it is said, the characters of the Monkey King in comic strips and TV plays will carry forward from one generation to another.

The former residence of ZHAO Hongben is located at No. 4 in Alley 148 on Middle Urumqi Road. Built in 1941, the house has a former name of Qimei New Village, which is of garden residence in alley. The house is of a three-storied structure of brick and wood with the first floor built on stilts, and the building plane is approximately rectangular. The facade of the house has paint veneer and the first floor has a layer of cement wainscot. The whole building has steel doors and windows. At the south facade, there are balconies with a structure of concrete cantilevered slab. Cornices, balcony and other parts have white long architrave; the roof has gentle slopes covered with flat tiles made by machines and the overhanging eaves are made of wooden structure. The entrance of the first floor is at the west side of the house. Both the small hall at the entrance and the aisle on the first floor have waterstone veneer. The layouts from the first to third floors are similar. Along the west side of the staircases are the garret, bathroom and living room. The interior aisles and room floors are basically made of hardwood stripes. The stairs are straight with landings in wooden structure with wooden steps and handrails.

赵宏本 （邬海佳画） ZHAO Hongben （By WU Haijia）

赵宪初
（1907—1998）

浙江嘉善人，教育家。1928年于上海交通大学毕业后，长期在南洋模范中学任教。1931年任校教务主任兼数学教师。中华人民共和国成立后，担任南洋模范中学副教导主任，1956年任副校长，1979年任校长，1984年任名誉校长。从教七十年培养了大量人才，是上海市第一批特级教师。1955年加入中国民主促进会，历任民进上海市委第七、八、九届副主任委员，第十届主任委员，第十一、十二届名誉主任委员；民进中央第六、七届委员，民进中央参议委员会第一、二届委员，第三届常委。先后担任徐汇区政协委员、常委，徐汇区人民政府副区长。1988年4月至1993年2月任上海市政协第七届副主席。曾担任上海市社会主义学院副院长、上海市中小学幼儿教师奖励基金会副理事长等。著有《赵宪初教育文集》等。

南模中学最独特的保留节目

初二年级数学教学中，代数和平面几何公式铺天盖地且易混淆，学生们叫苦不迭，而牢记公式方可为下阶段更深入地学习奠定扎实的基础。赵宪初潜心钻研教学艺术，孜孜不倦地探索数学教学规律和方法，逐渐形成了独特的教学风格。

有一次授课时，赵宪初手持倾注大量心血自编的教材，用上海话“有腔有调”地念一元二次方程求根公式：“x/ 等于 /2a 分之 / 负 b/ 正负 / 开方 /b 方 / 减 4ac”。同学们愣了一下，继而哄堂大笑，觉得赵老师不像是在念公式而像在唱滑稽戏，而且还煞有介事地拖长音，听起来实在太可笑了。然而，平日里笑容可掬的赵宪初此刻却神情庄严肃穆，他一本正经地继续这样“滑稽”地念公式。念第二遍时，笑声渐渐稀疏了，有一些学生还侧耳聆听。他微笑着环视教室，慈祥地观察每位学生的神情，有些学生难掩笑意，有些心领神会地点头，还有些迷茫地望着他。念第三遍时，好几位学生轻声地跟着赵宪初以上海话念起一元二次方程求根公式。赵宪初向他们投去赞赏的目光，继续以独特的音调及节奏念第四遍。这次，深受感召的学生们纷纷模仿赵宪初，用上海话摇头晃脑、异口同声地跟念。和蔼可亲的微笑在赵宪初的脸庞荡漾，在谈笑风生中，连原本厌烦数学公式的学生们也能准确无误地记住那一连串复杂的公式，并灵活地运用于解题了。

学校组织联欢晚会时，同学们总会起哄他们爱戴的赵老师，请他表演节目。赵宪初落落大方地走上台去，对着麦克风以不紧不慢的上海话一口气吟诵一大串公式，颇具江南小调的韵味，他还动员台下的学生们跟他一起吟诵，这被誉为南模最独特的保留节目。

赵宪初钟爱教育事业，自嘲“终日忙忙，不甘碌碌，常年辛辛，不觉苦苦”。他寓教于乐、生动有趣的授课场景成为一代又一代学生心中难以忘怀的美好回忆。南模48届学生钟万励在纪念赵宪初先生从教七十周年之际，特地请擅长演奏小提琴的上海同乡将赵老师独创的沪语版一元二次方程求根公式的音调谱上曲子以便流传。被誉为“中华之光”的南模54届校友王选院士称颂赵宪初先生“领头背数学公式的有趣声调是半个多世纪被几代学生所津津乐道的”。

建筑简介：永福路86弄3号

赵宪初旧居位于永福路86弄3号。永福路86弄1至6号占地5333平方米。该地最初为荒地，池塘小河分布其间，仅有陈姓几户居民。中华人民共和国成立前为三兴花园园址。1963年由国家征用。翌年在此建成混合结构五层公寓楼五幢，二层附屋一幢，建筑面积共5580平方米，取名伯乐大院。

ZHAO Xianchu

ZAHO Xianchu (1907—1998), an educator, has his ancestral family from Jiashan in Zhejiang province. After graduating from Shanghai Jiaotong University in 1928, he taught in Nanyang Model High School for a long time. In 1931 he served as director of teaching affairs and mathematics teacher. After the founding of the PRC, he served as assistant director of Nanyang Model High School, vice president in 1956, president in 1979 and honorary president in 1984. Teaching for seventy years, he cultivated a large number of talents and was one of the first special-grade teachers in Shanghai. In 1955, he joined the China Association for Promoting Democracy and served as vice chairman of the 7th, 8th and 9th congresses, chairman of the tenth congress and honorary chairman of the eleventh and twelfth congresses of its Shanghai Municipal Committee. In addition he served as member of the sixth and seventh congresses of its Central Committee as well as member of the first and second sessions and permanent member of the third session of its Central Senate Committee. Also he served as member and permanent member of the Xujiahui District CPPCC and deputy head of Xujiahui District People's Government. From April 1988 to February 1993, he served as vice chairman of the seventh session of Shanghai Municipal CPPCC. Once he also served as vice president of Shanghai Institute of Socialism and vice chairman of Shanghai Elementary Education Teacher Award Foundation. He authored such books as *Education Paper Collection by ZHAO Xianchu.*

The Most Unique Repertoire in the High School

In the mathematics teaching of the junior students, the formula of algebra and planar geometric are overwhelming in number and easily confusing. Students constantly complained, but it was necessary to firmly keep the formula in mind to lay a solid foundation for further study in the next stage. ZHAO Xianchu painstakingly studied the art of teaching and tirelessly explored the laws of mathematics teaching methods, gradually forming a unique teaching style.

赵宪初
ZHAO Xianchu.

Once in a class, he took hold of a self-edited textbook for which he spent a lot of painstaking efforts and used the Shanghai dialect to read with accent a rooting formula in a quadric equation, "x / equal / 2a / negative b / positive and negative / open square / b square / minus 4ac". Students felt stunned for a moment and then the whole classroom burst into laughter. They thought that the teacher was not reading a formula, but playing a funny opera. Moreover, he also pretended to be serious and dragged on to produce a long sound, which seemed too ridiculous. However, he was all smiles in his daily life, but looked solemn at the moment. He solemnly continued this "funny" reading of the formula. When he read for the second time, the laughter became gradually sparse and some students pricked up their ears to listen. He looked around the classroom with smiles, kindly observing the expression of each student. Some students could not conceal their smile; some appreciated his thought with nods and some looked at him at a loss. When he read for the third time, several students softly followed him to read the formula in Shanghai dialect. He cast a look of appreciation on them and continued to read with a unique tone and rhythm for the fourth times. This time the students were deeply impressed and imitated him to shake their heads and read with the Shanghai dialect with one voice. The amiable smiles rippled on his face. In cheerful and humorous talk, even the students who were bored with mathematical formulas could remember the complex formulas accurately and apply them flexibly in solving problems.

When the school organized evening parties, the students always stir up their favorite teacher and asked him to give a performance. He took the stage in a natural and graceful way and spoke to the microphone, chanting a long list of formulas in one breath in Shanghai dialect at an unhurried pace, which had the flavor of a popular tune in the south of China. He also mobilized the students to recite with him, known as the most unique repertoire of the Nanyang Model High School.

He loved the cause of education, saying with self-deprecating humor that I was "busy all day, unwilling to be commonplace, laborious all year round and feeling no hardships". His teaching together with pleasure and entertainment through lively activities became unforgettable memories for students one generation after generation. In order to commemorate his 70th anniversary, ZHONG Wanli, a student of the forty-eighth year of the school, specially invited a native of Shanghai who was adept at playing violin to compose a piece of music for the formula of the quadratic equation for the purpose of its spreading. Academician WANG Xuan, who was an alumnus of the fifty-fourth year students of the school and honored as the "Light of China", praised Mr. ZHAO Xianchu "for his interesting class to guide students to recite mathematical formulas has been talked about by students for several generations".

The former residence of ZHAO Xianchu is located at No. 3 in Alley 86 on Yongfu Road. Apartments from No. 1 to No. 6 in Alley 86 on this road cover an area of 5,333 square meters. This land was formerly a wasteland, dotted with ponds and rivers and only a few families with the name CHEN. Before the founding of the People's Republic of China, it was the site of a park. In 1963, it was confiscated by the country. In the following year were constructed five apartment buildings of five stories in a mixed structure and one attached building of two floors, with a total construction area of 5,580 square meters, which was named as Bole Courtyard.

赵宪初 （桑麟康画） ZHAO Xianchu （By SANG Linkang）

赵焕章
（1930— ）

山东利津人，电影艺术家，国家一级导演。1952 年于山东大学艺术系毕业后，进入上海联合电影制片厂。1972 年开始电影导演工作。1980 年、1983 年、1985 年三次被评为上海市劳动模范。1988 年获“新时期全国影视十佳导演”称号。曾任上海市政协常委、上海市徐汇区人民代表大会代表。导演的电影有《战船台》《风浪》《海之恋》《喜盈门》《咱们的牛百岁》《咱们的退伍兵》《这不是误会》《八仙的传说》等。其中《喜盈门》《咱们的牛百岁》《咱们的退伍兵》被誉为中国农村电影“三部曲”，先后荣获百花奖、金鸡奖以及文化部、广电部颁发的优秀影片等各类奖项十余项。

永福路上的灯光

20 世纪 80 年代，上海电影制片厂在五年中连续推出由赵焕章导演的电影《喜盈门》《咱们的牛百岁》《咱们的退伍兵》，一时红遍全国。这些被称为农村电影“三部曲”的优秀剧本就诞生在永福路 52 号。

1979 年，山东作者辛显令在赵焕章的鼓励下，写出了《喜盈门》。辛显令在文化馆工作，平时写诗歌，还搞小戏。因过去习惯于为政策服务，所以《喜盈门》的最初稿基础不错，但图解政策的痕迹很深。于是，辛显令被请到了上海，住进永福路 52 号上影文学部招待所。

一见面，赵焕章就对辛显令来了个“约法三章”，说自己缺乏农村生活经验，改的难免凭想当然，他会不断地贡献点子，但要符合实际的才能用，最终由作者定夺。招待所里的灯光常常彻夜通明。足足改了两个月，一部以北方农村一个家庭婆媳之间的争端为主要内容，充满喜剧色彩的电影剧本在这里诞生了。

《咱们的牛百岁》的作者袁学强，本身就是个农民，一手把锄，一手写作。1982 年，袁学强也被请到了永福路。袁学强有丰富的农村生活经验，但真正“触电”却刚开始。为使他放下包袱，赵焕章鼓励引导他，尽力帮他修改剧本。初稿完成后，赵焕章的父亲在济南去世。于是他一边奔丧，一边帮着改剧本。

1985 年，曾合作《高山流水》《泪痕》《几度风雪几度春》等电影剧本的“山药蛋派”代表人物马烽、孙谦又写出了《咱们的退伍兵》。赵焕章对其一见钟情，顷刻就被剧中洋溢的浓厚的农村气息和贴近现实的新生活所吸引。老作家的剧本十分精彩，但从文学本到真正拍摄，有些地方还得改动。于是“为分镜头剧本提意见”，赵焕章也把二老请到了上海。招待所门卫一见赵焕章来了，就笑着说，赵导来了，今晚不到深夜 12 点是关不了门的。姜是老的辣，二老认真修改外，还不停地给剧本贡献金点子。赵焕章和编辑们快马加鞭，夜以继日，很快完成了修改和定稿。

赵焕章说，“十年磨一戏”，戏演了还可以不断修改。影视是遗憾的艺术，拍好了“磨”也难。为此，每个剧本的“通关”慎之又慎：《喜盈门》五易其稿，《咱们的牛百岁》七易其稿，《咱们的退伍兵》出于老作家的手笔，但为定稿也足足花了半个月。

建筑简介：五原路281弄16号

赵焕章寓所位于五原路281弄16号。五原路281弄为花园里弄，15号与16号是利用空地所建造的两幢新式里弄住宅。15号为电影表演艺术家杨在葆寓所。

ZHAO Huanzhang

ZHAO Huanzhang (1930–) has his ancestral family from Lijin in Shandong province. He is known as a film artist and is a national first-grade director. After graduating from the Department of Art of Shandong University in 1952, he entered Shanghai United Film Studio. In 1972, he started the work as a film director. In 1980, 1983 and 1985, he was elected Shanghai Model Worker for three times respectively. In 1988, he won the title of "Ten Best Directors of New Era National Film and Television". Once he served as member of the Standing Committee of the CPPCC Shanghai Committee and representative of Shanghai Xuhui District People's Congress. The films he directed include *In The Shipyard*, *The Stormy Sea*, *Love Of The Sea*, *In-Laws*, *Our NIU Baisui*, *Our Demobed Soldier*, *This is Not a Mistake* and *The Legend of Eight Immortals*. Among them *In-Laws*, *Our NIU Baisui* and *Our Demobed Soldier* are regarded as the "trilogy" of China's rural films, which have won over ten awards including Hundred Flowers Award, Golden Rooster Award and Excellent Film Award issued by the Ministry of Culture and the Ministry of Radio and Television.

Lighting on Yongfu Road

In the 1980s, the Shanghai Film Studio produced such films as *In-Laws*, *Our NIU Baisu*i and *Our Demobed Soldier* in five consecutive years directed by ZHAO Huanzhang, which became popular throughout the country in a short while. These excellent scripts known as the "trilogy" of rural films were born at No. 52 on Yongfu Road.

In 1979, XIN Xianling, the author from Shandong, finished the writing of *In-Laws* under the encouragement of ZHAO Huanzhang. The former was working in the cultural center, wrote poems and also dialectal operas in his spare time. Because he used to serve in government agencies, the first draft of *In-Laws* had a good foundation. But the traces of graphic explanations of policy were too clear. Later he was invited to Shanghai and was admitted to stay at the literary guest house of Shanghai Film Studio at No. 52 on Yongfu Road.

As soon as they met, ZHAO made a few simple rules with XIN, saying that he lacked rural life experience and his changes could inevitably be made by taking it for granted. Nevertheless he would continue to contribute ideas, but only those in line with the actual facts could be of use, which would be finally decided by the author. The light in the hostel used to be bright and clear all night.

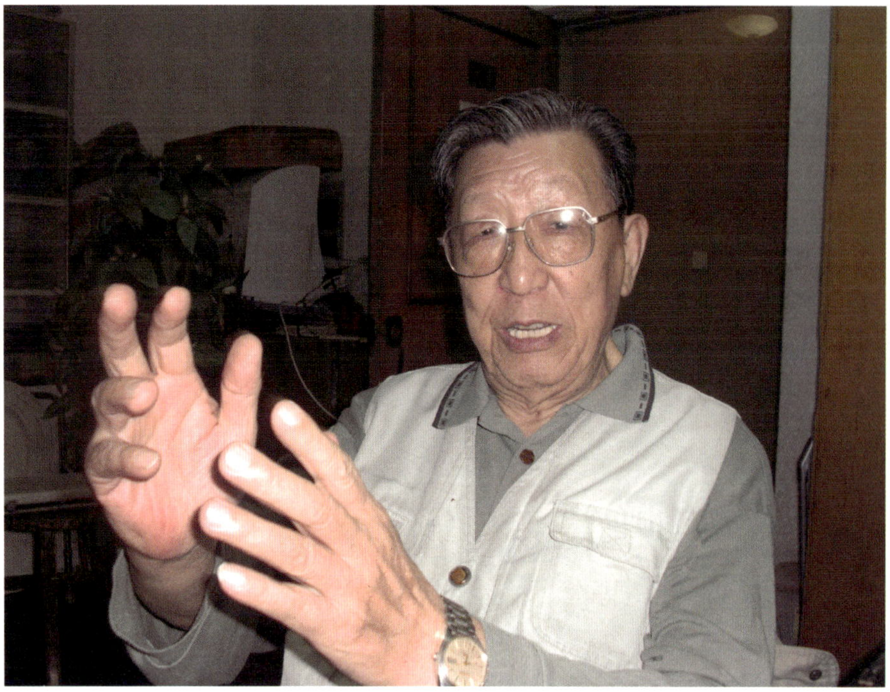

赵焕章
ZHAO Huanzhang.

Modification lasted for two months so that a film script was born here, which was mainly about the family dispute between mother-in-law and daughter-in-law in rural north China, and which was richly comic.

YUAN Xueqiang, the author of *Our NIU Baisui*, was a farmer himself with a hoe in one hand and with a pen in the other. In 1982, he was also invited to Yongfu Road. He had rich rural life experiences, but that was just the beginning of real "shock". To enable him to lay down the burden, ZHAO encouraged and guided him, and tried his best to help him modify the script. After the completion of the first draft, ZHAO's father passed away in Jinan. So he helped with the modification of the script while he hastened home for the funeral.

In 1985, MA Feng and SUN Qian, representatives of the "Potato School" and co-authors of the film scripts including *Lofty Mountains and Flowing Water*, *Tear Stains* and *Several Springs with Snowstorms*, again finished the writing of *Our Demobed Soldier*. ZHAO fell in love with it at first sight and was instantly attracted because it was filled with strong rural atmosphere and close to the reality of the new life. The script of the elderly writers was very exciting, but when it was changed from literature to film, some points had to be modified. In order to "seek advice for the film script", ZHAO also invited the two elder writers to Shanghai. At sight of ZHAO, the guest house guard said with a smile that Director ZHAO came so that it was impossible to close the gate until twelve o'clock. Old ginger is always spicy. Two writers not merely made modifications carefully, but also contributed golden ideas to the script. ZHAO and editors worked at top speed day and night and quickly completed the revision and finalized the script.

ZHAO once said, "It takes ten years to perfect a play", which could also be constantly modified after its debut. Film is the art of regret, since it is also difficult to perfect after its production. To this end, it could never be overestimated to be cautious with the finalization of each script. The first script of *In-Laws* was revised for five times, and that of *Our NIU Baisui* for seven times. The script of *Our Demobed Soldier* was out of veteran writers, but its finalization also took a full half month.

The apartment of ZHAO Huanzhang is located at No. 15 in Alley 281 on Wuyuan Road. The alley is one of a garden. No. 15 and No. 16 are the two new residential buildings in an alley which were built by making use of open space. No. 15 is the residence of YANG Zaibao, a film performing artist.

赵焕章 （桑麟康画） ZHAO Huanzhang （By SANG Linkang）

唐绍仪
（1860—1938）

广东香山（今中山）人，字少川，一作绍怡。曾留学美国。1881年回国。1885年赴朝鲜办理税务，任袁世凯的书记官。1894年袁内调后，代理袁在朝鲜的职务。1895年回国。后历任清政府天津海关道，外务部侍郎，沪宁、京汉铁路督办，邮传部侍郎、尚书，奉天巡抚等职。武昌起义后，充任袁世凯内阁全权代表，参加南北议和。1912年袁世凯就任临时大总统，被任命为第一任内阁总理，并加入同盟会。6月，因袁破坏责任内阁制，愤而辞职。1917年参加护法军政府，任财政部长，后被推为七总裁之一。1919年任护法军政府代表，与北洋军阀政府代表在上海议和。1922年第一次直奉战争后，被黎元洪提名为国务总理，因直系军阀反对未能就职。不久退居故里。1931年在汪精卫、孙科组织的广州政府中任常务委员兼中山县县长。九一八事变后，任国民党中央监察委员、国民政府委员。1938年在上海遇刺身亡。

变节疑云

1938年9月30日上午9点左右，一辆黑牌汽车抵达唐绍仪住处。这栋建筑位于法租界的洋房门口，有巡捕和密探负责安保。车里几人自称向唐绍仪出售古董，其中一人取出名片，说是唐绍仪特别约见。值班门卫认出他是谢志磐，于是让他与其余三位貌似古董商的陌生人入内。一行人被领至会客室。唐绍仪下楼会见，一如往常与有交情的客人见面，他让家人回避。

十几年前，唐绍仪便与谢志磐相识，他担任中山县县长时，谢志磐是国际通讯社社长，为他创办过广州《新晚报》。年初，日伪曾多次劝说唐绍仪出山为其效力，他以年迈无心问政为由拒绝出任伪职。日本军部及外务省顾问不断前来拉拢他，就在此前不久，日本驻中国特务总机关长土肥原贤二也对他劝说，但他始终未答应，宁愿寄情古董。

箱子里的古董深深吸引着他的目光，他捧起一件古瓷瓶仔细端详，心满意足地想要买下，便让仆人上楼取款，注意力依然停留在瓷瓶上……突然，一道寒光闪过，斧头劈下，唐绍仪倒在沙发上，鲜血如注。仆人赶到时，来客已不知所踪，唯有凶器还留在唐绍仪头部。

唐绍仪伤重去世，凶案令舆论哗然。对案发现场找到的所印“谢志磐”的名片调查与通缉无果而终，被拘的嫌疑人因证据不足全部获释。汪伪南京政府将唐绍仪记录在所谓的《殉难先烈名单》中，表示悼念。远在重庆的国民政府发表政府令，其中写道：“不幸猝遘惨变，遽失老成，眷怀勋旧，震悼良深。著拨给治丧费五千元，并将生平事迹存备宣付国史，用彰政府笃念勋耆之至意。”而国民党军统特务组织则把暗杀事件作为成功“锄奸”实例列入《行动术》教材，向学生传授。

历史迷雾终飘散，1986年12月和1989年4月在珠海举办的两次“唐绍仪史料研讨会”公开澄清了唐绍仪的晚节问题。唐绍仪晚节未失的清白终被证实。

建筑简介：武康路40弄1号

唐绍仪旧居位于武康路40弄1号，建于1932—1933年，华籍建筑师董大酉设计，建筑面积约350平方米，属西班牙式建筑风格的花园住宅。建筑为三层砖木结构，主入口朝北，券形拱门，两侧是科林斯绞绳纹立柱。二层设三联券柱落地窗，檐下饰连续双拱券。双坡硬山顶，黄色混水拉毛墙面，红色筒瓦双坡屋顶，其壁炉、烟囱尖端呈哥特式。二楼东西向正中及两侧延伸置有三座大阳台，呈曲折状。1933年成为诸昌年的寓所，诸昌年是唐绍仪的女婿，1937年唐绍仪曾在此居住。1999年9月23日上海市人民政府公布其为市优秀历史建筑。

TANG Shaoyi

TANG Shaoyi (1860–1938) has a courtesy name of Shaochuan or Shaoyi, with his ancestral family from Fragrant Hill (now Zhongshan) in Guangdong province. Once he studied abroad in the United States and returned to China in 1881. In 1885, he went to North Korea for the purpose of taxation, serving as the secretary of YUAN Shikai. When the latter came back in 1894, he worked as his deputy in North Korea. After returning in 1895, he served in succession as intendant of the Tianjin Customs of the government of Qing Dynasty, assistant minister of Ministry of Foreign Affairs, supervisor of Shanghai-Nanjing and Beijing-Hankou Railway Administration, assistant minister and minister of the Postal Department, as well as governor of Mukden (now Shenyang). After the Wuchang uprising, he acted as the full-fledged delegate of the cabinet of YAUN Shikai to participate in the peace negotiation. In 1912, when YUAN became the interim president, he was appointed as the first premier and joined the United League of China. In June, he resigned due to the fact that YUAN demolished the cabinet system. In 1917, he joined the government of the Law Protection Army and served as minister of finance. Later he was elected as one of the seven presidents. In 1919, he acted as one of the representatives of the government of the Law Protection Army to participate in the peace negotiation in Shanghai with the representatives of the Northern Warlords government. In 1922, after the first war between the Warlords from Hebei and Mukden, he was nominated as the premier, but failed to take office due to the opposition of warlords from Hebei province. Soon he went back to live in his hometown. In 1931, he served as a member of the standing committee in the Guangzhou Government organized by WANG Jingwei and SUN Ke, as well as the head of Zhongshan County. After the September 18 Incident, he served as a supervisor of the KMT Central Committee and a member of the National Government. In 1938, he was stabbed to death in Shanghai.

The Suspicious Treason

At about 9 in the morning of September 30, 1938, a car of black plate arrived at the apartment of TANG Shaoyi. At the gate of this foreign building located in the French Settlement, there were policemen and detectives in charge of security. A few people from the car claimed to go to sell antiques to him and one of them took out the name card, saying that they had made a special appointment

唐绍仪（左）与孙中山
TANG Shaoyi (left) and SUN Yat-sen.

with him. The guard on duty recognized him as XIE Zhipan, so he allowed him in with the rest of the three persons who seemed to be antique dealers. They were brought to the reception room. Then TANG came downstairs to meet them. As usual when he met his friend guests, he did not allow the family members to be present.

More than ten years ago, TANG got to know XIE. When he served as head of the Zhongshan County, XIE was director of the international news agency and founded the New Evening News for him in Guangzhou. At the beginning of the year, the Japanese invaders had repeatedly tried to persuade TANG to work for them, but he refused on the ground of being old. The advisors from the Japanese army office and the Ministry of Foreign Affairs constantly came to pull him over. Not long before that, the chief head of the Japanese spy agency in China also came to persuade him, but he never agreed, preferring to devote his energy to antiques.

This time, the antiques in the box deeply attracted his attention. He picked up an ancient porcelain bottle and carefully looked at it. Contented with it he wanted to buy it and told the servant to go upstairs to get money. At this time his attention was still on the porcelain... Suddenly a flash of light passed by and an axe struck him swiftly. TANG fell on the sofa and blood ran down. When the servant arrived, the visitors had disappeared, but only the axe was still on the head of the master.

TANG died of severe injuries and the murder stirred up the public opinion. All the investigation on the basis of the name card with the name of "XIE Zhipan" found on the spot finally came to nothing. The arrested suspects were all released due to lack of evidence. The puppet government of Nanjing recorded his name in the so called *List of Martyrs* as a token of mourning. The National Government far in Chongqing issued a government decree, which wrote that "he unfortunately suffered from the sudden disaster, leaving us with the abrupt loss of such an elderly person. We deeply miss the nobility. Here is the order that five thousand yuan be allocated for the funeral cost and his lifelong deeds be kept in the national history to represent the will of the government in honoring those senior celebrities". In the meanwhile the KMT spy organization took the assassination as an example of "eliminating traitors" and included it in the textbook to teach students.

The misty process in history could be eventually clear. In both December 1986 and April 1989, the two symposia concerning the historical data of Tang publicly helped clarify his integrity in his later years. That he did not lose his loyalty was confirmed in the end.

The former residence of TANG Shaoyi is located at No. 1 in Alley 40 on Wukang Road. Built in the years between 1932 and 1933, and designed by a Chinese architect, it has a construction area of about 350 square meters and is a garden residence of Spanish style. The building is of a three-storied structure of brick and wood. The main entrance faces north and the doors are arch-shaped. At both sides are columns decorated with Corinthian patterns of twisted ropes. On the second floor there are French windows and continuous double arches under eaves. The roof has two slopes with red tiles and hard gable walls which have yellow napped stucco veneer. The fireplace and chimney tops are of gothic style. In the middle and at the two sides of the second floor are three large balconies of curved shape. In 1933, the building became the residence of a son-in-law of TANG, and in 1937 TANG himself once lived here. On September 23, 1999, it became a Heritage Architecture issued by the Shanghai Municipal People's Government.

唐绍仪（桑麟康画） TANG Shaoyi （By SANG Linkang）

峻青
（1922— ）

山东海阳人，原名孙俊卿，作家。1941 年开始发表作品。1946 年加入中国共产党。历任胶东《大众报》记者，新华社前线分社随军记者，昌潍地区武工队小队长，《中原日报》编辑组长，中南人民广播电台编委兼宣传科长，中国作家协会上海分会副主席、代理党组书记，《文学报》主编，上海市炎黄文化研究会副会长等。其作品具有坚实的生活基础和革命浪漫主义精神，故事动人，人物形象鲜明。代表作品有《黎明的河边》《党员登记表》。另著有长篇小说《海啸》，短篇小说集《最后的报告》《怒涛》《海燕》等，散文集《欧行书简》《秋色赋》《雄关赋》《沧海赋》等，评论集《峻青谈创作》与《峻青文集》（6 卷）。

含泪写下战争名篇

峻青的小说《马石山上》《黎明的河边》《党员登记表》等，都曾风靡文坛，影响深远。其作品为什么有那么强的震撼力和亲近感？原来，他的作品是在枪林弹雨中“打”出来的，他是亲历者，真枪真刀地同敌人战斗过。也因此，他写的小说里边有他的血，有他的泪，更有他写作时一颗滚烫的心。

马石山是屹立在峻青故乡的一座英雄的山，在抗日战争年代里，这里的军民用自己的血肉之躯一次又一次地挫败日寇的扫荡和围剿，曾发生过八路军的十壮士为保护老百姓突围，一次又一次冲入敌人“火网”的壮举。峻青是这场战斗的亲历者，也是被十壮士救出来的人员之一。他说，本来这十位战士完全可以一起撤走，但走了不远，忽又听到山谷中有老乡呼救声，于是，立即又返回敌人的“火网”中，最后拉响了手榴弹与敌人同归于尽。马石山战斗刚刚结束，山头上还冒着硝烟，十壮士和乡亲们的尸体还没来得及掩埋的情况下，峻青在逆风呼啸、大雪纷飞的山麓含着热泪，在粗糙的笔记本上写下了这场战斗，时为 1942 年 12 月。1951 年，他修改加工当年的草稿。1954 年，他在上海的家中又重写，终于完成这一战争文学名篇。

同样，当年一个八路军的通讯员曾护送峻青等五六个人过潍河，拂晓时遭遇了敌人。当他们全部渡过潍河安全转移后，却发现通讯员为掩护他们壮烈牺牲了。解放后，峻青又回到当年战地，遍寻潍河两岸的十几个村庄，终于打听到了这个小战士的坟墓。他站在这座坟墓前鞠躬、流泪，默哀了良久。让峻青深为遗憾和不安的是，小通讯员死得如此悲壮，却至死也没留下名字，直到今天，这里仍是一座无名烈士墓。就在找到小通讯员墓的当天夜里，峻青的心再也无法平静，在一间小屋子里的煤油灯下，含泪写下了《黎明的河边》，其主人公小陈的原型就是这位小通讯员。

峻青的战争文学作品的共同特点是，作者善于用浓重的笔墨，从正面描绘革命斗争的艰难、残酷，刻画在艰苦的环境中人民大众对革命事业的无比坚贞，为我们绘制了一幅幅色彩绚丽、气吞山河的历史画卷。而正是这些革命斗争题材小说的创作，确立了峻青在 20 世纪后半期中国文学史上的地位。

建筑简介：复兴西路34号

峻青寓所位于复兴西路34号卫乐公寓，原名卫乐精舍，建于1934年，赉安洋行设计，占地面积1720平方米，建筑面积3797平方米，汽车间附屋802平方米，属现代点式建筑风格的公寓住宅。建筑为十三层钢筋混凝土结构，两翼跌落一层，立面对称，竖三段布置，中间凸出，设一串挑出的半圆阳台为构图中心，两边为卧入式阳台形成竖向线条；水泥砂浆外墙，立面中部竖线条及突出的半圆阳台为暗红色粉刷，其余部分为浅黄色粉刷，山墙顶部及南侧有重复线条装饰。楼前有小花园。中华人民共和国成立后，吕蒙与黄准夫妇、陈鲤庭、吴强、赖少其、峻青、王西彦等一批文化人在此居住。1994年2月15日上海市人民政府公布其为市优秀历史建筑。

JUN Qing

JUN Qing (1922–) has his ancestral family from Haiyang in Shandong province and has a former name of SUN Junqing. He is known as a writer. In 1941 he started to get works published. In 1946 he joined the CPC. Successively he served as correspondent of *The Masses Daily* in Shandong, war correspondent of the front office of the Xinhua News Agency, leader of an armed work team in Changwei area, editorial team leader of *The Central Plains Daily*, editorial director of South Central People's Broadcasting Station and publicity section chief, vice chairman and acting party secretary of the Shanghai branch of China Writers Association, editor-in-chief of *Literary Newspaper* and vice president of Shanghai Yanhuang Culture Research Association. His works have a solid foundation of life, and the spirit of revolutionary romanticism, with moving stories and vivid characters. His representative works include *The Riverbank at Dawn* and *Party Member Registration Form*. His other works include a novel *Tsunami*, short story collections like *The Final Report*, *Angry Billows* and *Sea Swallows*, prose collections like *Essays about a European Travel*, *Ode to Autumn*, *Ode to Brave Pass* and *Ode to Wide Sea,* and criticism collections *JUN Qing on Creative Writing* and *Collected Works by JUN Qing* (6 volumes).

Famous Works on War Written with Tears

Novels by JUN Qing, such as *On Mount Horse Stone*, *The Riverbank at Dawn* and *Party Member Registration Form*, were once popular in the literary circle and exerted far-reaching impact. Why did his works have such strong shocking value and sense of affinity? It turned out that his works were hammered out in the hail of bullets. He was a witness of battles and fought with the enemy with real guns. As a result, he wrote into his novels his blood and his tears and all the more his hot heart during his creative writing.

Mount Horse Stone is a heroic mountain standing in the hometown of JUN Qing. During the War of Resistance against Japan, soldiers and civilians here defeated the Japanese raids and encirclement again and again with their own flesh and blood. There had been the heroic feat of ten heroes from the Eighth Route Army who broke again and again into the "fire net" of the enemy to protect

抗战时期，峻青在胶东前线
During the War of Resistance, JUN Qing was at the battlefront in Jiaodong Peninsula.

the people in the process of breakthroughs. He was not only a witness of this battle, but also one of the people rescued by the ten soldiers. He said that the 10 soldiers could have been able to withdraw together with others, but when they were still not far away, they suddenly heard the villagers' cry for help in the valley. They immediately returned to the enemy's "fire net". Finally they pulled the pins of hand grenades and perished together with the enemy. When the battle at Mount Horse Stone had just ended, smoke still rose on the top of the hill, and the ten heroes and villagers had not been buried, JUN Qing recorded the battle in a rough notebook in the whistling wind and floating snow at the foot of the hill, his eyes being full of tears. It was in the December of 1942. In 1951, he modified the draft made years ago. In 1954, he rewrote it at home in Shanghai and finally completed his famous literary works on war.

Similarly, once a correspondent of the Eighth Route Army escorted five or six persons including JUN Qing to cross a river. At dawn they encountered the enemy. When they all crossed the river and transferred securely, they found that the correspondent heroically sacrificed his life in order to shield them. After the liberation, JUN Qing went back to the battle field, searching all over a dozen villages at the riverbank and finally found the tomb of this little soldier. He stood before the tomb, bowing, shedding tears and standing in silent tribute for a long time. To his deep regret and anxiety, the correspondent died such a solemn death, but his name remained unknown. Until today, here is still a tomb of a nameless martyr. At the very night of the day when he found the tomb of the little correspondent, JUN Qing's heart could keep calm no longer. Under a kerosene lamp in a small room, he started writing the novel *The Riverbank at Dawn* with his eyes full of tears. Its protagonist is the correspondent.

The common feature of JUN Qing's war literature is that the author is good at depicting in details the hardships and cruelty of the revolutionary struggle from the positive perspective, portraying the immense faith of the masses in the revolutionary cause even in a difficult environment and depicting for us vivid and majestic pictures of history. It is precisely the creation of these novels with the revolutionary struggle theme that established his status in the history of Chinese literature in the late 20th century.

The apartment of JUN Qing is located in Willow Apartment at No. 34 on West Fuxing Road, formerly known as Willow Court. Designed by Leonard-Veysseyre-Kruze Architects and built in 1934, it covers an area of 1,720 square meters with a construction area of 3,797 square meters and attached rooms of 802 square meters for garage. It is an apartment of point construction and modern architectural style. The building has thirteen floors with a reinforced concrete structure. Its facade is symmetrical with three sections with the middle standing out and the two wings being one floor lower than the middle. A series of projected semi-circular balconies form the center of the composition. At both sides the receding balconies form vertical lines; exterior walls are coated with cement mortar; the vertical lines and prominent semi-circular balconies in the middle section have a color of dark red, and the remaining parts are of light yellow. At the top and the south side of the gable, parallel lines are used for decoration. In addition, a small garden is in front of the building. After the founding of the People's Republic of China, a number of cultural people once lived here. On February 15, 1994, it became a Heritage Architecture issued by the Shanghai Municipal People's Government.

峻青 （邬海佳画）　　JUN Qing （By WU Haijia）

徐玉兰
（1921—2017）

祖籍浙江富阳，越剧表演艺术家。1933 年进新登东安舞台科班学艺，同年到上海。1939 年与吴月奎等组建兴华越剧社。1947 年，自组玉兰剧团。1952 年率团参加中央军委总政治部文工团越剧队。1954 年加入上海越剧院。表演富有激情，善于塑造人物，尤擅扮演风流倜傥的角色，独步越坛。唱腔除继承越剧传统老调外，广泛吸收京、绍、杭等剧种的声腔成分，具有高昂激越的特色，被称为徐派。代表作有《红楼梦》（饰贾宝玉）、《西厢记》（饰张珙）、《追鱼》（饰张珍）、《北地王》（饰刘谌）等。1989 年获首届“金唱片奖”。2013 年获中国戏剧奖终身成就奖。2014 年获上海文艺家终身荣誉奖。著有《徐玉兰艺术生涯八十年》。

徐王舞台并蒂莲

恰如越剧《红楼梦》“宝黛初会”中所唱：“眼前分明是外来客，心底恰似旧时友。”1948 年秋，徐玉兰见到了比自己小 5 岁的王文娟，大有相见恨晚的感觉。9 月 22 日，两人在上海明星大戏院首演《风萧萧》，自此开启了徐王半个多世纪的舞台合作生涯。

到中华人民共和国成立，两人已合作推出了《荆轲刺秦王》《红娘子》《吕布与貂蝉》《信陵公子》《玉面狼》等剧目。1951 年，她们克服家庭困难，一起带团北上参军，并于 1953 年参加赴朝慰问团。

在朝鲜，整整 9 个月，徐玉兰和王文娟同睡一个铺，同吃一锅饭，逢到演出还互打背包。一天，王文娟牙齿发炎，痛得半边脸红肿。徐玉兰拦车送她去部队医院。那时正是六月天，她们顶着烈日到了医院。医生给王文娟打针，王文娟一阵剧痛惊叫。徐玉兰在旁安慰，又急又累，竟中暑晕了过去。待到醒来，王文娟反在一旁劝慰照顾徐玉兰了。

1960 年，徐王在广州演出《追鱼》。最后演“分别”时，徐玉兰有个“抢背”动作，本应将昏倒在地的“鲤鱼精”——王文娟扶起，可这时她却站不起来。王文娟一见徐玉兰脸色苍白，汗珠直冒，连忙反过来扶起徐玉兰。到后台，当发现锁骨从肩胛处突出，方知是锁骨骨折，王文娟心疼得直掉眼泪，赶紧送她去医院。

用她俩自己的话来说：“我们在一起生活、演出的时间要多于家庭生活的时间。”几十年来，两人足迹遍及全国和海外。20 世纪五六十年代，是徐王越剧艺术的成熟期。她们此时合作的精品《追鱼》《春香传》《西厢记》《北地王》《关汉卿》等如繁花吐蕊，最终《红楼梦》将她们的艺术推向高峰。1962 年这部越剧被搬上银幕。

令人高兴的是，就在拍摄《红楼梦》期间，王文娟找到了自己的人生伴侣——电影表演艺术家孙道临。这桩良缘是黄宗江和徐玉兰促成的。徐玉兰一直说，“王文娟和孙道临，我是大媒。”在《红楼梦》拍摄结束后，王文娟和孙道临去庐山度蜜月，而徐玉兰和她的先生俞则人高兴地随之同行，分享幸福。

1985 年，徐王组建红楼剧团。两人壮心不已，决心为越剧艺术后继有人再创辉煌。

建筑简介：复兴西路44弄6号

徐玉兰旧居位于复兴西路44弄玫瑰别墅6号。玫瑰别墅建于1940年，由七幢风格类似的住宅式公寓组成，占地面积4393平方米，建筑总面积3175平方米。七幢建筑均为平屋顶，水泥砂浆外墙，三层砖木结构，平面每层都有厨房间、备餐间、卫生间、客厅、卧室等，形体简洁，体现现代建筑风格，屋前有花园。孙科二夫人蓝妮亲自督工建造，7幢房子用7种不同的颜色，十分醒目、别致，因弄口地面上砌有“玫瑰”两字，老上海人称之为“玫瑰别墅”。2号曾住过孙科、蓝妮夫妇，金焰、秦怡夫妇；周小燕曾住过7号。

XU Yulan

XU Yulan (1921–2017) has her ancestral family from Fuyang in Zhejiang province and is known as a performing artist of Yue Opera. In 1933, she became an apprentice in Dong'an professional training class in Xindeng and in the same year she went to Shanghai. In 1939, she set up the Xinghua Yue Opera Society together with WU Yuekui and other people. In 1947, she started up her own troupe called Yulan Troupe. In 1952, she led her members to join the Yue Opera troupe of the General Political Department of the Central Military Commission. Since 1954, she joined the Shanghai Yue Opera House. Her performance is greatly abundant in passion, and she is adroit at the characterization of figures, especially those who are handsome and debonair, which earns her a leading role in Yue Opera. Apart from the succession to the traditional tunes of Yue Opera, her aria is characterized by high spirits and has extensively absorbed the tune elements of Beijing Opera, Yue Opera, Hangzhou Opera and other types of operas, which is widely recognized as the XU Style. She boasts a large number of representative works, including *A Dream of Red Mansions* (acting as JIA Baoyu), *West Chamber* (acting as ZHANG Gong), *Chasing Fish* (acting as ZHANG Zhen), and *The King of the North* (acting as LIU Chen). She won the first Golden Record Award in 1989 and the Chinese Drama Award for Lifetime Achievement in 2013 as well as the Lifetime Honorary Award of Shanghai Artists in 2014. *Eighty-year Art Career of XU Yulan* is one of her remarkable works.

Twin Flowers on the Stage

Just as what was sung during Bao and Dai's first meeting in the opera *A Dream of Red Mansions*, "although apparently, JIA Baoyu was a young man whom LIN Daiyu had never met before, she still felt familiar with him." XU met WANG Wenjuan, who was 5 years younger than her in the autumn of 1948. Both of them regretted that they had not known each other before. On September 22, they made their debut performance in *The Wind Withers* in Shanghai Star Theater, which opened a new chapter for their cooperation on stage for more than half a century.

By the time when the People's Republic of China was founded, they had co-starred some famous operas, including *The Emperor and the Assassin, Red Lady*, *LÜ Bu and DIAO Chan*, *Prince Xinling* and *Jade Face Wolf*. In 1951, they led members to proceed northward to join the army regardless of objection of their families and took part in the relief team to North Korea in 1953.

徐玉兰（左）饰贾宝玉，王文娟（右）饰林黛玉
XU Yulan (left) as JIA Baoyu and WANG Wenjuan (right) as LIN Daiyu.

During a period of 9 months in North Korea, XU and WANG shared one bed and had meals together, and also helped each other to pack when they had performance. One day, WANG was caught by dental inflammation and was so painful that half of her face swelled. XU quickly sent her to a military hospital. It was a day in June when they went to the hospital under the scorching sun. When doctor gave Wang an injection, Wang screamed out of the severe pain. Standing aside, anxious and tired, XU kept comforting Wang patiently. However, she fainted due to heatstroke and when she woke up, Wang in turn comforted and attended to her.

In 1960, XU and WANG performed in *Chasing Fish* in Guangzhou. At the end of the opera when performing the scene of departure, XU had an action of falling forward in which she should have lifted up WANG who pretended to faint on the ground when playing the role of evil spirit of carp. However, it was at the very moment that XU could not stand up. Seeing her pale and sweaty face, WANG quickly held her up in turn. They immediately arrived at the backstage, only to find the clavicle was out of the scapular. It was not until that time that they realized it was the clavicle fracture. WANG was so heart-broken that she couldn't stop shedding tears and quickly sent XU to the hospital.

They once said, "We spend more time on performance than on our family." In several decades, they performed around the country and even the entire world. The 1950s and the 1960s were the mature period of their opera. At that time, they cooperated to compose a large number of operas, including *Chasing Fish*, *Chunxiang*, *West Chamber*, *The King of the North*, *GUAN Hanqing* and other works. These works appeared one after another, all of which can be regarded as masterpieces in their career. Finally, *A Dream of Red Mansions* was played on the screen in 1962 and pushed their art to the peak.

Happily, it was during the very period when A *Dream of Red Mansions* was produced that WANG Wenjuan encountered with her life partner SUN Daolin, a film artist. This predestined affinity was contributed by HUANG Zongjiang and XU Yulan. XU always said that she was the matchmaker for WANG Wenjuan and SUN Daolin. After the shooting of *The Dream of Red Mansion*, WANG Wenjuan and SUN Daolin went to Lushan Mountain for their honeymoon with the company of XU Yulan and YU Zeren, her husband, who shared their happiness.

In 1985, XU and WANG cooperated to establish the Red Mansions Troupe. They were still in high aspirations and determined to gain another glory for the succession of Yue opera.

The former residence of XU Yulan lies in building No. 6 Alley 44 on West Fuxing Road (also called Rose Villa), which was built in 1940. It consists of seven residential apartments of similar style, covering an area of 4,393 square meters with a total construction area of 3,175 square meters. These seven buildings have flat roofs, exterior walls composed of cement and mortar, as well as the structure of three-story brick and wood. Each floor is equipped with a kitchen, pantry, bathroom, living room, bedroom, etc. The buildings boast themselves a concise form with a garden in front of the house, reflecting a style of modern architecture. The construction of the seven houses was supervised by LAN Ni, the second wife of SUN Ke, with seven different colors, making the houses not only eye-catching but also quite chic. Old Shanghai people called it Rose Villa for the word "Rose" carved on the ground of the alley entrance. The building No. 2 once housed the couple SUN Ke and LAN Ni, and JIN Yan and QIN Yi as well. The building No. 7 once housed ZHOU Xiaoyan.

徐玉兰 （戴晓明画）　　XU Yulan （By DAI Xiaoming）

聂耳
（1912—1935）

原籍云南玉溪，生于昆明，原名守信，字子义，后改紫艺。自幼喜好音乐。1927 年考入云南省立第一师范学校。1928 年加入中国共产主义青年团。1930 年到上海。1931 年进入明月歌舞团，开始从事专业音乐工作。1932 年参加北平左翼音乐家联盟的组建工作。1933 年初加入中国共产党，同年任中国电影文化协会常委兼组织部秘书。曾与任光等发起组织中国新兴音乐研究会。1934 年 4 月进入百代唱片公司，创作、发行了大量革命歌曲。1935 年 1 月进入联华影业公司，任二厂音乐部主任，同年 4 月取道日本赴苏联学习，7 月 17 日在日本藤泽鹄沼海滨游泳时不幸溺水去世。创作有歌曲《大路歌》《毕业歌》《义勇军进行曲》等 30 余首，对唤起民众、开展抗日救亡运动起了很大的推动作用。

《义勇军进行曲》的诞生

1935 年 2 月，田汉等左翼文艺工作者被捕入狱。当时日本已侵占东北，仍不断扩张。在此生死存亡的危急关头，与中国共产党有很深渊源的电通影片公司，决定将田汉创作的《凤凰再生》剧本梗概交由时为中共地下党“电影小组”组长的夏衍赶写成电影文学剧本，更名为《风云儿女》，展现中国青年在日寇入侵、国家与民族面临危难之时勇敢走上前线的英雄气概。

聂耳得知此事，询问夏衍：“听说《风云儿女》的结尾有一个主题歌？”夏衍给他看了电影剧本，他一拿到便直奔最后一首歌，念了两遍说，“作曲交给我。”“我干，田先生一定会同意的！”还没等夏衍回答，就和他握手，仿佛他早已认可。

《风云儿女》的主题歌被命名为《义勇军进行曲》。为了这首歌曲的创作，聂耳几乎废寝忘食，在他位于霞飞路的住所（今淮海中路 1258 号）内，夜以继日地忘我投入对曲调节奏的构思中。他时而在桌上打节拍，时而弹奏钢琴，时而来回踱步酝酿，时而又高声吟唱。房东以为这位房客发了疯，跑上楼将他训斥了一番。

4 月的一天清晨，聂耳前往荆州路 405 号电通影片公司摄影棚，敲响了导演许幸之的房门，一进门便举着乐谱高兴地说：“好啦！《义勇军进行曲》谱好了。”然后手持乐谱，一边在桌上打起拍子，一边嘹亮地唱起这首歌：“起来，不愿做奴隶的人们！……冒着敌人的飞机大炮前进，前进，前进，前进！”一遍遍地唱，直到他停下征求导演的意见。“整个曲子谱得很好，激昂、轻快，但起句显得低沉了一些，而最后一句还不够坚强有力。是否应当减少一些装饰音，形成一个坚强有力的煞尾？”聂耳沉吟片刻，拿起铅笔，将起句修改得更为奋发昂扬，又把末尾田汉原作的词改为“冒着敌人的炮火前进！前进！前进！进！”，两人不约而同一起唱起来。

1935 年 4 月 15 日清晨，为躲避国民党当局追捕，聂耳取道日本赴苏联学习。他携带着已完成的《义勇军进行曲》初稿，于 4 月末修改定稿后，从东京邮寄回国。

1949 年，《义勇军进行曲》成为中华人民共和国代国歌。2004 年 3 月 14 日中华人民共和国第十届全国人民代表大会第二次会议正式将《义勇军进行曲》作为国歌写入《中华人民共和国宪法》。

建筑简介：淮海中路1258号

聂耳于 1934 年底至 1935 年 4 月中旬赴日前租住在淮海中路 1258 号三楼。这幢近代公寓住宅具装饰艺术派风格。底层沿街为商铺，二、三层为住宅，屋顶南端有女儿墙，设置有折线形山墙和壁柱，柱头饰竖向条形浮雕，檐下有花瓣状雕饰板。每户单元立面均设有悬挑的阳台，铸铁围栏，开落地钢窗，窗裙及窗楣贴棕褐色泰山面砖，北侧三层有晒台。室内结构紧凑，各楼层皆设有卫生间，正房有壁炉。建筑由比商义品地产公司挂旗经租，至今仍由中方物业公司代收租金。目前该单元住宅部分由四户居民合用。

NIE Er

NIE Er (1912–1935) has his ancestral family from Yuxi and he was born in Kunming, both in Yunnan province. He had a former name of Shouxin with a courtesy name of Ziyi (literally children's righteousness) and later changed into Ziyi (literally purple art). He loved music since his childhood. In 1927, he was admitted to the First Normal School in Yunnan province. In 1928, he joined the Chinese Communist Youth League. In 1930, he arrived at Shanghai. In 1931, he entered the Bright Moon Song and Dance Troupe and began to engage himself in professional work of music. In 1932, he participated in the formation of Beijing Left-Wing Musicians Union. At the beginning of 1933, he joined the CPC and served as member of the Standing Committee as well as secretary of the Organization Department of Chinese Film Culture Association in the same year. Once he worked with others in initiating and organizing China's Xinxing Music Research Institute. In April 1934, he entered EMI Company and composed and issued a large number of revolutionary songs. In January 1935, he joined Lianhua Film Company and served as director of music department of its second factory. In April the same year he went to the Soviet Union to study via Japan. On July 17, he unfortunately passed away of drowning when he was swimming at Kugenuma Beach of Fujisawa in Japan. He composed over 30 songs such as *Song of the Broad Road*, *Graduation Song* and *March of the Volunteers*, which contributed to arouse the people to carry out the campaign against Japanese invasion for national salvation.

The Birth of *March of the Volunteers*

In February 1935, some left-wing writers and artists were arrested and imprisoned. At that time the Japanese invaders had occupied the Northeast and were still expanding. At this crucial moment of life and death, the Dentsu Film Company, which had a close relationships with the CPC, decided to hand over to XIA Yan the outline of the play *Phoenix Rebirth* created by TIAN Han in order that it could be adapted into film script since XIA was the film team leader of the underground Communist Party of China. The script was renamed as *Children of Trouble Time*, which showed the heroic spirit of the Chinese youth who bravely marched to the

1934 年夏天，聂耳（左）与田汉在上海合影
A photo of NIE Er (left) and TIAN Han in Shanghai in the summer of 1934.

front during the national crisis because of the Japanese invasion.

When NIE Er got to know that, he asked XIA Yan, "I happen to hear that there is a theme song at the end of film, right?" XIA showed him the film script while he directly jumped to the last song. After reading twice, he said, "I'll be responsible for music composition." "I'll do it. Mr. TIAN will agree!" Before XIA replied, he shook hands with him, as if XIA had already agreed.

The theme song of *Children of Trouble Time* was named as *March of the Volunteers*. For its creation, NIE Er lived a life of almost sleepless nights. In his residence at Xiafei Road (now No. 1258 on Middle Huaihai Road), he devoted himself day and night to the conception of the melody and rhythm of the song. He now beat on the desk for meter and now played the piano and now paced back and forth to consider and now sang aloud. The landlord thought the tenant had gone mad and ran upstairs to rebuke him a lot.

On an early morning one day in April, NIE Er went to Dentsu film studio at No. 405 on Jingzhou Road and knocked at the door of the director. No sooner had he entered than he held a sheet of music, saying happily, "It's done! The music of *March of the Volunteers* is ready."After that, holding the sheet of music in his hand and playing the beat on the desk, he sang the song in a loud and clear voice, "Arise! All those who don't want to be slaves!... Brave the enemy's planes and cannons, March on! March on! March on! March on!" He sang again and again until he stopped to seek the views of the director. "The song is very good as a whole, being passionate and resilient. But the first sentence seems to be a bit low-spirited while the last sentence is not strong and forceful enough. Would it be better to reduce the number of decorative sound to form a strong and powerful ending all of a sudden?" He pondered for a moment, picked up a pencil and modified the first sentence to be more high-spirited. Furthermore, he changed the ending of the original words by TIAN Han into "Brave the enemy's fire, March on! March on! March on! On!" Spontaneously the two sang the song together.

In the early morning of April 15, 1935, he went to the Soviet Union by way of Japan to study music in order to escape from the hunting of the KMT authority. Bringing with him the first draft of the song *March of the Volunteers*, he made the final revision of it at the end of April and sent it back home from Tokyo by mail.

In 1949, the song became the national anthem of the country. On March 14, 2004, the Second Session of the Tenth National People's Congress of the People's Republic of China formally wrote it as the national anthem into the *Constitution of the People's Republic of China*.

From the end of 1934 to the mid-April 1935 and before he went to Japan, he lived by rent on the third floor at No. 1258 on Middle Huaihai Road. This modern apartment residence is of Art Deco style. At the bottom along the street are shops and the second and third floors are for residence. The roof has a parapet at the southern end with fold-lined gables and pilasters, at the top of which are column headdresses with reliefs of vertical strip. Under the eaves are petal-shaped and carved panels. The front of each section is equipped with cantilevered balconies, cast iron railings and open landing windows of steel. Window spandrels and lintels are affixed with brown bricks of Taishan brand. At the north side there are balconies on the third floor. The indoor structure is compact and all floors are equipped with bathrooms. The main room has a fireplace. The building was leased by Crédit Foncier D'Extréme-Orient, a real estate company and the rent is now still collected by the Chinese property management company instead. At present the residential section of the apartment is shared by four families.

聂耳 （钱定华画）　　NIE Er （By QIAN Dinghua）

莫觞清
（1871—1932）

浙江吴兴（今浙江湖州）人。幼入私塾，后进学堂。1900 年，入苏州延昌永丝织厂，两年后到上海勤昌丝厂任总管车。1903 年，与王笙甫等人创办上海久成丝厂，生产“玫瑰”和“金刚钻”牌生丝。次年任上海宝康丝厂经理。1910 年后，先后开设久成二厂、又成丝厂、恒丰丝厂、久成三厂、德成丝厂等。到 1913 年，投资开设或任经理的丝厂达 10 余家，成为上海缫丝业最大的资本家之一。同时兼任美商蓝乐壁洋行买办。1917 年，同汪辅卿及美国人蓝乐壁合资开设美亚织绸厂，两年后停办。1920 年春，与天生锦绸庄合作，再度开设美亚织绸厂，聘请从美国留学回国的蔡声白任经理。晚年辞去蓝乐壁洋行买办职务，过寓公生活。1932 年病故于上海。

丝业巨擘的经营之道

茅盾小说《子夜》里民族资本家吴荪甫的原型便是上海丝业大亨——莫觞清，但与吴荪甫以破产崩溃告终截然不同的是，莫觞清的丝厂经营有方，虽历经起起落落，却仍保持业界领先的势头。在他去世前两年，他独资的美亚织绸厂有丝织机 1200 台，为全国规模最大的丝织厂。

莫觞清早年对外语产生兴趣，其父为他请了英语教师，好学的他利用在父亲的土丝行里当帮工之余暇，手不释卷。成年后，抽检厂丝，检查条纹均匀与否、是否有断头或糙块等丝厂工作，他都游刃有余，并凭借熟练的英语兼任翻译。

积累管理丝厂的经验后，他与王笙甫、杨孚生等人合伙，在上海徐家汇开办久成丝厂，尔后丝厂由他独资经营，1910 年又增加厂房扩展规模。1903—1928 年的 25 年间，莫觞清在上海独资经营的丝厂达到十家之多，一年可生产厂丝约 6000 担。他的经营之道在于：一来他有灵通的信息，因他兼任蓝乐璧洋行买办，能第一时间看到国外发来的丝业行情电报，如行情看涨便囤货不放、待价而沽，若有下跌势头则尽快抛售。其二，他十分重视生丝质量，针对丝厂的意大利式坐缫车设备，特意聘请意大利的专业人员担任总工程师专负检验产品质量之责，对投放的丝茧数量极尽苛刻，确保丝织的条纹粗细恰到好处，莫觞清的丝厂产品由此热销。其三，他知人善任，聘用职员唯才是举，如经理毛益群、汤也钦等人，都是因为精通业务、认真能干而为莫觞清赏识，并且莫觞清在经营过程中能悉心听取他们的意见，及时调整决策从而规避风险。例如 1929 年受世界经济危机影响，丝业亦不景气，适逢此时国外寄来一张要货单，汤也钦劝说莫觞清抛售 2000 担，这一举措挽救了莫觞清的企业。

莫觞清旧居位于武康路2号，建于1922年，占地面积约2400平方米，建筑面积937平方米。建筑为假三层砖混结构，主体立面对称，中部阳台为半圆形平面；入口立两根塔司干式柱；长方形窗，红色木窗框，米色水泥拉毛外墙；红瓦坡顶，出檐较浅，开老虎窗，有三个白色烟囱突出屋面。房前有大花园。20世纪50年代，上海市委书记柯庆施曾在此居住。2005年10月31日上海市人民政府公布其为市优秀历史建筑。

MO Shangqing

MO Shangqing (1871—1932) has his ancestral family from Zhejiang Wuxing (now Huzhou in Zhejiang province). In his childhood, he entered into an old-style private school and later went to a modern school. In 1900, he got into the Suzhou Yanchangyong Silk Mill and two years later transferred to the Shanghai Qinchang Silk Mill and served as general manager of spinning wheels. In 1903, he founded the Shanghai Jiucheng Silk Mill along with WANG Shengfu and others, producing raw silk of the brands "Rose" and "Diamond". The next year he served as manager of Shanghai Baokang Silk Mill. After 1910, he founded successively the Second Jiucheng Silk Mill, Youcheng Silk Mill, Hengfeng Silk Mill, the Third Jiucheng Silk Mill and Decheng Silk Mill. By 1913, the number of mills which he invested or where served as manager amounted to over ten, becoming one of the largest capitalists of silk reeling industry in Shanghai. Also he served as comprador of the American business R. Lang & Co., Inc. In 1917, he founded a joint venture Mayer Silk Mill with WANG Fuqing and an American businessman R. Lang, which closed down two years later. In the spring of 1920, he re-established Mayer Silk Mill in cooperation with the Tianshengjin Silk Store, inviting CAI Shengbai to serve as manager who came back from the United States. In his later years, he resigned from the position of comprador in R. Lang & Co., Inc. and lived a rich life. In 1932, he passed away of illness in Shanghai.

Way of Operation of a Silk Industry Giant

The prototype of the national capitalist WU Sunfu in the novel *Midnight* by Mao Dun was the silk tycoon MO Shangqing in

莫觞清（后排左六）全家合影
A family photo of Mo Shangqing (sixth from left in the back row).

Shanghai. However, totally different from the bankruptcy and collapse of WU, the silk factory of the latter was well run. After its ups and downs, it still kept the momentum of the leading role in the field of industry. Two years before his passing away, the Mayer Silk Mill with his exclusive investment had 1,200 silk looms, which was the largest silk factory in the whole country.

In the early years he had interest in foreign languages and his father invited an English teacher for him. Eager to learn, he was very studious in his spare time when he was a helper in his father's native silk business. In his adulthood, he was at ease with such work in the silk mill as random check of filature silk, checking the uniformity of stripes, and broken ends or rough blocks. In addition, he served as part-time translator with his proficient English.

After the accumulation of experience in the management of silk factory, he co-founded the Jiucheng Silk Mill in Xujiahui District in Shanghai together with WANG Shengfu, YANG Fusheng and others. Later he invested and operated the mill solely by himself. In 1910, workshops were added for expansion. During the 25 years from 1903 to 1928, the number of mills which he independently invested and operated amounted to over ten, the annual production reaching 6,000 *dan* of filature silk. The knacks of his business included several aspects. First, he was able to get quick information due to his position of comprador in R. Lang & Co., Inc. and get in the first time silk market telegrams sent from foreign countries. If the market prices were expected to rise, he would be hoarding goods and wait for the highest bid; if the prices told the tendency to fall, he would close out. Second, he attached great importance to the quality of raw silk. Given the Italian-style reeling car equipment in his silk factory, he specially hired Italian professionals to serve as the chief engineer in charge of testing product quality. He was extremely rigorous with the number of silk cocoon to ensure that the thickness of silk stripes was just right so that the silk products from his factory sold like hot cakes. Third, he knew his subordinates well enough to assign them jobs commensurate with their abilities. In addition his employment was only talent-oriented, such as the employment of the managers MAO Yiqun, TANG Yeqin and others, who were proficient in business, earnest and capable and therefore were appreciated by the boss. Moreover he carefully listened to and accepted their views in the process of operation and made timely adjustment of decision-making to avoid risks. For example, due to the influence of the world economic crisis in 1929, the silk industry was also sluggish. Just at that time, an order of products was sent to him from abroad. TANG Yeqin persuaded him to sell 2,000 *dan* of silk, which saved his enterprise.

The former residence of MO Shangqing is located at No. 2 on Wukang Road. Built in 1922, it covers an area of about 2,400 square meters with a construction area of 937 square meters. With a nominally three-storied structure of brick and concrete, it has a symmetrical facade. The central balcony has a semi-circular plane; at the entrance stand two Tuscan-style columns; it has rectangular windows, red wooden window frames and cream-colored cement napped walls; its roof has gentle slopes with red tiles, short eaves, tiger windows and three white chimneys standing out on the roof. There is a big garden in front of the building. In the 1950s, KE Qingshi, party secretary of the CPC Shanghai Committee, once lived here. On October 31, 2005, it became a Heritage Architecture issued by the Shanghai Municipal People's Government.

莫觞清 （齐亚明画）　　MO Shangqing （By QI Yaming）

袁一灵
（1917—1992）

祖籍江苏，出生于上海，原名袁国良，曲艺表演艺术家。1934年加入癸酉社学习文明戏，师从滑稽艺人赵希希，有“唱派滑稽”之称。先后在艺锋滑稽剧团、蜜蜂滑稽剧团、上海人民艺术剧院滑稽剧团、上海滑稽剧团任演员。擅长扮演机智“小人物”，在《前说后忘记》《钱笃笤求雨》《笑着向昨天告别》等滑稽戏中均有不俗表演。1980年后与荧屏结缘，主演喜剧电视片《颠倒主仆》。美国著名喜剧专家鲍勃·霍甫非常欣赏其表演才华，特邀其合拍喜剧片《通向中国之路》。自1934年创编演出《金铃塔》后，经数十年营造构筑，在唱念中融合了“快口”“绕口”技巧，成为上海绝唱，流传至今不衰。

上海绝唱《金铃塔》

谁能相信，滑稽名家袁一灵还曾是个口吃患者。原来，袁一灵幼年时的确患有口吃，讲话期期艾艾。初学文明戏时先生还不肯收他，是袁一灵“保证上台不打‘格楞’”，先生才同意试试。可袁一灵是个倔性子，明知自己口吃，偏偏专攻口吃患者最为忌讳的绕口令。功夫不负有心人，他不仅创编演出了令口齿伶俐的人都感到为难的《金铃塔》，而且居然基本消除了口吃。

那是1934年，17岁的袁一灵进癸酉社学戏不久，就参加文明戏《过关》的演出。《过关》是《孟姜女》中一场过场玩笑戏，明令任何人过关必须献艺。那天，袁一灵第一次登台，饰演过关人。当他过关时很是为难，因为他初学戏，拿不出绝活。无奈之中他突然想到平时学来的绕口令片段，那是民间流传后被苏州滩簧吸收的一个曲艺小段，叫《孩儿莲花落》。他大着胆子上台演了，没想到，不仅关官听得捋须抚掌频频点头，而且观众中也爆发出一阵阵掌声。从此，袁一灵便以毕生精力潜心构筑他的《金铃塔》。

几十年来，袁一灵不断地更换、调整绕口令的内容，在七段绕口令的结构、难度、速度上都作了精心的锤炼，终于形成一个完整的整体。他咬字准确、吐字清晰、舌如鼓簧、语似连珠、快而不喘、一气呵成，特别是他说绕口令时速度快得惊人，有人曾做过一次测试，他演唱最快时，击板人一秒钟要击板7次。

《金铃塔》终成袁一灵的经典代表作，在上海家喻户晓。“一曲金铃成绝唱，灵仙人间留轻音。”1992年袁一灵病逝，有人写了这样的对联来评价他。袁一灵的一生是营造构筑金铃宝塔的一生，金铃塔离不开袁一灵，袁一灵就是金铃塔。

1993年，袁一灵家人特地去浙江选择了一个以宝塔为背景的墓地，让袁老在宝塔旁安息。那天家人带去了录音机，再一次播放袁老生前演唱的《金铃塔》……

建筑简介：乌鲁木齐中路148弄1号

袁一灵旧居位于乌鲁木齐中路148弄1号。乌鲁木齐中路148弄原名琪美新村，建于1941年，为花园里弄住宅。房屋为三层砖木结构，建筑平面近似凹字形。东立面和南立面为面砖饰面，其余立面主要为涂料饰面，机制平瓦不规则坡屋面。一层入口位于房屋南侧，入口小门厅及一层走道地面均为水磨石饰面，小门厅地面饰有“FORDA”字样，走道地面饰有树叶图案（据调查，该图案与房屋建造者叶智化有关）；走道西侧原为库房和锅炉间，现为居住房间，东侧原为店面，现为沿街商铺。二至三层平面布局相似，沿中部楼梯间分布有卫生间、厨房间、亭子间和居住房间。室内走道及房间楼面基本为硬木长条地板。木结构双跑楼梯，木踏步，木扶手。门框、护墙板等线脚部位局部保留有精美的木雕花饰。

YUAN Yiling

YUAN Yiling (1917–1992), native of Jiangsu province, was born in Shanghai with a former name of YUAN Guoliang and was known as performance artist of folk art. In 1934 he joined the Guiyou Society to learn new style dramas under the instruction of the farce artist ZHAO Xixi and was known as “Singing Style Farce”. Successively he served as actor in Yifeng Farce Troupe, Bee Farce Troupe, Farce Troupe of Shanghai People’s Art Theater and Shanghai Farce Troupe. Good at playing witty “small persons”, he made impressive performances in all such comic operas as *Forget Before Speaking, QIAN Dutiao Praying for Rain, Bidding Farewell to Yesterday with Smiles* and others. After 1980, he got attached to the screen, starring comic TV series *Upside Down of Master and Servants*. The famous American comedy expert Bob Hope appreciated his performance talent very much and specially invited him to co-produce the comedy *The Road to China*. Since 1934 when he created and performed in *Golden Bell Tower*, decades of construction witnessed the integration into the reading and singing of such techniques as “quick speech” and “tongue twister”, which has become the peak of its category in Shanghai and spread far and wide up to date.

Golden Bell Tower: A Peak in Shanghai

Who could believe that the well-known comic artist YUAN Yiling was also a stuttering patient? Actually, he was indeed suffering from stuttering in his childhood, stammering in his speech. When he intended to learn new style dramas, his teacher refused to accept him. Only when he “promised not to make any hesitations on the stage” did the teacher allowed him to have a try. Nevertheless he had a stubborn temper. Clearly knowing his own stuttering, he still deliberately specialized in tongue twister from which those who stammered abstained. Efforts paid off. He not only created and performed in *Golden Bell Tower*, which was difficult

袁一灵表演《金铃塔》
YUAN Yiling performed in *Golden Bell Tower*.

for people who had a ready tongue, but also actually eliminated stuttering basically.

It was in 1934 when YUAN Yiling entered into Guiyou Society at the age of 17 that he participated in the performance of the drama *Getting Through a Pass*. It was an interlude of comedy from *MENG Jiangnü* in which it was ordered explicitly that any person must demonstrate his talents before getting through the pass. That day was the first time he appeared on stage to play the role of a person who went through a pass. It was very difficult for him because he was at the first stage of learning to perform and did not have any unique skill. In desperation, he suddenly thought of the tongue twister he learned. It was a short section of quyi which was circulated among the folk before it was absorbed by tanhuang, a form of folk art in Suzhou. It was called *Children's Melody*. He tried to be brave to get onto the stage. Out of expectation, not only the pass officer was satisfied since the officer stroked his beard, clapped his hands and nodded frequently, but also the audience burst into applause. Since then he devoted his life to the construction of his *Golden Bell Tower*.

For decades, he constantly changed and adjusted the contents of the tongue twister, made elaborate tempers of the structure, difficulty and speed of seven tongue twisters, and finally formed a complete whole. He was accurate in pronouncing characters and articulate in expression with his tongue being like a spring and his speech being in rapid succession like a chain of pearls. He was fast, but not breathless, accomplishing tongue twisters at a stretch. In particular his tongue twister was surprisingly swift. Some people once did a test to find out that the striker had to beat 7 times within one second when he sang the fastest.

In the end *Golden Bell Tower* became his classic representative, known by one and all in Shanghai. "A song of the bells turns into a peak; An immortal leaves behind him light sound." In 1992 he passed away of illness and such a couplet was written to evaluate him. His lifetime is one to create a golden bell pagoda, which cannot be separated from him. He is the very *golden bell tower*.

In 1993, his family specifically went to Zhejiang province to choose a cemetery for him with a pagoda as its background so that he could take a forever rest next to the pagoda. That day his family members brought a tape recorder with them and once again played the *Golden Bell Tower* which he sang in his lifetime...

The former residence of YUAN Yiling is located at No. 1 in Alley 148 on Middle Urumqi Road, which was formerly known as Qimei New Village and was built in 1941. It is a garden residence in an alley. The three-storey house has a brick-wood structure and the building plane is approximately concave. The east and south facades are decorated with face bricks and the rest is mainly finished with paints. The irregular slopes of the roof are covered with machine-made flat tiles. The entrance on the first floor is located at the south side of the house with the small hall at the entrance and the hallway covered with terrazzo. The floor of the small hall is decorated with "FORDA" and the floor of the hallway is decorated with patterns of leaves (which is associated with the builder YE Zhihua according to investigation). The west side of the hallway was for warehouse and boiler and is now for residence room; the east side was for store and is now for street shops. The layout of the second and third floors is similar; along the middle of the staircase are bathroom, kitchen, garrets and living rooms. The indoor hallway and the floor of rooms are basically covered by hardwood. The double stairs are of a wooden structure with wooden steps and handrails. Door frames and wall panels are locally decorated with fine wood carvings.

袁一灵 （钱定华画） YUAN Yiling （By QIAN Dinghua）

浙江嵊州人，越剧表演艺术家。11岁入越剧科班，工青衣、闺门旦。1942年，与新文艺工作者在大来剧场倡导编、导、演、音、美五位一体的越剧改革。1946年出演越剧《祥林嫂》。1953年主演的我国第一部大型彩色戏曲影片《梁山伯与祝英台》获第八届卡罗维发利国际电影节"音乐片奖"。2006年荣获首次设立的"白玉兰表演艺术终身成就奖"。2008年被授予"国家非物质文化遗产传承人"荣誉称号。她的表演和唱腔柔婉细腻、朴实深沉、韵味醇厚、节奏明快，重视刻画人物性格和内心活动，被誉为"袁派"。1978年起历任上海越剧院院长、名誉院长，上海对外友好协会副会长，全国政协常委等。

袁雪芬
（1922—2011）

钟爱雪松　德艺双馨

1992年，袁雪芬在华东医院结识的友人陈女士送给她一株雪松，袁雪芬十分喜爱这株为庭院带来绿意的雪松。家中的阿姨偶尔为了晾晒衣物想在树上绑一根绳子，袁雪芬担心会影响雪松的自然生长，总会耐心地加以劝阻。她常常在阳台上久久地凝视雪松，在她的心目中，雪松就像她在国外的三个儿子，她天天看着雪松茁壮成长，就像看着不在身边的三个儿子的成长。十多年后，苍翠挺拔的雪松为新康花园带来源源不断的盎然生机，浓荫下袁雪芬儿孙满堂。

客厅靠近书架的墙壁上，悬挂着20世纪60年代末，画家颜文梁特意为袁雪芬历经三年创作而成的风景画《秋岭》，画中郁郁葱葱的树木与庭院中苍翠挺拔的雪松遥相呼应，宁静幽远的画风与新康花园雅致的氛围十分契合。

钟爱雪松的袁雪芬拥有雪松般高洁正直的品格。从1995年起，她连任15届上海"白玉兰戏剧表演艺术奖"评委会主任，她把"清清白白做人，认认真真演戏"的座右铭带到了白玉兰奖的评奖过程中，立下了"吃饭勿到，送礼勿要"的铁律并以身作则严格践行。有一年评奖前，一位上海越剧院的同事带着家乡剧团的客人，一起来到新康花园探望袁雪芬，希望她能多多关照他们的剧目和演员。临走时他们欲向袁雪芬送上一条沉甸甸的金项链，向来和蔼可亲、平易近人的袁雪芬当即沉下脸把他们全都轰了出去。她义正词严地告诫他们："这是对我的污辱！要评奖，就把艺术水平拿出来！"在袁雪芬的带领下，没有黑幕的白玉兰奖始终如雪松般正气凛然、冰清玉洁，成为"最公正、最纯洁"的艺术奖项之一。

建筑简介：淮海中路1273弄

袁雪芬旧居位于淮海中路1273弄新康花园，建于1934年，新马海洋行设计，英商新康洋行投资建造，占地面积12987平方米，建筑面积9318平方米，属花园里弄住宅。新康花园南北贯通淮海中路与复兴中路，由11幢砖木结构二层西班牙式花园住宅和4幢混合结构五层公寓式里弄住宅组成。花园住宅立面竖三段式，中间凸出阳台，券柱式，顶层辟为平台，阳台置螺旋纹柱，缓坡红瓦屋面，檐口有齿形饰。灰色水泥外墙。在坊内中段设集中车库。花园里弄内南北主通道宽6.5米，八条次通道宽5.5米。北部11幢西班牙式公寓分别布置在主通道的两侧，分层分户进出，互不干扰。每户有两套浴室，宅前有较大花园。南部4幢为五层现代式公寓，围合状布局，一至三层每层为两套二室户，四、五层为两套跃层四室户。电影表演艺术家赵丹、画家颜文梁也曾在此居住。1989年9月25日上海市人民政府同时公布其为上海市文物保护单位和市优秀历史建筑。

YUAN Xuefen

YUAN Xuefen (1922–2011), a performing artist of the Yue Opera, has her ancestral family from Shengzhou in Zhejiang province. At the age of 11 she attended the Yue Opera class, specializing in black cloth roles and maidenly female roles. In 1942, she advocated reform of the Yue Opera together with new artists in the Dalai Theater in order to integrate editing, direction, performance, music and art. In 1946 she played a role in the Yue opera *Xiang Lin's Wife*. In 1953, *The Butterfly Lovers*, China's first large-scale color opera film in which she starred, won the "Music Film Award" in the Eighth Karlovy Vary International Film Festival. In 2006 she won the "Magnolia Performing Arts Award for Lifetime Achievement" which was set up for the first time. In 2008 she was awarded the honorary title of "a successor of the National Intangible Cultural Heritage". Her acting and singing were soft and mild, graceful and delicate, and plain and deep with mellow flavor and lively rhythm, which focused on the depiction of the character's personality and inner activities. Her style was known as "The Yuan Style". Since 1978 she served in succession as dean and honorary dean of Shanghai Yue Opera House, as well as vice president of the Shanghai Foreign Friendship Association and member of the Standing Committee of CPPCC.

Her Love for Cedar and Her Excellence in Both Performance and Morality

In 1992, YUAN received a cedar from a friend she got to know in East China Hospital. She was very fond of this tree which brought green to the courtyard. Even when the nanny occasionally wanted to tie a rope to it for drying clothes, she would patiently discourage her for fear of the bad effect on the natural growth of the tree. She used to stand in the balcony for a long time to gaze at it. In her mind, the pine tree was like her three sons in foreign countries. Every day she looked at the pine grow up healthy and strong, as if she were looking at her three sons who were not around. After 10 years, the green and tall tree brought endless vitality to her

袁雪芬
YUAN Xuefen.

New Health Garden. Under the shade she enjoyed the happy company of a big family of children and grandchildren.

On the wall near the bookshelf in the living room hangs a landscape painting *Autumn Ridge*, specially created for her at the end of the 1960s by the painter YAN Wenliang in three years. The green and luxuriant trees in the painting echoed the green and tall pine tree in the garden. The quiet and secluded style of the painting agrees perfectly with the elegant atmosphere of the New Health Garden.

She had a special love for cedars which reflected her personality of nobleness and integrity. Since 1995, she was elected in succession for 15 years as director of judges of "Shanghai Magnolia Performing Arts Award". She took it as a motto "to be innocent in behavior and to be serious in acting" and put it into practice in the process of deciding on the magnolia awards. For that purpose she set down an iron principle of "never being present at entertaining meals and never taking gifts" and she took the lead to put it into strict practice. In a year before the decision was made on awards, a colleague of Shanghai Yue Opera House came with guests from a theater in his hometown to visit her in her garden house, expecting that she could give much consideration to their repertoire and players. Before leaving they wanted to give to her a heavy gold necklace. Though always amiable and easy-going, she immediately looked serious and turned them all out. She told them with justice that "this is an insult to me! Awards depend on art!" Under her leadership, the Magnolia Award without shady deals were always as righteous and pure as the white pine tree, and turned out to be one of "the fairest and the purest" awards for art.

The former residence of YUAN Xuefen is located in New Health Garden in Alley 1273 on Huaihai Road. Built in 1934, it was designed by the New Mahai Foreign Business and was invested by the New Health Foreign Business from Britain. The building covers an area of 12,987 square meters and a building area of 9,318 square meters, which is of garden residence in alleys. The New Health Garden runs across the Middle Huaihai Road and Fuxing Road from north to south. It is composed of 11 two-storied Spanish style garden residences of brick and wood structure and 4 five-storied residences of mixed structure in lanes. The front of the garden has three vertical sections. The middle one projects to form balconies; the top is made into a terrace. The balconies have columns with swirl marks. The roof has gentle slopes covered with red tile and the eaves are decorated with dentel. The exterior walls are coated with grey cement. In the middle of the building are garages. In the garden, the main passages from north to south are 6.5 meters in width and the 8 minor passages are 5.5 meters wide. In the north the 11 Spanish style apartments are located on the two sides of the main passage, with each household enjoying separate passage in and out without any interference with each other. Each household has two sets of bathrooms and a large garden. In the south the 4 five-storied modern apartments form a surrounding area. From the first to the third floors, two households occupy the two apartments on the same floor; on the fourth and fifth floors, four households occupy the four apartments, each of which crosses two floors. Both ZHAO Dan, the film performance artist and YAN Wenliang, the well-known painter, once lived here. On September 25, 1989, it became a Cultural Relics Protection Unit and a Heritage Architecture issued at the same time by the Shanghai Municipal People's Government.

袁雪芬 （戴晓明画）

YUAN Xuefen （By DAI Xiaoming）

郭泰祺
（1888—1952）

湖北广济人，字保元，号复初。1904年被选送留学美国，后入宾夕法尼亚大学攻读政治学。1911年获奖学金进研究院学社会学。1912年回国，加入国民党，任湖北都督府外交股长。1919年1月，以中国代表团专门委员名义出席巴黎和会。1921年孙中山任非常大总统，郭泰祺任总统府参事兼宣传局长。1932年作为中国首席代表，与日方代表重光葵议订《淞沪停战协定》，同年任驻英公使。1935年任第一任驻英大使兼国联中国代表。抗战期间，多次照会国联，要求采取措施制止日本侵略，并努力争取国际援助。1938年，英国牛津大学授予郭泰祺名誉法学博士学位。1941年回国任外交部长，12月调任立法院外交委员会主任委员。1946年2月，出任中国驻联合国安全理事会首席代表（3至4月任安理会主席），又任联合国原子能委员会委员。1947年12月出任驻巴西大使。1949年退隐美国。

打通滇缅公路禁区

抗战期间，郭泰祺作为中国驻英全权大使，以宽广的人脉和良好的亲和形象，积极开展公众外交，充分利用各种机会发表讲演，声明“我国此次抗战乃为争民族之独立自由，非至敌人放弃其侵略政策，绝无和平可言”的立场。

滇缅公路是抗战期间中国军事重要的补给线。1940年6月24日，日本通过正式外交途径向英国提出停止通过滇缅公路运送武器弹药以及诸如燃料、卡车及铁路器材等物资的要求。郭泰祺非常关注事态的进展。6月28日，他前往英国外交部，向英国外长指出一味退让徒增纠纷，希望英国就滇缅公路运输给中国一个切实的保证。7月1日，在访问英国外交部政务次官巴特勒时，郭泰祺重申滇缅运输事关中国抗战及英国自身利益，希望英国慎重考虑。日本的屡次威胁与中国的一再抗议使英国政府左右为难。7月10日，英国驻日大使克莱琪“在雨季关闭滇缅公路三个月，停运一些货物，将难题留到三个月后”的提议获英国内阁通过。

郭泰祺义愤填膺地以政府的名义向英国发出书面抗议：“八年来致力增进中、英友谊，所以对我政府报告，总以英国重道义决不负我为言，此次英方处置，使祺痛惜深于愤懑。”在之后的两个多月时间内，郭泰祺发动了强有力的外交攻势，为重新开放滇缅公路奔走。8月初，郭泰祺首先解决了药品、急救车辆在滇缅公路的运输问题，随后要求将汽油纳入非禁运行列，并以日本在中国大肆搜捕英国侨民的事实，力证英国对日本绥靖所带来的危害。8月13日，郭泰祺会晤英国外长，义正辞严地陈述利害关系，提醒英国政府三个月期满后滇缅公路若延期开放，以后开禁会加倍困难。

10月4日，郭泰祺访问英国首相丘吉尔时，终于获得了丘吉尔重新开通滇缅公路的承诺。推动英国开放对中国抗战意义重大的军事补给线滇缅公路，郭泰祺功不可没。

建筑简介：武康路376号

郭泰祺旧居位于武康路376号，建于1928年，占地面积约600平方米。建筑为新古典主义风格的花园住宅，三层砖混结构，清水红砖外墙，人字坡红瓦屋顶。主立面三段式划分，左右结构布局完全对称，局部有欧洲古典元素。南面底层为塔斯干柱廊，二层内阳台为简化的爱奥尼克券柱结构，建筑主入口门楣具巴洛克风格。建筑内部用材考究，制作精良，整体保存较好，多数室内装饰和卫浴设备仍在使用。中华人民共和国成立后一度作为超声波仪表厂和长江计算机厂的办公用房，现为民居。

GUO Taiqi

GUO Taiqi (1888–1952) has his ancestral family from Guangji in Hubei province. He also has a courtesy name of Baoyuan and style name of Fuchu. In 1904 he was sent to study in the United States and later entered University of Pennsylvania to study politics. In 1911, he was awarded a scholarship to study Sociology in the Graduate School. In 1912 he returned to join the KMT and served as chief of foreign affairs in the governor's office in Hubei province. In January 1919, he attended the Paris Peace Conference in the name of commissioner of the Chinese delegation. In 1921, when Sun Yat-sen took office of Extraordinary President, he served as presidential counselor and publicity director. In 1932 he served as chief representative of China to talk with the Japanese ones and signed "Shanghai Armistice Agreement". In the same year he served as minister stationed in Britain. In 1935 he was appointed as the first ambassador of China to the United Kingdom and the Chinese representative in the League of Nations. During the War of Resistance against Japanese Invasion, he repeatedly presented diplomatic notes to the League of Nations, asking it to take measures to stop the Japanese aggression and striving for international aid. In 1938, he was awarded honorary doctorate degree by Oxford University in Britain. In 1941 he returned to serve as the foreign minister and was transferred in December to serve as chairman of the foreign affairs committee of Legislative Yuan of the KMT government. In February 1946, he was appointed as the Chinese chief representative in the Security Council in the United Nations (as its president from March to April) and also as member of the United Nations Atomic Energy Commission. In December 1947 he served as ambassador of China to Brazil. In 1949 he retired to live in seclusion in the United States.

Breaking through the Burma Road

During the War of Resistance, he served as ambassador plenipotentiary of China to Britain. With a broad connection and amiable image, he actively carried out public diplomacy and made full use of various opportunities to deliver speeches, declaring the position that "this war of China is for the independence and freedom of the nation. Before the enemy was forced to abandon its aggressive policy, there would be no peace at all".

Burma Road was an important military supply line during the War of Resistance. On June 24, 1940, Japan requested through

郭泰祺
GUO Taiqi.

formal diplomatic channels to the United Kingdom to stop the transport of arms and ammunition by means of the Burma Road as well as fuels, trucks, railway equipment and other materials. GUO was very concerned about the development of the situation. On June 28, he went to visit the British Foreign Office, pointed out to the British Foreign Minister that blind concession would only result in increasing disputes and hoped that the United Kingdom should present a practical guarantee to China on the Burma Road transport. On July 1, when visiting Butler, deputy minister of the British Foreign Office, he reaffirmed that the transport on Burma Road was related to the war in China and Britain's own interests and expected British careful consideration. With the repeated threats from Japan and repeated protests from China, the British government was left in a dilemma. On July 10, Sir Robert Craigie, British ambassador to Japan, made a proposal that "the road should be closed in the rainy season for three months and transport of some goods should be stopped so that the problem remained until after three months", and this proposal was approved by the British Cabinet.

In his indignation, he sent a written protest to the United Kingdom in the name of the government: "In the past eight years, I have made great efforts to promote the friendship between China and Britain. Therefore, my report to the Chinese government has always focused on the point that the Britain values justice and will never betray China. The position adopted by Britain this time has left me more in regret than in anger." In the next two months, he launched a strong diplomatic push, running for the re-opening of the Burma Road. At the beginning of August, he first resolved the transport issue of medical drugs and emergency vehicles on the Burma Road. Later he requested that gasoline should be put into the list of non-prohibited items. In addition, he took advantage of the fact that the British people in China were wantonly arrested by the Japan invaders in order to prove that the British appeasement to Japan would only result in dangers. On August 13, he contacted the British Foreign Minister and expressed sternly from a sense of justice the advantages and disadvantages of its decision, reminding the British government that, if the opening of the road was postponed at the expiry after three months, it would be doubly difficult to lift the ban.

On October 4, when he visited Winston Churchill, the British Prime Minister, he finally got a promise that the Burma Road would be re-opened. In promoting the Britain to re-open the Burma Road, a military supply line which was of great significance to the war in China, he contributed his bit.

The former residence of GUO Taiqi is located at No. 376 on Wukang Road. Built in 1928, it covers an area of about 600 square meters. As a garden house of the neo-classical style, it is of three-storied brick structure with exterior walls of water red bricks and a roof of gable slopes and red tiles. The main facade has three sections with the left and right ones being completely symmetrical and parts enjoying European classical elements. The bottom floor has Tuscan colonnades at the south side. The inner balconies at the second floor have the structure of simplified Ionic columns. The lintel at the main entrance witnesses a Baroque style. The interior of the building makes use of elegant materials of excellent quality. The building is well preserved as a whole and most of the interior decoration and bathroom equipment are still in use. After the founding of the People's Republic of China it was used as the office of Ultrasonic Instrument Factory and the Yangtze River Computer Factory. It is now for folk residence.

郭泰祺 （邬海佳画）　　GUO Taiqi （By WU Haijia）

广东香山（今中山）人，生于澳大利亚悉尼。1918年回国，入岭南大学学习。后赴美国留学。1927年回国后，任上海永安纺织公司工程师、副经理、副总经理。中华人民共和国成立后，先后任上海市人民政府委员、华东财经委员会委员、上海市侨联主任、广东省副省长、广东省政协副主席、广东省人大常委会副主任、民建中央副主任委员、全国侨联副主席、全国政协常委、中国工商经济开发公司董事、香港特别行政区基本法起草委员会委员。1986年4月9日在广州病逝。

郭棣活
（1904—1986）

一片冰心在玉壶

1947年，在日本侵略战争带来重重磨难后，又遭受国民党政府的强征暴敛，上海许多工商界人士纷纷移居香港，永安纺织公司的诸位董事也商议迁厂香港事宜，但维护和发展先辈在上海创立的纺织产业，是郭棣活执着的信念。他反复研究赴港设厂的可行性，发现气候潮湿的香港不适宜纺纱，如果安装空调，将增加许多成本，不利于公司的长远发展。郭棣活在给公司总监督郭乐和总经理郭顺的信中，提出对迁厂香港宜“详加研究，再行决定”的意见。

1949年初，随着解放上海的号角声越来越嘹亮，负隅顽抗的国民党反动派企图破坏城市建设。郭乐、郭顺等前辈担忧他的人身安全，多次致电力促他立即离沪赴港，但始终未能动摇郭棣活“洛阳亲友如相问，一片冰心在玉壶”的坚定信念。他千方百计克服原料紧缺、货币贬值等困难，以超群的胆略毅然驻守上海经营永安纺织公司，终于迎来了上海的解放。

1949年5月的一天，陈毅市长在中国银行大厅内，召集上海各界代表人士开会。在酒会上，陈毅市长特地找到郭棣活，亲切地握着他的手说：“共产党是了解你的。解放前夕，有许多人劝你离开上海，而你决定留下来，你做得对。”陈毅市长和蔼的谈话使郭棣活感受到党的温暖，深受鼓舞。时任上海市副市长的潘汉年负责统一战线工作，他多次专程前往郭宅探望郭棣活，一方面宣传共产党的政策，鼓励他大胆地搞好棉纺生产，另一方面又帮助他解决生产过程中原材料购置的困难和交通运输上的问题，从而使永安纺织公司迅速恢复生产。

1950年6月，郭棣活应邀参加第一届全国政协第二次会议，聆听了国家领导人所做的政府工作报告，心潮澎湃，回沪后即写信给二伯父郭乐，提出把从国外订购的一批纺织机械和原材料运回上海，此举获得了郭乐等前辈的支持。这批包括瑞士制造的7000千瓦汽轮发电机组和1万锭纺纱机器全套设备及6000多包美国棉花，价值共计250万美元的物资顺利地运回国内，为祖国工商业的发展提供了有力的支持。

建筑简介：华山路893号

郭棣活旧居位于华山路893号，有东西两幢，占地面积893平方米，建筑面积800平方米，属现代派建筑风格的花园住宅。建筑为钢筋混凝土结构，西楼建于1938年，建筑平面呈不对称布局，以东南立面为构图中心，作圆角处理。底层入口挑出圆形雨厦，二层曲尺形退为阳台，挑出舌形雨厦。平屋顶，方形门窗，灰色水泥拉毛墙面，四坡挑檐屋顶，螺旋楼梯。室内采用宽大的走廊、圆弧形大楼梯和玻璃屏风隔断。客厅通向花园，落地玻璃门。客厅和餐厅间以推拉移门相隔，拉开移门即为一个很大的舞厅。所有门窗均采用双层玻璃，里层为透明玻璃，外层为磨砂玻璃，暖气片上有青铜铸花护罩，楼梯装青铜铸花栏杆。东楼建于1947年，风格相似。1994年2月15日上海市人民政府公布其为市优秀历史建筑。

GUO Dihuo

GUO Dihuo (1904–1986) was born in Sydney, Australia with his ancestral family from Xiangshan (now Zhongshan) in Guangdong province. In 1918, he returned from abroad to study at Lingnan University. Later he went to study in USA. In 1927 he came back to work in Shanghai Yong'an Textile Company as engineer, vice manager and vice manager general in succession. After the founding of the New China, he successively worked as commissioner of Shanghai Municipal People's Government, commissioner of the East China Financial and Economic Committee, director of Shanghai Municipal Federation of Returned Overseas Chinese, vice-governor of Guangdong province and vice chairman of the CPPCC Guangdong provincial committee and vice director of the Standing Committee of the Guangdong provincial People's Congress, assistant director of the Central Committee of China Democratic National Construction Association, vice chairman of All-China Federation of Returned Overseas Chinese, member of the Standing Committee of the National Committee of the CPPCC, director of China Industrial and Commercial Economic Development Corporation, and member of the committee for drafting the basic law of the Hong Kong Special Administrative Region. On April 9, 1986, he passed away of illness in Guangzhou.

A Pure and Noble Personality

Owing to the numerous hardships brought about by the Japanese invaders and also due to the forced and cruel imposition of taxes by the KMT government, many public figures from the circles of industry and commerce in Shanghai moved to Hong Kong in succession in 1947. The directors of Yong'an Textile Company were also discussing to move the factory to Hong Kong. However, maintenance and development of textile industry founded by predecessors in Shanghai had been the ever-pursued faith of GUO Dihuo. He repeatedly investigated the possibility of establishing a company in Hong Kong, only to find that the wet climate in Hong Kong was inappropriate for spinning. The installment of air-conditioners would increase cost a lot which went against the long-term development of the company. In his letters to both the general inspector and the general manager of the company, he put forward his opinion with regard to moving their company to Hong Kong that "there is the necessity to do detailed investigation before a decision is made."

永安纺织厂
Yong'an Textile Factory.

In the beginning of 1949, with the accelerating pace of the liberation of Shanghai, the desperately struggling KMT reactionaries attempted to destroy the city construction. Some of his predecessors, including his uncles, were afraid of his personal security and called him several times to urge him to leave Shanghai for Hong Kong. But they failed to shake his firm faith in "A Pure and Noble Personality". He made use of every possible means to overcome the difficulties of material shortage and devaluation, determinedly and courageously staying in Shanghai to manage the Yong'an Textile Company. In the end he witnessed the liberation of Shanghai.

One day in May, 1949 and in the hall of the Bank of China, CHEN Yi, mayor of the city, convened a meeting of representatives from various circles in Shanghai. In the banquet the Mayor specially went up to GUO, warmly shaking hands with him and saying, "Our Party knows you well. On the eve of the liberation quite a few people persuaded you to leave Shanghai while you chose to stay here. You are right!" The warming words of the mayor enabled GUO to feel the warmth of the Party and left him deeply inspired. PAN Hannian, vice mayor of Shanghai at that time, was in charge of the sector of the United Front. For several times, PAN made special trips to pay visits to GUO, explaining to him the policies of the Party to encourage him to bravely actualize the cotton textile production, and on the other hand giving him a hand to overcome the difficulty of material purchase in the process of production and solve the problems in transportation. Subsequently the Yong'an Textile Company quickly renewed its production.

In June 1950, GUO was invited to attend the second meeting of the first session of the CPPCC to listen to the report on the work of government by state leaders. He was full of excitement. After returning to Shanghai he immediately wrote to his second uncle and proposed to ship back to Shanghai the textile machines and raw materials ordered from abroad. This move got support from some of his predecessors including his uncle. The 7 thousand kw turbo-generator set manufactured in Switzerland, the complete set of 10 thousand ingots spinning machine and 6 thousand bags of American cotton—all these, worth 2.5 million US dollars, were shipped back to China successfully, which supplied a mighty support for the development of industry and commerce of the country.

The former residence of GUO Dihuo is located at No. 893 on Huashan Road. It has two buildings with one in the east and one in the west, covering an area of 893 square meters and a building area of 800 square meters. It is a garden house of modern style of architecture. Its structure is of steel concrete. The west building was built in 1938 and its building plane is of an asymmetric layout with the south-east facade as the center treated as a circular corner. Over the entrance on the first floor is a projected circular penthouse and the second floor has an L-shaped recess as the balcony with a tongue-shaped canopy. The building has a flat roof, square windows, grey cement napped walls, a roof with four slopes and cornice, and spiral staircase. The inside adopts a wide corridor, a circular arc shaped staircase and glass screen partition. The living room leads to the garden and has a French door of glass. The living room and dining room are separated with sliding doors, behind which is a large ballroom. All doors and windows have two layers of glass with the transparent one as the inside and the frosted one as the outside. Over the radiators are bronze shields with cast flowers and the staircase is equipped with bronze railings also with cast flowers. The east building was built in 1947 with a similar style. On February 15, 1994, it became a Heritage Architecture issued by the Shanghai Municipal People's Government.

郭棣活 （吴耀明画）　　GUO Dihuo （By WU Yaoming）

陶金
（1916—1986）

江苏苏州人。1934年考入济南戏剧训练班学习话剧。1936年加入上海天一影片公司当演员。1937年加入上海业余实验剧团。"八一三"事变后加入上海救亡话剧四队，从事抗日宣传工作。1940至1945年，在重庆主演《胜利进行曲》《青年中国》等影片。1945年回上海加入昆仑影业公司，1947年与白杨等联合主演《八千里路云和月》《一江春水向东流》而成名。1948年赴香港加入家华影业公司，主演《国魂》《山河泪》等影片。1949年导演第一部故事片《诗礼传家》。中华人民共和国成立后回上海。1956年任上海电影制片厂导演，导演昆曲艺术片《十五贯》、故事片《护士日记》《苗家儿女》等。1958年调任武汉电影制片厂导演。1961年调任珠江电影制片厂导演。1976年后导演故事片《斗鲨》、戏曲片《西园记》等。1981年赴美参加旧金山国际电影节。为中国影协理事。

发自内心的表演

陶金对于做作虚假的表演非常反感，他在电影表演中坚决摒弃事先设计表演方法，避免预先规定形体动作、表情神态。他也不喜欢把自己的主观设计强加于别人，更是对摄影机抢镜头、拖片子的恶习深恶痛绝。他认为，重要的是正确理解剧本、人物、人物关系，弄清自己扮演角色的目的，但演员切忌以演角色为目的，而应该从内心的体验去交流、反映与呈现。在影片《一江春水向东流》中，他扮演的张忠良既有人生理想，又屈服于生活现实；既不乏热血，又软弱怯懦。他的表演，鲜活呈现了一个黑暗社会环境里缺乏坚定人生观、内心矛盾、随波逐流的悲剧人物。

陶金表演中的发自内心，与他一直以来对中国电影事业发自肺腑的热忱与挚爱密不可分。1935年12月，抗日救亡运动如火如荼，中国旅行剧团因演出话剧等弘扬爱国主义而受反动当局查抄，陶金也一度被捕。出狱后，他依然活跃于话剧舞台，并投身银幕。1937年，"八一三"事变后，他辗转到武汉，参加《春寒》《芳草天涯》《蜕变》《日出》等话剧演出，宣传抗日。当武汉失守，他便到重庆继续将一个个饱满的人物形象献给观众。在各地辗转跋涉、不辞辛劳的演出途中，市井村庄各式各样的生活体验，成为他艺术灵感的源泉。

1951年，陶金毅然放弃在香港的演艺事业与宽裕生活，随大光明电影公司集体重返上海，为中华人民共和国的电影事业而努力。抗美援朝时期，他谢绝香港电影公司的高薪邀约，全身心投入根据话剧《当祖国需要的时候》改编的电影《和平鸽》的执导和演绎中。1956年，由他导演的电影《十五贯》上映后，周恩来总理称赞为"一出戏救活了一个剧种"。

建筑简介：高邮路5弄34号

陶金旧居位于高邮路5弄34号。高邮路5弄是上海少有的具有丰富历史文化底蕴的弄堂，曾经住过不少名人。弄堂里有十几幢独立的老洋房，斑驳的墙面，红砖烟囱，别有洞天。弄内25号是著名作家、文史学者、首任国家文物局局长郑振铎的旧居。7号曾住过赵四小姐赵一荻的六哥赵燕生和夫人吴靖。“美丽牌”香烟的广告女郎、京剧名伶吕美玉曾住在50号二楼。此外还有袁世凯的孙子袁玮和孙媳朱章秀等。弄堂最南端通往湖南别墅的后门。

TAO Jin

TAO Jin (1916–1986) has his ancestral family from Suzhou in Jiangsu province. In 1934 he was admitted to Jinan drama training class to learn drama. In 1936, he joined Shanghai Tianyi Film Company to work as an actor. In 1937, he joined Shanghai Amateur Experimental Troupe. After the “August 13” Incident, he joined the Fourth Team of Shanghai National Salvation Troupe and engaged himself in the publicity against Japanese invaders. From 1940 to 1945, he starred in Chongqing such films as *Victory March* and *Young China*. In 1945 he went back to Shanghai to join Kunlun Film Company. In 1947 he co-starred with others such films as *Thousands of Miles* and *A Spring River Flows East*, for which he made his fame. In 1948 he went to Hong Kong to join Jiahua Film Company, starring *The National Genius* and *A Farmer Tragedy*. In 1949 he directed his first feature film *A Family of Scholars*. After the founding of the New China he went back to Shanghai. In 1956 he served as director of Shanghai Film Studio, directing Kunqu opera film *Fifteen Strings of Cash*, as well as feature films including *Nurses Diary* and *Children of Miao Nationality*. In 1958 he was transferred to Wuhan Film Studio to serve as director. In 1961 he was further transferred to work as director in Pearl River Film Studio. After 1976 he directed films such as *Fighting Sharks* as well as opera film *The Story of Western Garden*. In 1981 he went to the United States to attend the International Film Festival in San Francisco. Once he was director of China Film Association.

Performance from the Heart

TAO Jin had a strong aversion to making a false performance. In film performance he resolutely abandoned the method of pre-designed performance and avoided pre-specified physical movements and facial expressions. He did not like to impose his own subjective design on others. He cherished a bitter hatred for the abuse of scene stealing and sluggish performance in front of the camera. In his view, it was important to correctly understand the script, characters and interpersonal relations, and clarify the purpose of the role one played, but actors should not take the performance of roles for its own purpose. Instead they should exchange, reflect and present with experience from their heart. In the film *A Spring River Flows East*, he played the role of ZHANG Zhongliang, who had ideal but also succumbed to reality; and who was an ardent youth but also a weak coward. His performance freshly showed a tragic figure who was lacking in firm outlook on life, experiencing inner contradictions and was carried along by the tide in a dark social environment.

陶金出演的《一江春水向东流》剧照
A photo of the film *A Spring River Flows East* TAO Jin starred.

He always performed from the bottom of his heart, which was closely associated with his heart-felt enthusiasm and love for Chinese film industry. In December 1935, the national salvation movement against Japanese invasion was in full swing. The Chinese Travel Troupe was confiscated by the reactionary authorities for its performance of drama to sing in praises of patriotism. He was also arrested. After his release, he was still active in the drama arena and threw himself into the field of film. After the "August 13" Incident in 1937, he was tossed about to come to Wuhan, participating in drama performances in *Spring Cold*, *Grass at the Horizon*, *Transformation*, *Sunrise* and others in the publicity of resistance against Japanese invasion. When Wuhan fell, he went to Chongqing and continued to dedicate full images to the audience one after another. His journey to various places, tireless performance on the way and a variety of village life experience—all this became sources of his artistic inspiration.

In 1951, he resolutely gave up his acting career and comfortable life in Hong Kong and returned to Shanghai together with the Grand Brightness Film Company to work for the film industry of People's Republic of China. During the Korean War, he rejected high-paying invitation of the Hong Kong Film Company and threw himself into the direction and performance of the film *Peace Dove* adapted on the basis of the drama *When the Motherland Needs Us*. In 1956, he directed the film *Fifteen Strings of Cash* and, after the release, Premier ZHOU praised it by saying that "a play serves to save a kind of drama".

The former residence of TAO Jin is located at No. 5 in Alley 34 on Gaoyou Road, which was a rare alley with rich historical and cultural heritage in Shanghai and where a lot of celebrities once lived here. In the alley are more than a dozen independent old houses with mottled walls and red brick chimneys, which was a world of its own. No. 25 in the alley is the former residence of ZHENG Zhenduo, a famous writer, scholar of literature and history and the first director of the State Bureau of Cultural Relics. No. 7 once accommodated the sixth elder brother and sister-in-law of ZHAO Yidi, Miss ZHAO the fourth sister. LÜ Meiyu, a showgirl for cigarette of the brand of Beauty and famous actress of Beijing Opera, once lived on the second floor of No. 50. In addition, the grandson and the granddaughter-in-law of YUAN Shikai once lived here also. The southern end of the alley leads to the back door of Hunan Villa.

陶金 （钱定华画） TAO Jin （By QIAN Dinghua）

陶勇
（1912—1967）

安徽霍邱人，原名张道庸。1929 年加入中国共产主义青年团，同年参加中国工农红军。1931 年加入中国共产党。红军长征时任红四方面军第 10 师 28 团团长。1938 年春调任新四军第 1 支队副参谋长。1940 年 7 月起任新四军苏北指挥部第 3 纵队司令员等。抗战胜利后，任华中野战军第 8 纵队司令员兼政治委员、第三野战军第 23 军军长等，参加了苏中、莱芜、孟良崮、豫东、淮海、渡江、上海等战役。他指挥作战英勇顽强，与叶飞、王必成并称第三野战军的三员“虎将”。中华人民共和国成立后，任第 9 兵团副司令员等。1950 年 11 月参加抗美援朝战争。1952 年任华东军区海军司令员等职。1955 年被授予中将军衔。1967 年在上海逝世。

抗美援朝战场上的灵活指挥

1950 年 10 月上旬一天上午，第三野战军第 23 军军长陶勇一身戎装，前往上海市人民政府市长办公室。陈毅市长告诉他，以美国为首的“联合国军”已越过“三八线”入侵朝鲜，并向朝中边境推进，轰炸中国丹东地区，严重威胁中国安全，朝鲜政府请求中国出兵援助。毛主席作出“抗美援朝、保家卫国”的决策，命令第 9 兵团赴朝作战，任命陶勇担任兵团副司令员。陶勇立即表态要到朝鲜打胜仗向首长报捷。

11 月上旬，第 9 兵团作为中国人民志愿军第二批参战部队抵达朝鲜战场。11 月下旬，美军总司令麦克阿瑟下令发起全面攻势，意欲东西线两军在江界会合后再向中朝边境推进以占领整个朝鲜。中国人民志愿军第 9 兵团于 11 月 27 日发起反击。陶勇赴前线指挥第 20 军、27 军战斗。他发现面对两个师的敌军，我军的兵力有些分散，当即决定集中第 27 军主力首先围歼美军第 7 师。调整部署后，于 29 日歼灭美军第 7 师两个团大部。第 20 军主力经过几天攻击，使号称“王牌军”的美军陆战队第 1 师主力伤亡惨重。12 月 1 日，美军被迫向南突围。陶勇召集各师师长研究对付美军坦克的战术，他提出：“对付敌人坦克不能靠死打硬拼，我们反坦克武器少，硬碰硬是不行的，要发动群众，采取破路，以小分队突击结合火力袭击的多种战法；要集中力量打击敌之摩托化步兵与坦克。”这一战略使突围的美军遭重创，沿途丢弃坦克，仓皇逃窜。我军乘胜追击，当面临后方供应离前线太远而粮弹供给不及时，陶勇告诉兵团指挥所就地借粮，并电报通知后勤部，命令各兵站向前延伸。部队进至咸兴、兴南港附近时，敌军借助海岸附近地形，利用舰队、坦克等的层层火力形成防御，陶勇立即命令各追击部队利用地形就地隐蔽，不可贸然前进以避免损失，趁对方火力懈怠时攻取咸兴和兴南港。

陶勇在东线战场指挥部队取得第二次战役最后胜利。毛泽东主席在 1950 年 12 月 17 日致电说：“9 兵团此次在东线作战，在极困难条件下，完成了巨大的战略任务。”

建筑简介：长乐路1221号

陶勇旧居位于长乐路1221号，建于1941年，属具有西方现代派建筑特征的独立式花园住宅。建筑共三层，外观由比较简单清晰的形体单元组合，底层门廊、外突窗框和平直檐口都强调水平向构图，与几处扁平小窗以及楼梯间弧形转角和简洁流畅的木扶手共同显现出流线型风格特征。底层门廊由简洁轻巧的圆柱支撑，立面上多次出现转角窗，是当时体现建筑走向现代的典型设计语汇，这意味着沉重的转角不仅从新型结构体系中解放出来，空间的室内外关系也因此开始了极大的转变。

TAO Yong

TAO Yong (1912–1967) has his ancestral family from Huoqiu in Anhui province and has a former name of ZHANG Daoyong. In 1929 he joined the Communist Youth League of China and in the same year he joined the Chinese Red Army of Workers and Farmers. In 1931 he became a member of the Communist Party of China and then played his part as the regimental commander of the twenty-eighth regiment of the tenth division for the Fourth Branch of the Red Army on the Long March. In the spring of 1938, he was transferred to serve as deputy chief staff officer of the First Detachment of the New Fourth Army. Since July 1940, he served as commander of the Third Column of the Northern Jiangsu Headquarters of the New Fourth Army. After the victory of the war, he served as commander and the political commissar of the Eighth Column of the Central China Field Army as well as commander of the Twenty-Third Army Corps of the Third Field Army, participating in campaigns at such places as the Central Jiangsu province, Laiwu, Mengliangu, Eastern Henan Province, Huaihai River, Crossing-Yangtze-River and Shanghai. He was brave and tenacious in commanding wars and was highly praised as the three "tigers" in the Third Field Army together with YE Fei and WANG Bicheng. After the founding of the People's Republic of China, he was appointed as deputy commander of the Ninth Army Corps. In November 1950, he participated in the War of Resisting US Aggression and Aiding Korea. In 1952, he served as commander of the Navy of the East China Military Area. He was awarded as lieutenant general in 1955 and passed away in Shanghai in 1967.

Flexible Command in the Korean War

In early October 1950, TAO Yong was commander of the Twenty-Third Army Corps of the Third Field Army. One morning, he headed in his military uniform to the mayor's office of the Shanghai Municipal People's Government. Mayor CHEN Yi told him that the "the United Nations Army" led by the United States had already crossed the 38th Parallel to invade North Korea and pushed forward to the DPRK-China border, bombing Dandong area of China and posing a grave threat to China's security. The DPRK government asked for military aid from China. Chairman MAO made the decision of "resisting US aggression and aiding Korea,

1950 年陶勇与夫人在上海合影
A photo of TAO Yong and his wife in Shanghai in 1950.

protecting homes and defending our countries", issuing an order that the Ninth Army Corps should go to North Korea to attend the war and appointing him as deputy commander of the Chinese army. He immediately made a promise to win the battle in the DPRK and report the success to the Head of State.

In the early November, the Ninth Army Corps arrived in the Korean battlefield as the second batch of troops in the Chinese People's Volunteer Army. In the late November, the US commander-in-chief MacArthur ordered the launch of a comprehensive offensive with an intention that thc East and West lines of military forces headed to the Sino-Korean border to promote the occupation of the entire North Korea after their rendezvous at the city of Jiangjie. The Ninth Army Corps of the Chinese People's Volunteer Army launched a counterattack on November 27. TAO Yong went to the frontline to command the battles of the Twentieth Army Corps and the Twenty-Seventh Army Corps. He found our military forces were scattered to some extent when they were in face of two divisions of the enemy. So he immediately decided to focus first on surrounding and annihilating of the US Seventh Division with the main force of the Twenty-Seventh Army Corps. After adjusting the deployment, they wiped out most of the two regiments of the Seventh Division of the US Army on November 29. After several days of attacking, the Twentieth Army Corps beat the US First Division which was known as "ace troops" of the US Marine Corps and caused them heavy casualties. On December 1, the US military forces were compelled to head south for breakthrough. In order to come up with tactics which could be used against the US tanks, TAO called for division commanders to make investigation. He proposed, "We can't beat enemy tanks in a reckless way. As we are lacking anti-tank weapons, we ought not to confront the tough with toughness. Instead, we'd better take tactics like mobilizing the general public to destroy the roads and adopting many ways such as squad assaults combined with firepower attacking. We should concentrate on fighting with the enemy's motorized infantry and tanks." Thanks to this strategy, the US army that tried to sally were hit badly and fled away in panic, abandoning tanks along the road while our army followed up victories to pursue the enemy. When we were faced with the tough situation that rear supply was too far from the front line and both grain and bullets supply couldn't reach the army timely, TAO told the Corps to borrow local grains and telegraphed logistics department to command the military stations to extend forward. When the troops marched close to Hamhung and Hungnam, the enemy took the advantage of the landform near the seacoast and formed a defense by using the fleet, tanks and other layers of fire. Instead of rushing forward, TAO immediately ordered the chasing troops to hide by using the landform to avoid losses and conquered Hamhung and Hungnam when the enemy's firepower got weak.

TAO Yong commanded the troops at the east battlefield and obtained the final victory in the second campaign. On December 17, 1950, Chairman MAO Zedong said in a telegraph, "the Ninth Army Corps fought in the Eastern Front and completed a huge strategic task in very difficult conditions."

The former residence of TAO Yong is located at No. 1221 of Changle Road. It was built in 1941. This building boasts itself an independent garden-style house with western modern architectural features. The three-storey building consists of a simple and clear combination of elements. For the porch at the bottom floor, protruding window frames and straight cornice, emphasis is laid on horizontal composition, which shows a streamlined style together with several flat small windows, staircase arc angle in addition to simple and smooth wood handrails. The bottom porch is supported by simple, lightweight cylinders. In the front, corner windows appear for many times. It is a typical design feature for modern architecture, which means that heavy corners are not only liberated from the new structure system, but also the space relations between the interior and exterior have experienced infinite changes.

陶勇 （杨宏富画）

TAO Yong （By YANG Hongfu）

高锟
（1933— ）

出生于上海，华裔物理学家。由于在光纤领域的特殊贡献，被誉为“光纤之父”。1970—1974 年，任香港中文大学电子学系教授、讲座教授和该系创系主任。1974 年返回 ITT 工作，在位于美国弗吉尼亚州的 ITT 光电产品部任主任科学家，后升为工程主任、光电产品部副经理。1982 年被 ITT 公司任命为首位“ITT 执行科学家”。1985 年在德国的 SEL 研究中心工作。与此同时，还任耶鲁大学特朗布尔学院兼职教授、研究员。1986 年，被任命为合作研究主任，并在标准电话与电缆公司的标准电信实验室作研究。1989 年，获得英国电机工程师协会院士称号。还是英国国际电话电报公司的研究总裁与总工程师，美国电话电报公司、英国电报与无线电公司的顾问。1990 年成为美国工程院院士。是北京邮电大学名誉教授。2009 年，与威拉德·博伊尔和乔治·埃尔伍德·史密斯共享诺贝尔物理学奖。

“光纤之父”的童年

高锟童年时期住在淮海中路 1670 弄中南新村一栋三层楼的房子里。10 岁时，入读上海世界学校（现世界小学），在上海度过了小学及初中一年级的时光。

高锟从小就对科技情有独钟，强烈的好奇心及求知欲驱使他想把什么都拆开来看看。六年级时，高锟接触到化学实验，他从教育书店购买化学品，大量阅读科普读物，兴致盎然地在自己家设立了“实验室”，尝试做各种稀奇古怪的实验。他曾自制灭火筒、焰火、烟花，甚至将红磷和氯酸钾加上水调成糊状，填塞进湿润的泥土里，搓成一颗颗泥球炸弹。

有一次，高锟在和父母一起逛商店时发现一盒无线电收音机的零件套，内含电磁圈、可调校的电容器、晶体棒、耳筒、电线及螺丝刀。他央求父母购买后如获至宝，一头扎进家里的“实验室”，废寝忘食地沉浸在未知的无线电世界中。然而任凭他怎么捣鼓，每当跃跃欲试地把耳筒塞进耳朵，却总是什么也没听到。他与对科学小实验也怀有浓厚兴趣的周同学一同探讨，通过参考有关无线电的书籍，他们知晓了无线电的原理，明晰了电容器和电磁圈可以在某一特定的频率接收到无线电信号。在“实验室”中，高锟屏息凝神，慢慢地调校电容器，以免错过了电台的波段。功夫不负有心人，经过反复调试，电台广播终于悠然响起，高锟体验着前所未有的奇妙感觉。“在什么也没有的空气里，竟然可以蕴藏音乐，简直是魔术。”迷上无线电的他再接再厉，在不分昼夜的刻苦钻研下，一部装有五六个真空管的收音机在年幼的高锟手中诞生了。

高锟在上海世界学校里，和同学们一起玩无线电、做实验，通过有趣的方法，探索更广阔的知识，在相互鼓励中共同遨游神奇的科学世界。对电机工程的浓厚兴趣在年幼的高锟心中悄然萌发，他从此与科学结缘，在光纤通信领域收获了累累硕果，成为荣获诺贝尔物理学奖的“光纤之父”。

建筑简介：淮海中路1670弄

高锟曾居住于淮海中路1670弄中南新村。中南新村建于1941年，建筑面积8402.35平方米，属新式里弄住宅。建筑为砖木结构，毗连式，前后错位，原有13栋，现存11栋。建筑入口架空为门廊，方形门窗，缓坡红瓦屋面，本色水泥外墙，横向窗间墙灰绿色面砖贴面，窗台上下有突出边框，强调水平线条，部分楼梯间外墙纵向窗间有几何图案装饰。每单元均有小庭院。当时多为商界人士及军政要员居住。1994年2月15日上海市人民政府公布其为市优秀历史建筑。

GAO Kun

GAO Kun (1933–), born in Shanghai and a physicist of Chinese origin. Due to his special contribution in the field of optical fiber, he got to be known as "the father of fiber". From 1970 to 1974, he worked as professor, chair professor and the first head of the department of electronics in the Chinese University of Hong Kong. In 1974, he returned to ITT in Virginia in the United States, where he served as director scientist in the department of optoelectronic products. Later he was promoted to director of engineering and vice manager of photovoltaic products. In 1982 he was appointed as the first "ITT executive scientist". In 1985 he worked in SEL Research Center in Germany. At the same time, he also served as part-time professor and researcher at Trumbull College of Yale University. In 1986, he was appointed as director of cooperative research and did research work at the Standard Telecommunication Lab of Standard Telephone and Cables. In 1989, he obtained the title of academician of the British Institute of Electrical Engineers. Also he was research president and chief engineer of the International Telegraph and Telephone Company of the United Kingdom as well as consultant of the Telephone and Telegraph Company of the United States and the British Telegraph and Radio Company. In 1990 he became an academician of engineering of the United States. Also he was honorary professor of Beijing University of Posts and Telecommunications. In 2009, he shared the Nobel Prize in Physics with Willard Boyle and George Elwood Smith.

The Child' s Tastes of "Father of Fiber"

In his childhood GAO Kun lived in a three-story house at Central-South New Village in Alley 1670 on Middle Huaihai Road. At the age of 10, he was enrolled in Shanghai World School (now World Primary School), spending his time of elementary and junior high school in Shanghai.

Since his childhood he had a deep love for science and technology so that a strong curiosity and thirst for knowledge drove him to dismantle anything in order to take a look. In the sixth grade of his schooling, he was exposed to chemical experiments. Buying chemicals from the education bookstore and reading a lot of popular science books, he set up a "laboratory" with great interest in his

高锟在标准电信实验室工作时的留影

A photo of GAO Kun at work in the Standard Communication Lab.

own home, trying to do all kinds of strange experiments. Once he made fire extinguishers and fireworks by himself. Moreover he even mixed the red phosphorus and potassium chlorate with water to make them into a kind of paste, which he filled into the moist soil and rubbed into bombs of mud ball.

On one occasion when shopping together with his parents, he found a box of radio components, including magnetic coils, adjustable capacitors, crystal rods, headphones, wires and screwdrivers. He begged his parents to buy them and got the support and encouragement of his father. As if finding out treasures, he headed into the "laboratory" at home and immersed himself in the unknown radio world even with sleepless nights. However, despite his fiddling, he could hear nothing whenever he tried eagerly to tuck headphones into his ears. He also discussed with students who also had a keen interest in scientific experiments. By referring to the books on radio, they got to know the principles of radio and made it clear that capacitors and electromagnets could receive radio signals at a specific frequency. In the "laboratory", he held his breath and concentrated his attention, slowly adjusting the capacitor so as not to miss the radio band. Hard work pays off. After repeated debugging, radio broadcast finally came out in a leisurely way. At this moment, he was experiencing the wonderful and unprecedented feeling. "In the air where there is nothing, music should be hidden there. This is simply magic." Fascinated by radio, he made persistent and assiduous efforts in his study day and night. Finally, a radio with a five or six vacuum tubes was born from the hands of the kid still young.

At the Shanghai World School, he together with other students played with radio and did experiments. They explored a broader scope of knowledge with interesting methods and traveled in the magic world of science under mutual encouragement. The interest in electrical engineering quietly budded in his young heart. Ever since then, he became attached to science, harvested fruitful achievements in the field of fiber optic communications and became "Father of Fiber" who won the Nobel Prize in Physics.

GAO Kun once lived in Central South New Village in Alley 1670 on Middle Huaihai Road. Built in 1941, the Central South Village is a new-style alley residence with a construction area of 8,402.35 square meters. The building complex is of the structure of brick and wood with buildings adjacent to each other in horizontal rows and mutually dislocated in longitudinal rows. There were originally thirteen buildings and only eleven of them are still extant. The building has an entrance with a porch built on stilts and has square doors and windows, a roof of gentle slope with red tile, and exterior walls coated with natural cement. The horizontal spaces between windows are coated with a veneer of gray green face bricks, above and under windowsills are installed with projected frames, laying emphasis on horizontal lines. Between the longitudinal windows on exterior walls of some staircases, there are decorations of geometric patterns. Each unit has a small courtyard. At former time, these buildings were mostly occupied by business people and military and political officials. On February 15, 1994, it became a Heritage Architecture issued by the Shanghai Municipal People's Government.

高锟 （桑麟康画） GAO Kun （By SANG Linkang）

高占非
（1904—1969）

天津人，原名高执欧。保定军官学校肄业。1923 年加入上海明星影片股份有限公司任演员。1928 年后因主演影片《小侦探》和《奇女子》而崭露头角。20 世纪 30 年代，先后在明星、联华、艺华、天一、新华等影片公司任演员。左翼电影运动兴起后，在《共赴国难》《劫后桃花》等影片中担任主角。1934 年《电声周刊》发起“中国电影明星选举”，高占非当选“影帝”。抗战胜利后去香港。1948 年，与顾而已、顾也鲁等共同创办大光明影片公司。1951 年，随大光明公司回到上海，在影片《方珍珠》中扮演角色。一生出演了近百部影片。

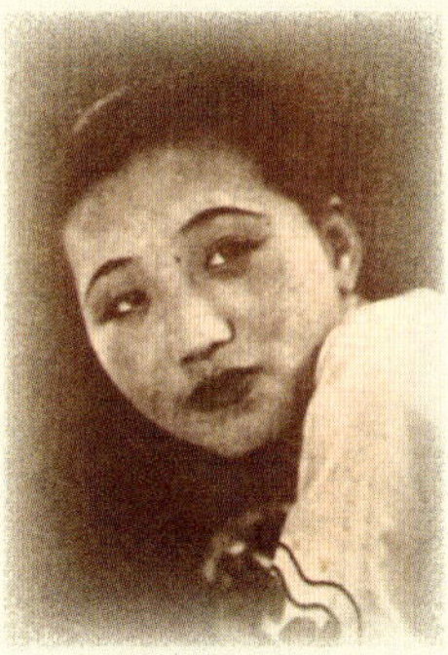

高倩苹
（1911—？）

演员。1928 年从影，在杨耐梅自组公司投拍的影片《奇女子》中任角色。次年在民新公司主演《风流剑客》，此后进入明星公司，主演《战地小同胞》《勇士救美记》《重婚》《乡愁》等。左翼电影运动兴起后，出演了《丰年》《二对一》《春蚕》等 30 余部影片。1936 年，在走红时毅然退出影坛，转而去上海政法学院攻读法律，四年后挂牌成为女律师。

柳暗花明又一村

1928 年，高占非和高倩苹曾一同参演女星杨耐梅自组公司投拍的影片《奇女子》，而后又同在上海明星影片公司任职。高占非体格魁梧，心地笃实，举止沉稳，故人称“老高”。高倩苹清新可爱，小鸟依人，故人称“小高”。“老高”和“小高”常常切磋表演艺术，日久生情，由同事发展为恋人，携手步入婚姻殿堂，成为影坛佳侣。婚后两人相敬如宾，育有子女数人。

明星影片公司是当时上海规模最大、最具影响力的影片公司，是演员们梦想启航的圣地。高占非在人才济济的明星影片公司，三年中只饰演了几个小角色，始终未能得到崭露头角的良机。老板张石川较为苛刻，常常在拍戏时责备高占非演技不到位，高大魁梧的“老高”在同仁们面前被骂得抬不起头来。受责备后的高占非愈加拘谨，演戏时愈加不自在，日渐抑郁消沉，开始质疑自己是否具备成为一名合格演员的潜质，甚至萌发了改行的想法。

高倩苹不忍目睹丈夫如此颓丧。她安慰丈夫，肯定他乃可塑之材，重振旗鼓必能一鸣惊人，并积极张罗筹备，帮助高占非联络上已经加入联华电影公司的好友蔡楚生。“联华”是当时刚刚崛起的一家新电影公司，拍摄的影片关注现实生活，格调清新自然，深受青年学生青睐。高占非加盟“联华”后不久，蔡楚生编导了他的导演处女作《南国之春》，并邀请高占非饰演男主角。高倩苹鼓励丈夫抓住这来之不易的契机，并悉心照料丈夫的生活起居，让他全心全意钻研表演艺术。功夫不负有心人，《南国之春》上映后，反响热烈，高占非饰演的洪瑜一角深受观众喜爱，兼具魁梧健硕身材和俊朗阳刚气质的高占非鲤鱼跳龙门，一跃而成为大明星。

建筑简介：新乐路100弄16号

高占非、高倩苹旧居位于新乐路（原名亨利路）100弄的永利村16号。建于1938年，单面行列式布置44幢，总建筑面积8902平方米，属新式里弄。砖木混合结构，三层，两幢连体，平面方形，立面对称，中间以一竖墙分隔，无阳台，相邻两个号码的主入口均设有方形雨厦。沿街住宅以褐色毛面砖贴墙，作竖直隔离装饰之用。弄堂主入口三层通高壁柱直达檐口。缓坡屋顶，挑檐较小，方窗，水泥砂浆外墙。永利村素有"影人村"之称，20世纪二三十年代，胡蝶、张织云等著名电影演员们云集于此。

GAO Zhanfei and GAO Qianping

GAO Zhanfei (1904–1969) has his ancestral from Tianjin with a former name of GAO Zhi'ou. He had his study in Baoding Army Officers School. In 1923, he joined Shanghai Star Film Co., Ltd. to work there as an actor. After 1928 he made a figure for himself due to his starring in the film *A Little Detective* and *A Strange Woman*. In the 1930s, he worked as actor in film companies including Star Film Company, Lianhua Film Company, Yihua Film Company, Tianyi Film Company and New China Film Company. After the rise of the left-wing film movement, he played leading roles in the *Share the Burden of National Crisis*, *Down-trodden Peach Blossom* and other films. In 1934 the *Film Sound Weekly* launched the "Chinese Movie Star Election", in which GAO Zhanfei ascended the throne of "Movie King". After the victory of the War against Japanese Invasion he went to Hong Kong. In 1948, he along with GU Eryi and GU Yelu co-founded the Ever Shining Film Company. In 1951, he returned to Shanghai with the film company and played a role in the film *Square Pearl*. In his lifetime, he performed in nearly a hundred films.

GAO Qianping (1911–?) was an actress. In 1928 she started her film career, playing a role in the film *A Strange Woman* invested and produced by a film company organized by YANG Naimei herself. In the following year, she starred in the film *Merry Swordsman* produced by Minxin Film Company. After that she joined the Star Film Company, starring films such as *Young Townsmen on the Battlefield*, *A Warrior Rescued the Beauty*, *A Bigamic Marriage* and *Homesickness*. After the rise of the left-wing film movement, she performed in over 30 films like *Harvest*, *Two to One*, *Spring Silkworm* and others. In 1936, she took upon herself to drop out from the field of film when she was having her moment, turning to study law in Shanghai Institute of Political Science and Law. Four years later she became a female lawyer.

Every Cloud Has A Silver Lining

In 1928, GAO Zhanfei and GAO Qianping participated together in the film *A Strange Woman* invested and produced by a film

高占非和高倩苹
GAO Zhanfei and GAO Qianping.

company organized by female star YANG Naimei and then they worked together in Shanghai Star Film Company. He was of a great stature and was honest and sincere and composed, so known as "Big GAO". She was a fresh and lovely girl, timid and innocent, so known as "Little GAO". They used to exchange the performing arts with each other. As the common Chinese saying goes, love would come in time. As time went by, they developed from colleagues to lovers and entered the marriage hall hand in hand, making a good companion in the field of film. After marriage, they were loving and had several children.

The Star Film Company was the largest and most influential in Shanghai and was also a holy land where actors and actresses started their dreams. In the film company filled with talented stars, the husband only played a few minor roles within three years and failed to have good opportunity to make a brilliant figure. The boss ZHANG Shichuan was comparatively demanding, often reproaching him for his insufficient acting in the process of shooting. The scolding only left the tall and burly "Big GAO" unable to lift his head in front of colleagues. After the blame, he became increasingly stiff and felt more uncomfortable in acting. Also he turned to be more depressed and gloomy and began to have doubts as to whether he had the potential to become a qualified actor. In the end, an idea even crossed his mind that he should change his trade.

The wife could not bear to see her husband so depressed. She consoled him, confirming that he had a great potential. If only he would dust himself down, he could definitely pull off a great coup. In the same time she actively made preparation and arrangements to help her husband to get into contact with CAI Chusheng, their good friend who had joined the Lianhua Film Company. It was a new film company which had just sprung up and produced films concerned about real life and characterized with fresh and natural styles. Therefore these films were deeply favored by young students. Shortly after the husband joined the Lianhua Company, CAI wrote and directed his first film *Spring of the South* and invited him to play the leading man. The wife encouraged her husband to seize this hard-won opportunity and carefully took care of his daily life so that he could wholeheartedly delve into the performing arts. Efforts paid off. After the release of *Spring of the South*, there was a warm response and the role of HONG Yu performed by the husband was deeply loved by the audience. With the combination of both strong build and handsome masculine, he made a success of himself and became a big star with one leap.

The former residence of GAO Zhanfei and GAO Qianping is located at No. 16 in Yongli Village in Alley 100 on Xinle Road (formerly Henry Road), which was built in 1938. As a new style alley, it has a one-sided layout of rows with 44 buildings with a total construction area of 8,902 square meters. The buildings have a mixed structure of brick and wood. Each having three stories, two buildings are connected. The horizontal plane is a square while the elevation one is symmetrical. The middle has a vertical wall to separate the two buildings, which have no balcony. The main entrances of two adjacent numbers are equipped with a square canopy. Residences along the street have walls with brown napped bricks for the purpose of decoration and vertical separation. The main entrance of the alley has high pilasters with a height of three stories reaching directly to the cornices. The roof has gentle slopes with smaller eaves. Windows are square and exterior walls have cement mortar. The Yongli Village is known as the "Filmmakers Village". In the 1920s and 1930s, famous film actors and actresses such as HU Die and ZHANG Zhiyun gathered here.

高占非、高倩苹 （钱定华画）

GAO Zhanfei and GAO Qianping （By QIAN Dinghua）

曹禺
（1910—1996）

祖籍湖北潜江，出生于天津，原名万家宝，剧作家。毕业于清华大学外国语文系和清华大学研究生院。1933 年创作话剧处女作《雷雨》，并于次年发表，1936 年和 1937 年分别出版重要剧作《日出》和《原野》，自此奠定了其杰出现代剧作家的地位，有“中国莎士比亚”之称。中华人民共和国成立后历任中央戏剧学院副院长、北京人民艺术剧院院长、北京市文联主席、中国文联主席、中国剧协主席、中国作家协会书记处书记等。著有剧本《北京人》《家》《王昭君》等，电影文学剧本《雷雨》《日出》，散文集《迎春集》，作品集《曹禺剧本选》《曹禺选集》等。

李玉茹
（1924—2008）

北京人，原名李淑贞、雪莹，京剧表演艺术家。1932 年考入中华戏曲专科学校，习青衣、工旦角，师承王瑶卿、梅兰芳、程砚秋等名家。1940 年组织“如意社”，先后与马连良、杨宝森、谭富英等合作演出。抗战胜利后定居上海，与周信芳、俞振飞等合作演出。上海解放后，组建李玉茹京剧团，后并入上海京剧院，任主要演员。曾任上海京剧院三团团长、院艺术顾问。主要作品有《小放牛》《玉人美》《鸳鸯泪》《白蛇传》《唐赛儿》等。

相知相思，30 年成眷属

1978 年是李玉茹一生中一个重要的年头，她与曹禺再次相遇。12 月 8 日她去宾馆看望来沪的曹禺。

与李玉茹见面点燃了曹禺内心的热情。原来他们相识于 1947 年。30 年前他不被李玉茹母亲欢迎、只得在楼下等待这位女演员的景象，以及两人在兆丰公园（今中山公园）散步讨论戏曲女伶人生活的话题，宛如发生在昨天一般。曹禺在沪几天，两人一起谈人生、谈痛苦，当然也谈幸福。

曹禺回到北京，开始天天往上海写信、打电话。其中有《如梦令·寄友人》为证，曹禺写道：三十年前旧梦，今日又来相抚。瞬息又离别，谁知何日再睹？再睹，再睹，春风小楼独主。在上海复兴中路 1462 弄 3 号小楼里，李玉茹读完曹禺的信，回应道：三十年已逝矣，今日大地春回。喜意外重逢，暂离相会有期。有期，有期，小楼坐待生辉。

“相知才相思啊！”李玉茹非常明白曹禺对自己的眷恋，也欣赏他那喷薄如火山岩浆一般的激情。1979 年 12 月 7 日，两人在北京办理了结婚手续。李玉茹终于在 55 岁时圆了做曹禺妻子的梦。没有等蜜月结束，李玉茹就回上海工作。这一段时间里，曹禺经常到上海来，甚至作为家属与她一起到外地去巡回演出，这让曹禺兴奋不已。

10 年快要过去了。1988 年，晴天霹雳，曹禺被诊断为肾功能衰退，住进北京医院。李玉茹二话没说，陪着老伴住进了医院，在一张钢丝小床上，一睡就是几年。人后，她哭得死去活来，当着曹禺的面，却显得信心百倍，鼓励曹禺跟她一起往前走。1996 年 12 月 13 日，曹禺去世。“于凌晨 3:55 分悄然离我走了……

家宝今天独自一人睡在北京医院太平间了，我不能陪他了，好人家宝，我舍不得你。”李玉茹黯然流泪。

李玉茹把对于曹禺的深深思念，投入到为老伴编书中。从曹禺去世一直忙碌到2000年底，《没有说完的话》终于出版。李玉茹在扉页上给孩子们写下了这么几句话：这是妈妈花了大心血出的一本集子。我尽量忠实地再现爸爸的真实情感，还原他本来面目，让人们更多一些了解曹禺其人。

建筑简介：复兴中路1462弄3号

曹禺、李玉茹旧居位于复兴中路1462弄3号。1938年由郑相衡投资在此建造砖木结构楼房15幢，原为假三层，占地1430平方米。中华人民共和国成立后改建成真三层楼房，建筑面积2620平方米，为新式里弄。建筑入口有雨篷，立面开方窗和长窗，铁窗框。双坡硬山屋顶，底层为红砖贴面，其他水泥本色粉刷。因业主系英国剑桥大学研究生，建筑又地处淮海中路与宝庆路、复兴中路围成的三角形地块，沪语中“角”与“阁”谐音，故名剑桥阁，也称剑桥角。

CAO Yu and LI Yuru

CAO Yu (1910–1996) has his ancestral family from Qianjiang in Hubei province. Born in Tianjin, he had a former name of WAN Jiabao and is known as a playwright. He graduated from the Department of Foreign Languages and the Graduate School of Tsinghua University. In 1933 he created his debut drama *Thunderstorm*, which was published the following year. In 1936 and 1937 he got published his major dramas *Sunrise* and *Wilderness*. Since then his status of outstanding modern playwright was laid and reputed as “Chinese Shakespeare”. After the founding of the New China he served in succession as vice president of the Central Academy of Drama, president of the Beijing People’s Art Theater, chairman of the Beijing Municipal Federation of Literary and Art Circles, chairman of the China Federation of Literary and Art Circles, chairman of the Chinese Drama Association, and secretary of the secretariat of the Chinese Writers Association. His works include plays such as *Beijing Native*, *Family* and *WANG Zhaojun*; film literature works such as *Thunderstorm* and *Sunrise*; prose collection *Anthology Greeting Spring*; work collections such as *Collection of Plays by CAO Yu* and *Anthology by CAO Yu*.

LI Yuru (1924–2008) is a native of Beijing with former names of LI Shuzhen and Xueying. She is known as a Beijing Opera performing artist. In 1932 she was admitted to the Chinese Opera School, learning the role of Black Clothes and good at roles of female actress under the teaching of such famous masters of Beijing Opera as WANG Yaoqing, MEI Lanfang and CHENG Yanqiu. In 1940 she launched the organization of Ruyi Society and cooperated successively in performance with MA Lianliang, YANG Baosen and TAN Fuying. After the victory of the War against Japanese Invasion, she settled in Shanghai and performed in cooperation with ZHOU Xinfang and YU Zhenfei. After the liberation of Shanghai, she launched the formation of LI Yuru Beijing Opera Troupe, which was later incorporated into the Shanghai Beijing Opera Theater with her as a leading actress. Once she served as head and art consultant of the third troupe of Shanghai Beijing Opera Theater. Her main works are *Little Cowboy*, *Jade Beauty*, *Lovers’ Tears*, *Story of White Snake* and *TANG Saier*.

曹禺(左)和李玉茹(右)
CAO Yu (left) and LI Yuru (right).

Understanding with Longing Means Final Marriage

The year of 1978 was an important time for LI Yuru in her lifetime because she met with CAO Yu for the second time. On December 8, she went to the hotel to visit CAO Yu who arrived in Shanghai.

The meeting with her ignited the passion in his heart. It turned out they got to know each other in 1947. But 30 years ago, he was not welcomed by her mother and could only wait downstairs for the presence of the actress; the two took a stroll in Zhaofeng Park (now Zhongshan Park) to discuss the life of a female actress of drama—it seemed as if all the scenes and the topics happened yesterday. CAO Yu stayed in Shanghai for a few days and they talked about life, about pains and, of course, about happiness.

After he returned to Beijing, he began to write to her or call her every day. Among them, one poem serves as evidence "To the Tune of Dream", in which CAO Yu wrote: Old dreams thirty years ago have come back to caress today. A moment of meeting was followed by parting away, but who knows what day to see again? Again, again, spring breeze witnesses lonely days. In the small building at No. 3 in Alley 1462 on Middle Fuxing Road in Shanghai, she finished reading his letter, replying: thirty years passed away and spring has come back today. Great happiness for accidental reunion anticipates temporary parting and meeting again. Again, again, the small building is waiting for radiating one day.

"Alas! Understanding means longings!" She was not merely aware of his sentimental attachment to her, but also appreciated his gushing passion like volcanic magma. On December 7, 1979, they got married in Beijing. She finally realized her dream of becoming his wife at the age of 55. When the honeymoon had not ended, she returned to Shanghai to work. During this period of time, he often came to Shanghai. Moreover, he even went with her as a family member to other places for road shows, which made him excited.

Nearly ten years passed. In 1988, a bolt came from the blue when he was diagnosed with renal failure and admitted to the Beijing hospital. She did not say anything, but accompanied her husband to go hospital. From then on she stayed on a small wire bed for a few years. Behind people, she wept her heart out, while she seemed very confident in his presence and encouraged him to go forward with her. On December 13, 1996, he passed away. "At 3:55 in the early morning he left me quietly... He slept alone in the hospital morgue in Beijing today. I could not be with him. A good person you are, but I could not bear without you." She shed tears sadly.

She devoted her deep missing for him to compilation of books for her husband. She was busy from his passing away to the end of 2000, The book *Remarks not Finished* was finally published. On the title page she wrote for the children a few words: This is a collection your mum spent a great effort on. I've tried my best to faithfully reproduce the true feelings of your dad and restore his true colors so that people could understand more of CAO Yu.

The former residence of CAO Yu and LI Yuru is located at No. 3 in Alley 1462 on Middle Fuxing Road. In 1938, ZHENG Xiangheng invested to construct 15 buildings here with a structure of brick and wood which was nominally three-storied. The residence covers an area of 1,430 square meters. After the founding of the New China it was restructured into a true three-storey building with a construction area of 2,620 square meters in a new style of alley. The entrance of the building has canopy awning and its facade has square window and long window with iron window frames. The roof has double slopes with hard gables. The bottom floor has red brick veneer and the other ones have walls whitewashed with cement color. Since its owner was a graduate student from the University of Cambridge and also since it is located in a triangle plot circled by Middle Huaihai Road, Baoqing Road and Middle Fuxing Road, it is also called the Cambridge Pavilion and the Cambridge Corner due to the similar pronunciation of the characters of "corner" and "pavilion" in Shanghai dialect.

曹禺、李玉茹 （邬海佳画）

CAO Yu and LI Yuru （By WU Haijia）

盖叫天
（1888—1971）

河北高阳人，原名张英杰，号燕南，京剧表演艺术家。童年入天津隆庆和科班，初学武生，后改学老生，倒嗓后复演武生。长期在上海、杭州一带演出。继承了南派武生创始人李春来的艺术风格，吸取京剧与昆曲、地方戏中各流派武生和其他行当表演艺术的长处，逐渐形成了独具特色的盖派表演艺术，有“江南活武松”和“武生宗匠”之誉。曾当选中国戏剧家协会浙江分会主席、第三届全国人民代表大会代表。拍摄有影片《盖叫天的舞台艺术》《武松》等。

触类旁通 潜心艺术

盖叫天爱收藏古玩，善于将古玩上的纹饰与京剧的身段、舞姿联系，从中寻求灵感与启迪。东湖路寓所内有两三间大房间专门用来放古玩，其中瓷器有几千件。有一只瓷瓶据说盖老是花重金买来的，盖老从这瓷瓶上“两边垂下、很匀称”的杨柳纹饰中获得启发，联想到《夜奔》中“刷喇喇风吹叶落”的舞姿可借鉴这杨柳的形态：剧中林冲双掌分开，由上而下，双掌颤动着模拟树叶纷纷落下所需的视觉艺术效果，与瓷瓶上杨柳从容不迫地徐徐下垂、两边匀称有弹性、又有点儿飘动的柔和形态正好吻合。故盖老将此瓷瓶视若珍宝，置于堂前桌上。

《夜奔》描述了在经历了遭人陷害、充军发配、野猪林脱险、火烧草料场等一系列坎坷之后的林冲只身一人夜奔梁山的故事。如何将林冲悲凉沧桑但不失大气豪迈的复杂心境通过演员的独唱、独舞传神地展现出来，盖叫天对此琢磨多年。精益求精、追求完美的个性使他在潜心钻研的过程中对自己的要求越来越严苛，迟迟不愿在舞台上公演这出自认为尚未研究透彻的高难度武生戏。

1956 年 11 月的一天下午，盖叫天东湖路的家中宾客满堂。北昆的名武生侯永奎专程拜访这位武生宗师，同行的还有京剧界、昆剧界的同仁们。寒暄之后，侯永奎谦虚地向盖老请教《夜奔》的表演艺术。宾客们力邀盖老现场示范。盛情难却，盖老在长衫上系上大带，挂上宝剑，“四击头”拟声中“林冲”出场了。

能在东湖路的盖府欣赏 68 岁的盖老献演《夜奔》，实乃可遇不可求的幸事。在场的宾客们屏息凝神，沉浸在对盖老每一个身段、动作及表情的艺术欣赏中。尤其是“回首西山日影斜”的“跨步回身”和“进庙”时的“挨身而进”两处身段，在盖老迅捷、舒展的演绎下，尽显雄浑、圆劲，其矫若游龙的表演令人叹服。盖叫天独揽唱、念、做、舞，一气呵成地演了大半出《夜奔》，令宾客们拍案叫绝。

盖叫天旧居位于东湖路56弄22号，为花园里弄住宅，二层砖木结构，建筑平面近似矩形。外立面为清水红砖墙面，机制平瓦四坡屋面，木结构挑檐，挑檐底面以白色涂料涂饰。一层为"骑楼"式样，并辅以巴洛克式的装修风格。一层入口位于房屋北侧，入户后有小门厅，东侧有厨房，南侧原为客厅和居室。旋转木楼梯，吊顶上悬挂欧式风格的水晶挂灯。通过旋转楼梯上到二层，三间大卧室朝南并排而立，推开百叶门，打通的阳台连廊豁然显现。室内走道及房间楼面基本为硬木长条地板。房前的庭院原为60余平方米的小花园，是盖老练功的地方。

GAI Jiaotian

GAI Jiaotian (1888–1971) has his ancestral family from Gaoyang in Hebei province. He had a former name of ZHANG Yingjie with a courtesy name of Yannan and was known as a Beijing Opera performing artist. In his childhood he entered into the Tianjin Longqinghe Opera Art School, learning the martial role in the beginning and later changed to study the role of old gentleman. After losing his voice, he went back to learn the martial role. He attended performance in Shanghai and Hangzhou for a long time. After inheriting the artistic style of LI Chunlai, the founder of the southern school of martial roles and absorbing the strengths of Beijing Opera, Kunqu, various schools of martial roles in the local operas and other performing arts, he gradually formed a unique performance art of GAI School. He has the reputation of "Southern Living Actor for Wu Song" and "Great Master of Martial Roles". Once he was elected chairman of the Zhejiang Branch of the Chinese Dramatists Association and representative of the Third National People's Congress. He participated in the performance of such films as *The Stage Art of GAI Jiaotian* and *WU Song*.

Comprehending by Analogy and Concentrating on Art

GAI Jiaotian had a liking for the collection of antique, good at the association of patterns on antique with Beijing Opera and dance postures, from which he tried to seek for understanding and inspiration. There were two or three large rooms in his apartment on East Lake Road dedicated to the storage of antiques, among which there are some thousands of pieces of porcelain. One porcelain vase was said to obtain by spending a lot of money. He got inspirations from the willow patterns of decoration "hanging on both sides and very well-proportioned" on the vase, associating them with the dancing of "blowing of wind and falling of leaves" in *Fleeing by Night* for which references could be made from this form of willow. In the opera, LIN Chong separated his two palms, moved from top to bottom and quivered to imitate the visual effects required by falling leaves, which well matched the soft shape of the willow patterns on the porcelain hanging slowly and casually, being symmetrical and elastic on both sides and fluttering a little bit. For all this, he took the vase as treasure and placed it on the table in the front of the house.

The opera *Fleeing by Night* describes the story of Lin Chong alone fleeing to Liangshan one night after the experience of a

盖叫天（右）与周信芳（左）、赵如泉（中）畅谈艺术
GAI Jiaotian (right) was happily talking about art with ZHOU Xinfang (left) and ZHAO Ruquan (middle).

series of ups and downs such as being framed, being exiled for penal servitude, getting out of danger at wild boar forest, and setting fire on grass yard. How to vividly exhibit the desolate vicissitudes of life and heroic complex state of mind of LIN Chong through the solo singing and solo dance—for this, he made comparisons and ponderings for many years. He had the personality to strive for excellence and pursue perfection so that he was increasingly stringent with himself in the process of his concentrated study. Therefore he was reluctant for a long time to put this difficult opera of a martial role on the stage for which he had not finished his research.

In the afternoon one day in November 1956, his home on East Lake Road was full of guests. HOU Yongkui, the well-known martial role actor in the northern Kunqu, made a special trip to visit the great master of martial roles, accompanied by colleagues of Beijing Opera and Kunqu. After greeting, HOU modestly consulted him about the performance art in *Fleeing by Night*. Guests invited him with open arms to make a demonstration on the spot. Difficult to refuse such kindness, he tied a big belt on the gown and put on a sword so that "LIN Chong" came out on the spot among the sound of the "four percussion musical instruments".

It was a lucky experience to enjoy his performance of *Fleeing by Night* when he was at the age of 68 in his house on the East Lake Road. All the guests at present held their breath and immersed themselves in the artistic appreciation of each of his postures, actions and expressions. In particular, for the postures of "approaching bit by bit" at such two scenes as "stepping and turning around" and "getting into the temple" in the act of "Looking Back at the Western Hills with Oblique Sun Shadows", he performed swiftly and stretched his body to demonstrate the vigor, firmness and forcefulness. His performance was brisk and nimble like swimming dragon, which found all the audience gasping in admiration. Also he alone covered singing, speaking, action and dance and performed a major half of the opera at one go so that all guests were overwhelmed.

The former residence of GAI Jiaotian is located at No. 22 in Alley 56 on the East Lake Road. As a garden house, it is a two-story structure of brick and wood and its architectural plane is approximately rectangular. The facade has walls of water red bricks and the roof has four slopes covered with flat tiles manufactured with machines. It has wooden structure canopy, at the bottom of which is washed with white paint. The first floor is the type of "riding building", supplemented by decorations of Baroque style. The entrance of the first floor is located on the north side of the house and there is a small hall behind the door. At the east side is a kitchen and at the south side were formerly living room and bedrooms; wood staircases rotate upward and under the suspended ceiling a crystal light hangs from it with a European style; the rotating stairs lead to the second floor, where three large bedrooms face south side by side; the shutter door lead to the continuous corridor formed by connected balconies; indoor walkways and rooms basically have a floor of long strips. The courtyard in front of the house was formerly a small garden of 60 square meters, a place for him to do physical exercises.

盖叫天 （钱定华画） GAI Jiaotian （By QIAN Dinghua）

黄兴
（1864—1916）

湖南善化（今长沙）人，原名轸，字廑午，号杞园，又号克强。1898年入两湖书院。1902年赴日本留学，和杨笃生等创办《游学译编》，次年参加拒俄义勇队。1904年2月和陈天华、宋教仁在长沙成立华兴会，任会长，同年策划长沙起义未成，逃亡日本。1905年与孙中山筹划成立中国同盟会。1907年起，先后参与或指挥钦州、防城起义和镇南关（今友谊关）起义，钦州、廉州、上思和广州新军起义。1911年4月与赵声领导广州起义（黄花岗之役）。武昌起义后，被推为革命军总司令。1912年南京临时政府成立，任陆军总长兼参谋总长。8月，同盟会改组为国民党，被推为理事。1913年二次革命时在南京任江苏讨袁军总司令，失败后流亡日本。1914年孙中山在日本组织中华革命党，因与孙意见不合，拒绝加入。不久后旅居美国，积极策动讨袁，与孙呼应。1916年回国，10月31日在上海病逝。遗著编为《黄兴集》。

生死之交

1916年7月4日，黄兴由日本回到上海，入住位于福开森路（今武康路393号）的"黄公馆"。黄兴将在这里接待他的挚友蔡锷。黄兴和蔡锷虽为湖南同乡，但他们的相识相知，却是在共同留学的东瀛日本。从此，他们共同致力于革命，为维护中华民族的独立奔走于四方。

1916年8月18日，"讨袁护国"的英雄蔡锷因喉疾辞去四川督军之职，赴日本就医，途经上海。黄兴派大儿子黄一欧到码头迎接蔡锷一行。黄兴也不远千里，从广东赶回上海看望蔡锷。8月31日，黄兴又抱病亲到码头送别蔡锷。两位老友依依惜别，再三互道珍重。此时，两人均已沉疴在身，深知这一次告别，恐怕今生再难相见了。9月20日，蔡锷到达日本，入福冈大学医院治疗。然而，为革命奋斗一生的黄兴，终因积劳成疾，于10月31日凌晨4时30分病逝于上海，时年52岁。

噩耗传来，远在日本福冈的蔡锷十分悲痛。他亲自拍发唁电，并托人代表自己前往祭奠，还抱病撰写祭文及挽联。挽联云："以勇健开国，而宁静持身，贯彻实行，是能创作一生者；曾送我海上，忽哭公天涯，惊起挥泪，难为卧床九州人。"不久，蔡锷又撰一副挽联："方期公挽我，不期我挽公，国事回思惟一哭；未以病为忧，竟以忧成病，大勇哪知世险夷！"这两副挽联情真意切，后人读之，无不击节而感叹！8天以后，即11月8日凌晨4时，蔡锷也因病危不治，病逝于日本，年仅34岁。

当黄、蔡逝世噩耗传出后，全国上下深为悲痛。以黎元洪为首的北京国民政府，经国会议决，为这两位民国元勋举行国葬，建墓于岳麓山麓。在岳麓山麓，黄兴墓紧挨着蔡锷墓，守望相依。伟大的史学家司马迁曾说过："一死一生，乃知交情。"这也是黄兴和蔡锷一生情谊的最好写照。

建筑简介：武康路393号

黄兴旧居位于武康路393号，建于1912年，英式古典主义花园住宅，占地面积740平方米。该组建筑平面由一个矩形和一个直角三角形相接而成。三角形部分临街，矩形部分位于南面。南面矩形为英国古典式，半露木构架，陡坡顶。临街三角形部分为典型的装饰艺术派风格，其立面强调水平线条和垂直线条的穿插构图，并以深褐色面砖衬托出浅色的横竖线条。此外，还有大量带有装饰艺术派特征的浮雕和装饰线脚。1916年7月，黄兴返沪并寓居此地，孙中山曾两次来黄兴寓所。黄兴逝世后，旧居花园内曾有大规模扩建，为世界社、上海国际图书馆使用，后改为世界学校。

HUANG Xing

HUANG Xing (1864–1916) has his ancestral family from Shanhua (now Changsha) in Hunan province with a former name of Zhen, a courtesy name of Jinwu and style names of Qiyuan and Keqiang. In 1898, he entered into the Two-Lake Academy. In 1902, he went to Japan to study abroad and co-founded *Tour Study Adaptation* with YANG Dusheng and others. In the following year he participated in the volunteer team against Russian forces. In February 1904, he co-established the Chinese Prosperity Society with CHEN Tianhua and SONG Jiaoren and served as its president. In the same year he made plans for the Changsha Uprising, but failed and fled to Japan. In 1905 he made plans with SUN Yat-sen to set up the United League of China. Since 1907, he successively participated in or commanded many uprisings in different places. In April 1911, he led the Guangzhou Uprising (Huanghuagang battle) with others. After the Wuchang Uprising, he was elected as commander in chief of the revolutionary army. When the Nanjing Provisional Government was established in 1912, he served as chief of staff of the army and chief of the general staff. In August, the League was reorganized as the KMT and he was elected as director. During the Second Revolution in Nanjing in 1913, he served as commander in chief of the army against YUAN Shikai in Nanjing, but failed and went to Japan in exile. In 1914, SUN Yat-sen organized the Chinese Revolutionary Party in Japan and he refused to join it because of disagreement. Soon he travelled to live in the United States and actively mobilized crusade against YUAN in response to SUN Yat-sen. He returned in 1916 and passed away in Shanghai on October 31. He authored a posthumous works *An Anthology by HUANG Xing*.

Friendship between Life and Death

On July 4, 1916, HUANG Xing returned from Japan to Shanghai and stayed at the “HUANG Xing Mansion” on Ferguson Road (now No. 393 on Wukang Road). He would receive his best friend CAI E in this mansion. Fellow countrymen from Hunan province as they were, they got to know each other when they studied abroad in Japan. Since then, they worked together in revolution and tossed themselves around to safeguard the independence of the Chinese nation.

On August 18, 1916, CAI E, hero in “crusading against YUAN to protect the country”, resigned from the post of governor of Sichuan because of throat disease and went to Japan for medical treatment by way of Shanghai. HUANG Xing sent his eldest son to the pier to greet CAI E and his party. The former also traveled far and wide from Guangdong back to Shanghai to visit the latter. On

黄兴（左四）与孙中山（左二）等
HUANG Xing (fourth from left), SUN Yat-sen (second from left) and others.

August 31, HUANG Xing went to the pier with illness to bid farewell to CAI who went to Japan for medical treatment. The two old friends were reluctant to part and exchanges best wishes to each other again and again. At this point, the two had severe illnesses within themselves, knowing that farewell this time might find it difficult for them to meet again in their lifetime. On September 20, CAI E reached Japan and entered into the Fukuoka University Hospital for medical treatment. However, after struggling for revolution during his whole life, HUANG Xing broke down from constant overwork in the end and passed away in the early morning at 4:30 on October 31 in Shanghai when he was 52 years old.

The sad news came where CAI E was all sorrows at Fukuoka. He personally sent a message of condolence and entrusted other to go on behalf of him to attend the memorial ceremony. Also he wrote in sickness an elegiac address and an elegiac couplet, which read, "With courage to start a new country and with serenity to cultivate morality, you put them into practice throughout to create a wonderful life; Once see me off and now I cried for you beyond horizon. I startled to shed tears, but it's hard to help people all over the country." Soon CAI E wrote another elegiac couplet, which read, "Once expecting elegy for me, I am now elegizing for you and I only have tears to shed when recalling the past of the state; not worrying about the disease and actually diseases visiting for worries, but how great courage could know risks in the world!" After reading these two elegiac couplets full of affection and thoughtfulness, all but sighed a long sigh! Eight days later, in the early morning at 4:00 on November 8, CAI E also passed away of uncured illness in Japan, when he was only 34 years old.

When the sad news came, the whole country fell into deep grief. The Beijing National Government led by LI Yuanhong made a decision approved by the Congress to hold a state funeral for the two of great merits for the Republic of China and their tombs were built at the foot of Mount Yuelu. At the foot of the mountain, two tombs are close to each other, keeping watch and clinging to one another. The great historian SIMA Qian once said, "Between life and death, intimate friends get mutual knowledge." This is the best portrayal of the friendship between HAUNG Xing and CAI E in their lifetime.

The former residence of HUANG Xing is located at No. 393 on Wukang Road. Built in 1912, it is a garden residence which occupies an area of 740 square meters. The building plane consists of a rectangle and a right-angled triangle. The triangle part faces the street and the rectangular part lies in the south. Rectangular in the south is of the British classical style with semi-exposed wooden frame and steep slopes. The triangle part at the street is of the typical style of art deco and its facade emphasizes the interspersed composition of the horizontal lines and vertical lines, also with dark brown bricks to bring out the light-colored vertical and horizontal lines. In addition, there are a large number of reliefs and decorative architraves with the characteristics of decorative arts. In July 1916, HUANG Xing returned to Shanghai and lived here and Sun Yat-sen paid visits to his residence twice. After his death, the garden of the former residence was once expanded in a large scale, for the use of the World Society and Shanghai International Library. Later it was transferred for the use of the World School.

黄兴 （桑麟康画） HUANG Xing （By SANG Linkang）

程十发
（1921—2007）

祖籍上海金山枫泾，生于上海松江城外莫家弄，海派书画大家。1941 年毕业于上海美术专科学校。20 世纪 40 年代末，创作完成了第一本连环画《野猪林》。1952 年进入华东美术出版社工作，主要从事连环画、年画创作和文学名著插图绘制。1956 年参加上海中国画院筹建，1960 年为画院画师。1984 年起任上海中国画院院长。其在山水、花鸟、人物领域都有别开生面的贡献，独创了具有个人艺术风格的“程家样”，深受百姓喜欢。代表作品有《胆剑篇》《阿 Q 正传》《画皮》《丽人行》《小河淌水》等。著有《程十发画选》《程十发近作选》《程十发花鸟习作选》等。国画《歌唱祖国的春天》获全国青年美展一等奖。《儒林外史》插图获莱比锡国际书籍装帧展览银质奖。连环画《孔乙己》获首届全国连环画绘画评奖二等奖。1993 年获第二届上海文学艺术杰出贡献奖。

程十发与《小河淌水》

“月亮出来亮旺旺，想起我的阿哥在深山。哥像月亮天上走，哥啊，山下小河淌水清悠悠……”这首幽婉的云南民歌《小河淌水》，程十发不仅爱听，而且会唱。

20 世纪 50 年代，中国绘画艺术面临新时代“转型”的课题。这时的程十发已创作了大量具有影响的连环画，令画坛刮目相看。但程十发自己心里明白，他还远远没有画出心中的画，他在等待。

1957 年春，程十发到云南德宏傣族景颇族自治州写生。保存着独特民俗风情和自然风光的云南的一切，对这个出生在江南的年轻人而言都是新奇。他发现，云南少数民族的服饰特别适宜于用中国写意画潇洒多变的笔墨线条来表现，这不仅可以充分展示自己的艺术个性和才情，同时又符合表现新时代生活的要求。就这样，他创作了具有创意且有民族风情的《召树屯和喃婼娜》《双身凤》等连环画。

当时，一曲云南少数民族情歌《小河淌水》让他痴迷。他哼唱着，一种用灵魂来演绎的爱情绝响和用生命来诠释的旷世恋歌的感觉油然而生。

回到上海延庆路 141 号的家中，他又反复听唱这首歌，每当听罢就以此作一幅画。1959 年 10 月的一个晚上，他听着歌，欣然挥毫，一个戴着斗笠，挑着担子和陶罐趟过小溪的傣族姑娘跃上画面。画中的姑娘怕水沾湿裙子，回头用手轻轻拎起了裙摆，栩栩如生。这就是后来让人过目难忘的佳作《小河淌水》。这幅画，他曾画了无数遍，每一个动作、每一根线条、每一抹色彩都苦心经营，直到此时，水到渠成，一挥而就，画面看上去是如此轻松洒脱。

在这片天地里，程十发找到了表达自己真性情和真笔墨的自由之境。他创作的少数民族题材作品在画坛一炮打响，开创了当代中国画的一大流派。令人感怀的是，程十发躺在医院的日子里，陪伴他以及送他走完最后一程的，依然是那首让他魂牵梦萦的《小河淌水》。

建筑简介：延庆路141号

程十发旧居位于延庆路141号。延庆路135至149号，由中国建业地产公司建于1934年，每幢房屋建筑面积360平方米。建筑为砖木结构三层花园住宅，住宅平面接近正方形，主立面竖三段布置，中间凸出，底层为方形大门，平缓四坡瓦顶，方形门窗。每幢前有花园。二层设券柱廊或半圆形敞廊，有室外楼梯通向花园。三层为阳台。沿街北面的室外楼梯直接进入二楼主入口，建筑南面左右对称的室外楼梯也直达二楼。底层原为车库和厨房。1999年9月23日上海市人民政府公布其为市优秀历史建筑。

CHENG Shifa

CHENG Shifa (1921–2007) has his ancestral family from the old town of Fengjing in Jinshan District of Shanghai. Born in the Mo Family Alley outside Songjiang City in Shanghai, he is known as a great painter and calligrapher of Shanghai School. In 1941 he graduated from the Shanghai Art Academy. In the late 1940s, he finished the creation of his first comic book *The Rescue in Wild Boar Forest*. In 1952 he entered the East China Fine Arts Publishing House, mainly engaged in the creation of comics and paintings for the Chinese New Year as well as drawing of illustrations for famous literary works. In 1956 he participated in the preparation of the Shanghai Chinese Painting Academy and he worked as a painting artist in the academy in 1960. Since 1984, he served as president of the Academy. In the field of landscapes, flowers, birds and figure paintings, he made unique contributions and created a personal art of "CHENG Style" popularly enjoyed by the common people. His representative works include *Warrior Courage Section*, *The True Story of Ah Q*, *The Painted Skin*, *Three Women*, *A Gurgling Stream* and others. Also he is the author of such books as *Selected Paintings by CHENG Shifa*, *Selected Recent Paintings by CHENG Shifa*, *Selected Practice Bird Paintings by CHENG Shifa* and others. His Chinese painting *Singing for the Spring of the Motherland* won him the first prize of the National Youth Art Exhibition. The illustrations in *The Scholars* won him Silver Award at the Leipzig International Book Binding Exhibition. His comic book *KONG Yiji* won the second prize of the First National Comic Painting Award. In 1993 he won the outstanding contribution award in the Second Session of Shanghai Literature and Art Award.

CHENG Shifa and A Gurgling Stream

"The moon comes out bright; I think of my elder brother in the mountain's height. Brother moves like the moon in the sky; Brother ah, at the mountain foot a stream gurgles..." CHENG not only liked listening to this serene and beautiful Yunnan folk song *A Gurgling Stream*, but also was able to sing it.

In the 1950s, Chinese painting art was facing a new era of "transformation". At this time he had created a large number of influential comic books so that he attracted a completely new appraisal in the field of painting. But he knew in his own mind that he was far from producing paintings from his hearts, so he was waiting.

程十发作品《小河淌水》
The painting *A Gurgling Stream* by CHENG Shifa.

In the spring of 1957, he went to Yunnan Autonomous Prefecture for writing sketches. Yunnan preserved a unique folk customs and natural scenes, which were novel to a young man born in the south China. He found that the clothes of ethnic minorities in Yunnan was particularly suitable for Chinese painting to make expressions with the smart lines of freehand brushwork. This can both help fully demonstrate the artistic personality and talent of one's own and also meet the performance requirements of a new era of life. In this way, he created such comic books both creative and filled with ethnic style as *Chaoshutun and Nannona*, *Joined Bodies Phoenixes* and others.

At that time, a Yunnan ethnic minority song *A Gurgling Stream* found him obsessed. He hummed the song when a kind of feeling rose within him naturally that the soul was used to explain the final sound of love and life was adopted to interpret the unequaled love song.

After coming back home at No. 141 on Yanqing Road in Shanghai, he repeatedly listened to and sang the song. Whenever he finished listening to it, he created a painting based on it. One night in October 1959, he listened to the song and cheerfully wielded the brush with the result that a girl of the Dai nationality wearing a hat, carrying a burden and pottery and wading through the creek jumped on the paper. The girl on the painting was afraid that water might wet her skirt and looked back to gently pick up the lower hem of her skirt with a hand, as natural as though it were living. This was the masterpiece *A Gurgling Stream* which was later unforgettable. He made this painting for countless times. For each action, each line and each tint of colors, he made painstaking efforts until this time when it was a matter of course and it was done at one go. The painting looked so easy and free.

In this world, he found the realm of freedom for a true expression of his nature with true brush and ink. His paintings on ethnic minorities made a hit in the field of artistic painting, creating a major school of contemporary Chinese painting. What was really moving was the story that it was still this song *A Gurgling Stream* on his mind that accompanied him to finish the last part of his life when he was lying in the hospital.

The former residence of CHENG Shifa is located at No. 141 on Yanqing Road. Buildings from No. 135 to No. 149 on Yanqing Road were constructed by the China Real Estate Company in 1934, each having a construction area of 360 square meters. The buildings are three-storey garden residence with a structure of brick and wood. The plane of the residence is close to a square and the main facade has a layout of three vertical sections. Its middle protrudes and at the bottom is a square gate. There are four roofs with gentle slopes covered with tiles and doors and windows are also square. In front of each building is a garden. At the second floor there is a corridor supported with arched columns or semi-circular open corridor. There are outdoor staircases leading to the garden. The third floor is for balconies. The outside staircase in the north side along the street leads directly to the main entrance of the second floor. The outside stairs at the south side are symmetrical and also lead directly up to the second floor. The bottom floor was originally for garage and kitchen. On September 23, 1999, it became a Heritage Architecture issued by the Shanghai Municipal People's Government.

程十发 （邬海佳画） CHENG Shifa （By WU Haijia）

童自荣
（1944— ）

江苏丹阳人，配音表演艺术家。1966年于上海戏剧学院表演系毕业后留校工作。1973年进入上海电影译制厂任配音演员，先后在《佐罗》《铁面人》《苔丝》《黑郁金香》《国家利益》《啊，野麦岭》《茜茜公主》《水晶鞋与玫瑰花》《摩菲斯特》《沉默的人》《莫斯科之恋》《纽约大劫案》《云中漫步》等译制片中为主要角色配音。其中，担任主配的《苔丝》《黑郁金香》《摩菲斯特》分别于1982年、1985年、1988年获文化部或广播电影电视部优秀译制片奖。为《安娜·卡列尼娜》《加里森敢死队》等电视连续剧的主角配音。近年来为《玩具总动员》《风云决》《西游记之大圣归来》等影片配音。为影视剧配音已累计近千部，被誉为“配音王子”。

为“佐罗”配音

童自荣在中学时代看了很多外国电影，被配音演员富有魅力的声音深深感染，立志成为一名优秀的配音演员。刚进上海电影译制厂，童自荣一时不太适应配音工作，因为他在上戏学的台词读法带有舞台腔，并不适合电影配音的要求。他以顽强的意志力每天坚持练习电影台词的读法，终于扭转了诵读习惯。

1979年，进入上译厂六年后，童自荣在上译厂老厂长陈叙一的支持下，在《佐罗》里为佐罗及假总督两个角色配音。机会来之不易，童自荣格外珍惜。录音棚外的小空地上留下了他反复思索推敲时来回踱步的足迹。他全身心地沉浸在对角色的体悟中，常常废寝忘食。在休息时间，他仍手捧剧本潜心研读台词，不时若有所思地喃喃自语。童自荣不仅能将每句台词倒背如流，他的配音还流淌着基于角色的情感。

他以千锤百炼的嗓音诠释着角色，帮助观众理解影片的剧情，引导观众领会英雄侠客高尚的情操，为他们带来艺术享受。他颇具磁性的嗓音传神而富有感染力，让身披黑袍、脸戴面罩的潇洒帅气的剑客“佐罗”这位伸张正义的英雄走进了国人心中。

为区分佐罗及假总督这两个配音角色，童自荣苦思冥想，终于豁然开朗。为个性懦弱、懒散无能的假总督配音时，童自荣会穿一双拖鞋。铁骨铮铮的佐罗俊朗帅气，为他配音时童自荣就脚蹬一双亮闪闪的皮鞋。穿着不同的鞋子为这两个截然不同的角色配音，童自荣称说台词时内心会有一种很微妙的感觉。

上译厂曾邀请“佐罗”的扮演者阿兰·德龙到厂里参观并欣赏由童自荣担纲配音的《佐罗》片段。在放映室里，这位严苛的世界级明星听着自己原本很粗犷的声音变得华美，嘴角边漾起了微笑。他欣赏童自荣的声音，并关切地提醒患有慢性咽炎的童自荣要保护好嗓子。

时光的细纹爬上了童自荣的额头，这位“配音王子”声音的魅力却并未消减。他说自己这辈子最大的爱好就是配音。

建筑简介：淮海中路1200弄15号

童自荣寓所位于淮海中路1200弄15号，为联列式花园住宅。整幢房屋共4个单元，15号为东端单元。房屋为三层砖木结构，建筑平面呈矩形。外立面采用黄色涂料饰面，南立面、北立面外窗上方分别设有特色窗券，窗角墙面局部设有菱形花饰，双坡屋面。一层南侧为廊式门厅，门厅立柱为爱奥尼克柱式；每层两开间，楼梯位于西开间，一层楼梯北侧为小门厅（现为洗手间），一层东北侧为厨房间，东侧为房间；二层和三层布局基本相同，西开间楼梯间北侧为厨房，东侧分布两个房间，东南间南侧设有悬挑阳台，水泥立柱、铁栏杆，阳台门设有百叶门。

TONG Zirong

TONG Zirong (1944–), native of Danyang in Jiangsu province, is a dubbing performance artist. In 1966 he graduated from the Department of Acting of Shanghai Theatre Academy and worked there after graduation. In 1973, he entered Shanghai Film Dubbing Studio to work as a dubbing actor, successively dubbing major roles in such dubbed films as *Zorro*, *The Man in the Iron Mask, Tess, The Black Tulip, National Interest, Oh! The Nomugi Pass, Sissi, The Slipper and The Rose, Mephisto, The Silent One, Moskva, Lyubov Moya, Die Hard With a Vengeance* and *A Walk in the Clouds*. Among them, *Tess, The Black Tulip* and *Mephisto* in which he dubbed major roles were awarded Outstanding Dubbed Films respectively in 1982, 1985 and 1988 by Ministry of Culture or Ministry of Radio, Film and Television. Also he dubbed protagonists in TV series including *Anna Karenina, Garrison's Gorillas* and others. In recent years he dubbed for films like *Toy Story, Storm Rider: Clash of the Evils, CUG: King of Heroes* and others. The films and television series he has dubbed amount to nearly one thousand and therefore he is known as "Dubbing Prince".

Dubbing "Zorro"

TONG Zirong watched a lot of foreign films when he was in high school and was deeply moved by the charismatic voice of the dubbing actors. Therefore, he was determined to become an excellent dubbing actor. When he just entered Shanghai Film Dubbing Studio, he was not accustomed to dubbing work for a while, because his methods of reading lines which he learned in Shanghai Theatre Academy were characterized with a stage style and which did not satisfy the requirements of film dubbing. With tenacious willpower he insisted on practicing methods of reading lines of films every day and finally changed the recitation habit.

Six years after entering the dubbing studio in 1979, he dubbed two roles of Zorro and the fake governor in the film *Zorro* under the support of CHEN Xuyi, the elderly factory director. The opportunity did not easily come by and he particularly cherished it. On the small space outside the studio were left his footsteps when he paced back and forth to ponder. He was immersed heart and sole in the understanding of roles, often forgetting to have meals and sleep. During the time for rest, he still held the script in his hands

童自荣在配音
TONG Zirong at dubbing.

to read lines with great concentration, mumbling to oneself from time to time as if deep in thought. He could not only remember lines thoroughly by heart, but his voice was full of emotions based on roles as well.

With a voice on the basis of much practice, he interpreted roles to help the audience understand the story of films, guide them to understand the noble sentiment of heroes and bring them artistic appreciation. His magnetic voice was both vivid and full of appeal so that "Zorro", a handsome swordsman with a black robe and a mask on his face, as well as a hero of justice, found his way into the hearts of the Chinese people.

To make a distinction between the two dubbed roles of Zorro and the false governor, he racked his brains for ideas and finally saw the light all of a sudden. When dubbing the fake governor with a cowardly personality and lazy incompetence, he would wear a pair of slippers. In contrast, Zorro was both firm and unyielding, and smart and handsome. When dubbing him, he put on a pair of shiny leather shoes. Wearing different shoes to dub two different roles, he said that he had a very delicate feeling when reading the lines.

The studio once invited Alain Delon, the actor who played the role of "Zorro", to visit the studio and enjoy a fragment from the film *Zorro* where TONG Zirong shouldered the important task of dubbing. In the screening room, when the harsh world-class star heard that his original rough voice became gorgeous, a smile crossed the corner of his mouth. He appreciated the voice of TONG Zirong and reminded him with concern of protecting his throat which suffered from chronic pharyngitis.

Fine lines of time climbed onto his forehead, but the charm of the voice of the "Dubbing Prince" did not diminish any bit. He said that his biggest hobby in this life was dubbing.

The apartment of TONG Zirong lies at No. 15 in Alley 1200 on Middle Huaihai Road, which is a garden residence with row houses. The whole building has a total of four units and No. 15 is one at the east end. The three-storey house has a brick-wood structure with a rectangular plane. The facade adopts finishes of yellow paint. At the south and north facades, the upper parts of the outside window are equipped with characteristic window arches. Walls at window corners are locally equipped with diamond ornaments. The roof has double slopes. At the south side on the first floor is a corridor-like hall, the columns of which are of Ionic style; each floor enjoys a breadth of two rooms and the stairs are at the west side. At the north side of the stairs on the first floor is a small hall (now the toilet). At the northeast side on the first floor is the kitchen and at the east side are rooms. The second and third floors are basically the same in layout. The north side of the staircase at the west end is for kitchen and at the east side are two rooms. The south side at the southeast end enjoys a cantilevered balcony with cement columns and iron railings, and the door at the balcony has shutters.

童自荣 （钱定华画） TONG Zirong （By QIAN Dinghua）

董竹君
（1900—1997）

江苏海门人，生于上海。幼年家境贫寒，父亲是一名人力车夫，母亲为人帮佣。13岁时由于父亲病重，被迫沦为青楼卖唱女。后结识革命党人夏之时，结为夫妇。1929年两人分居，董竹君带着4个年幼的子女返回上海，先后创办富祥女子织袜厂、飞鹰公司、群益纱管厂。1934年董竹君与夏之时正式离婚。1937年底，董竹君在上海法租界大世界附近的华格臬路（今宁海西路）创办锦江川菜馆、锦江茶室。1951年两店奉公，迁移至长乐路华懋公寓，扩建为锦江饭店，董竹君担任董事长兼经理。1957年至1991年，任全国政协委员。

自強不息

1932年，“一·二八”事变后，群益纱管厂被炸毁，董竹君又因“私藏革命宣传品”被捕入狱。取保释放后，行动不自由，她无法再寻投资人继续开工。1933年，负债累累的董竹君为节省开支，从甘斯东路（现嘉善路）甘村迁到位于上海西区的美华里20号，这里当时比较荒凉，房租便宜。董竹君在晒台四周围上芦席，夏季当浴室使用，她和几个女儿住三楼一间，其余房间出租。时任《金陵日报》编辑的中共党员陈同生为房客之一，董竹君的孩子们常于晚饭后在弄堂外荒地上边乘凉边听他讲故事。此间，董竹君受限于巡捕房而不便露面，仍尽力为中国共产党地下领导的电影制片厂“电通影片公司”提供帮助，并吩咐女儿国琼为影片承担大提琴伴奏。

母亲、父亲相继病逝，使董竹君悲痛不已，但她并未一蹶不振，省吃俭用操持着家务与生计，当铺是她当时常去的地方，有次为付两个女儿的校服费，只好把大提琴拿去临时押当。即使如此困苦，她仍自强不息，从未向前夫求助，正如当初她与丈夫在思想上产生分歧，便毅然决然带着孩子离开。

1934年年底，来自四川的军火采购商李嵩高拜访董竹君，听说了她的故事，十分钦佩，对她说：“听说你也会经商，我愿意从买枪支的款内借给你两千元，先做点生意，把生活问题解决。”以这两千元，她创办了锦江川菜馆，很快悉数偿还借款。1936年，又建锦江茶室，作为上海地下党的联络点，支持夏衍、于伶、章泯、钱杏邨等开展工作。在美华里的生活虽短暂且艰辛，却见证了董竹君的人生转折和“锦江”的诞生。

中华人民共和国成立之初，周恩来总理宴请董竹君时赞扬她道：“多年来你为党做了不少工作，我敬你一杯。身为督军夫人，抛弃荣华，单枪匹马，参加革命，真难得！”1951年，董竹君响应国家号召，使“锦江”两店归为国有。为缩紧家庭开支，她从愚园路的花园洋房迁往复兴西路147号公寓租住。1957年董竹君当选为全国政协委员。复兴西路的住所，是她从上海迁至北京前最后的居住地，也寄托着她的爱国热忱。

建筑简介：复兴西路147号

董竹君旧居位于复兴西路 147 号，为带有西班牙建筑风格特征的公寓住宅，建成于 1933 年，由中国现代主义建筑师奚福泉主持建造。建筑为三层混合结构，设计简洁、紧凑，一底带三楼，外加朝北亭子间，有半圆形券门、螺旋柱券窗，以及铁艺装饰、米黄色水泥砂浆拉毛外墙、红色屋面筒瓦。此间，董竹君的房客和邻居有：柯灵、陈国容夫妇，陈同生，刘连波，廖沫沙，白薇，陈子展，钟南夫等革命老干部和知名人士。1933 年至 1934 年，董竹君曾在安福路（原名巨泼来斯路）191 弄 20 号（美华里 20 号）居住，1951 年迁此。1960 年底，董竹君由沪迁至北京。考虑到她以后来沪居住方便和身体状况，上海市委决定为她留下复兴西路 147 号房子并代付房租直至 1966 年。

DONG Zhujun

DONG Zhujun (1900–1997) was born in a poor family in Shanghai with her ancestral family from Haimen in Jiangsu province. Her father was a rickshaw puller and her mother a servant. At the age of 13 when her father was critically ill, she was forced to become a singer in a whorehouse. Later she got to know a revolutionist and got married with him. In 1929, the couple separated and she returned to Shanghai together with the four children at their young ages. After that, she successively set up the Fuxiang Female Socks Plant, Flying Eagle Company, and Qunyi Bobbin Factory. In 1934, she officially got divorced with her husband. At the end of 1937, she established Jinjiang Restaurant and Jinjiang Teahouse on Huagenie Road (now West Ninghai Road) which was near the Big World of the French Settlement in Shanghai. In 1951, the restaurant and the teahouse were presented to the government and she moved to Huamao Residential Area on Changle Road. They were expanded and renamed as Jinjiang Hotel. She assumed the office of board chairperson and manager. From 1957 to 1991, she had been member of the CPPCC.

Constant Self-improvement

After the Japanese invasion of Shanghai on January 28, 1932, the Qunyi Bobbin Factory was bombed down. DONG Zhujun was arrested and put into prison for the pretext of “privately storing revolutionary publicity materials”. Though bailed and released, she had no freedom of action, unable to find investors to restart work in the factory. In 1933, she was then deep in debt and, in order to save money, moved from East Gansi Road (now Jiashan Road) to No. 20 in Meihua Alley in the west area of Shanghai. This area was quite desolate at that time and the rent was inexpensive. She surrounded the roof terrace with reed mat which was used as bathroom in summer. She and her daughters lived in one room on the third floor and the other rooms were leased. One of the tenants was CHEN Tongsheng, a member of the CPC and the editor of *Jingling Daily* at that time. Her kids often listened to him telling stories

董竹君创办的锦江川菜馆
Jinjiang Restaurant established by DONG Zhujun.

after supper while they were relaxing in the coolness in the open wild land outside the alley. During this period of time, DONG was restricted in action by the police of the foreign settlement so that it was not convenient for her to turn up. But she still did her possible to provide assistance for the "Dentsu Film Company", a film studio run by the CPC underground organization. Also she asked one of her daughters to play cello for films produced by the studio.

The passing away of her father and mother in succession had left DONG in bitter grief, but she was not unable to recover from the difficulty. She managed her housework and livelihood by saving money on food and expenses. Pawnshop was one of the places she frequented. Once she had no choice but to pawn a cello in order to pay for the school uniforms of her two daughters. In spite of her hardships to such an extent, she still strived to be stronger, never seeking help from her former husband, just as she determinedly chose to leave together with her kids when ideological differences took place between her and her husband.

At the end of 1934, a military merchant paid a visit to her. After listening to her story, the dealer felt great admiration for her, saying, "I've got to know that you once did business and I would like to lend you 2,000 yuan out of the money for buying guns, so that you will be able to do some business to overcome your difficulty of livelihood." With this sum of money, she opened her restaurant and soon refunded all of it. In 1936, she also opened her teahouse, which functioned as a contact office for the CPC underground organization, supporting the underground work of some party members. Though short and hard, life in Meihua Alley witnessed a turning point of the life of DONG Zhujun and the birth of "Jinjiang Hotel".

In the beginning after the founding of the New China, ZHOU Enlai, the Premier, invited DONG Zhujun to a banquet and praised her, saying, "For years, you have done a lot for the CPC and I would like to make a toast to you. As the wife of a warlord, you cast away wealth and position to take part in revolution single handed. It's hard to come by!" In 1951, she contributed the restaurant and the teahouse to the government in answer to the national call. To reduce her family expenses, she moved from her garden villa on Yuyuan Road to an apartment at No. 147 on West Fuxing Road. In 1957, Dong was elected as a member of the national committee of CPPCC. Though in illness, she still promised to do it well against any difficulty. Her residence on West Fuxing Road was her last home before she moved from Shanghai to Beijing, hence bearing her zealous love for the nation.

The former residence of DONG Zhujun is situated at No. 147 on West Fuxing Road. It was built in 1933 by a modern architect of China. It is an apartment with the stylistic characteristics of Spanish architecture. The building is of a three-storied composite structure with concise and compact design. There is a garret facing north besides the main building, which has a semi-circular arc gate and arc windows fringed with screw pivots, in addition to wrought iron decoration, exterior walls napped with stucco veneer and the red roof covered with pantiles. During this period of time she had neighbors of quite a few elderly revolutionary leaders and well-known public figures. From 1933 to 1934, she once lived at No. 20 (No. 20 in Meihua Alley) in Alley 191 on Anfu Road, and moved to the former residence in 1951. At the end of 1960, she moved to Beijing. Considering her health condition and the convenience for her to stay on her coming to Shanghai, the municipal committee of the CPC decided to keep for her the house at No. 147 on West Fuxing Road and paid the rent for her until 1966.

董竹君 （齐亚明画）　DONG Zhujun （By QI Yaming）

韩敏
（1929— ）

浙江杭州人，连环画家、国画家。幼年时随父亲学习中国传统绘画技艺，深得其教诲。中华人民共和国成立后，先后进入长征出版社、上海新美术出版社、上海人民美术出版社任连环画创作员。1958 年一度改画年画。改革开放后，先后绘制出多部连环画，并转向中国画的创作。其绘画风格独特，在人物、山水、花鸟、书法等诸方面均有造诣。现为上海书画研究院院长、上海文史馆馆员。连环画代表作品有《白毛女》《郑板桥》《林家铺子》《焦裕禄》《苏武》等。水墨连环画《幸福的童年》获上海市第一届连环画评奖绘画二等奖，单线白描连环画《谢瑶环》获全国美术作品二等奖，宣传画《毛主席和我们心连心》获全国年画宣传画画展一等奖。

源于生活，高于生活

出生于书香世家的韩敏，幼年时即随父亲韩小梅学习中国传统绘画，并打下了扎实的基础。韩敏认为，绘画技法固然重要，但要使自己的作品富有生命力，那创作就离不开生活。

孩提时代，韩敏随父母从西子湖畔的杭州迁至沪上的泰安路。那时此处还是城乡接合处，有青青的田野、潺潺的小河及篱笆墙上爬满牵牛花的农家小院。这片田园可是他童年时的乐园，抓蝈蝈、掏雀窝、捕蟋蟀、粘知了。而今一个多甲子过去了，童心不泯的他将这儿时记忆中的花鸟草虫再现于笔端。那本洋溢着浓郁生活气息的《韩敏花鸟草虫集》（上海书画出版社出版），正是他对自然和生命的独特的感悟。

在韩敏的花鸟画里，最常见的题材是墨竹。他善画墨竹是因为从小生在竹乡，所以他笔下的墨竹，不是来自画谱，而是来自生活，能含风带露，自成面目。他的竹画里有时以竹子作为主体，小鸟穿梭其间，或浅吟低唱，或沉静传神；有时以竹子作为画面的布景，与笔下人物相伴成趣，不论是文人高士，还是仕女佳人，墨竹画意境跃然而至。

源于生活，高于生活，韩敏深得其理。他从年轻时就养成深入生活、观察体验的良好习惯。20 世纪 70 年代，为创作芭蕾舞剧《白毛女》连环画，他专门去芭蕾舞团观看演员排练。他一一研究舞蹈中展现的三十几个动作，对每一个动作的体位造型了然于胸。他说："如果对舞蹈本身茫然无所知，不深入实践，仅靠想象是画不出来的。"

他这种对事物细致的观察习惯直到今天也未丝毫改易。他认为，在继承传统绘画的精华外，应坚持立足当下，深入现实生活，向生活讨教。已经年逾八十的他，仍与很多年轻人一样，还常看《非诚勿扰》等生活综艺节目。娱乐之外，他比别人多了一份在绘画上的思考与借鉴。"我是画仕女的，台上正好站着 24 个姑娘，研究她们的出身、经历、性格和面相之间的关系，是为我的创作积累素材，" 他总结说，"如果不了解人们现在的审美观，我的画就是画得再好也是不合时宜的。"

建筑简介：淮海中路1326号

韩敏寓所位于淮海中路1326号。该公寓由浙江兴业银行于1934年建造，凯泰建筑师事务所黄元吉设计，张裕记营造厂承建，建筑面积12305平方米。建筑为钢筋混凝土结构，中间六层，两翼四层，平面沿道路转角布置，转角立面为对称中轴，饰竖向线条。两侧以连续玻璃窗和窗间墙构成水平线条。形体由中央向两侧跌落。水泥拉毛外墙，平顶。底层为商铺。20世纪80年代公寓进行改建，加高后中间和两翼分别达到七层和五层，外形仍基本保持原风格。该公寓原名帝国公寓，现底层为商用，二层以上为民居。1994年2月15日上海市人民政府公布其为市优秀历史建筑。

HAN Min

HAN Min (1929–) has his ancestral family from Hangzhou in Zhejiang province and is known as a comic artist and artist of Chinese painting. When he was young, he studied Chinese traditional painting techniques after his father and got the essence of his teachings. After the founding of the People's Republic of China, he entered the Long March Press, Shanghai New Fine Arts Publishing House and Shanghai People's Fine Arts Publishing House to serve as creator of comic pictures. In 1958, he once shifted to draw New Year paintings. After the reform and opening up, he finished successively quite a number of comic books and turned to the creation of Chinese paintings. He had a unique style of painting and made accomplishments in such fields as figures, landscapes, flowers and birds and Chinese calligraphy. Now he is president of Shanghai Academy of Painting and Calligraphy and librarian of Shanghai Research Institute of Culture and History. His representative comic works include *The White-Haired Girl*, *ZHENG Banqiao*, *The Lin Family Shop*, *JIAO Yulu*, *SU Wu* and others. His ink comic painting *Happy Childhood* won the second prize for painting of the Shanghai First Comic Book Award; his single-line sketch comic painting *XIE Yaohuan* won the second prize of the National Art Award; and his picture poster *Chairman MAO Closely Linked with Our Hearts* won the first prize at the National New Year Picture Poster Exhibition.

From Life and Higher than Life

Born in a scholarly family, HAN Min learned traditional Chinese painting with his father HAN Xiaomei in his childhood and laid a solid foundation. He believed that, though painting techniques were important, creation of artistic works full of vitality could not be separated from life.

In his childhood, he moved with his parents from Hangzhou at the West Lake to Tai'an Road in Shanghai. At that time, this place was a joint point of the urban and rural areas where there were green fields, gurgling rivers and fence walls of small farm courtyard covered with morning glories. This pastoral area was a paradise for his childhood, where he snapped at grasshoppers,

韩敏在书房
HAN Min in his study.

searched bird nests, caught crickets and stuck cicadas. Now over 60 years passed, but he still retained the innocence from is childhood and reproduced his memories the flowers, birds and insects in his works. The work *Painting Collection of Flowers, Birds, Grass and Insects by HAN Min* (published by Shanghai Painting and Calligraphy Press) filled with a strong flavor of life represents his unique understanding of nature and life.

In his paintings of flowers and birds, the most common theme is ink painting of bamboo. He is good at painting bamboo because he lived in an area of bamboo since his childhood so that his ink paintings of bamboo are not from painting copybooks, but from life. Therefore his paintings have unique features as if they contain wind and dew. Sometimes bamboo paintings are dominated by bamboo with birds shuttling, or chanting and singing, or keeping quiet. Sometimes bamboos are used as the background, which form a pleasing contrast with the figures. Either literati and excellent scholars, or ancient ladies and beauties, enable artistic effect of ink bamboo to leap on the paper of painting.

He has a profound understanding of the idea that paintings are from life and higher than life. In his young age, he formed the good habit of immerging deep in life to observe and experience. In the 1970s, for the creation of the comic for the ballet *The White-Haired Girl*, he went to the ballet troupe to watch its rehearsal and studied over 30 movements reflected in the dance. In the end he remembered each movement and posture. He made a comment, saying, "If you know nothing about dance itself and do not have in-depth practice, it is impossible to paint only by imagination."

His habit of making meticulous observations of things has remained until today without the slightest change. He has inherited the essence of traditional painting and also adhered to the contemporary basis, indulgence into real life and turning to life for advice. Now over 80 years old, he is still like many young people and often watches life variety show programs such as "You Are the One". Besides entertainment, he has an additional thinking and reference about painting in comparison with others. "I am an artist painting ancient ladies. On the stage are standing just 24 girls. A study of the relationship between their origins, experiences, characters and faces serves to accumulate materials for my creation." He reached s conclusion, "If I did not know the aesthetic outlook of modern people, my painting would be outdated in spite of their quality."

The apartment of HAN Min is located at No. 1326 on Middle Huaihai Road. Built by Zhejiang Industrial Bank in 1934, the apartment was designed by HUANG Yuanji from Kaitai Architects and constructed by ZHANG Yu Construction Company with a construction area of 12,305 square meters. It has a structure of reinforced concrete with six floors in the middle and four floors at the two wings. The building plane lays out along the corners of roads and the corner facade is symmetrical along the central axis with decorations of vertical lines; both sides make use of continuous glass windows and walls between windows to form horizontal lines. The total structure falls from the center to the sides. Walls are cement napped with a flat top. The bottom floor is for shops. In the 1980s, the apartment was renovated and heightened so that the middle part reached seven floors and the two sides rose to five floors respectively and the original shape was still basically maintained. The apartment was formerly known as Empire Mansions and now the bottom floor incorporates the Department Store and floors above the second are for residence. On February 15, 1994, it became a Heritage Architecture issued by the Shanghai Municipal People's Government.

韩敏 （邬海佳画） HAN Min （By WU Haijia）

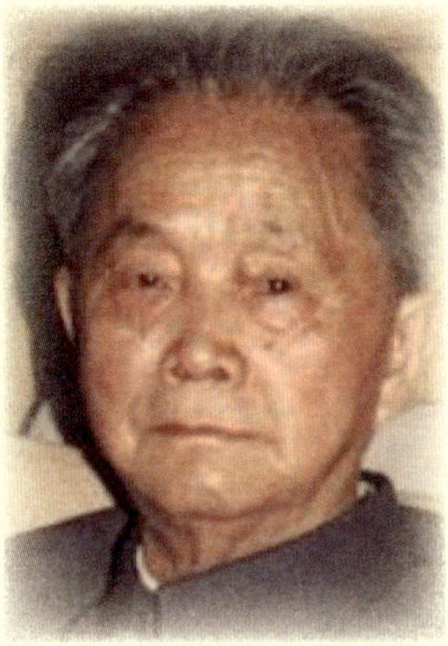

舒同
（1905—1998）

江西东乡人，书法家、政治家。1926 年加入中国共产党，1930 年加入中国工农红军并参加长征。抗日战争和解放战争时期，曾任八路军总部秘书长、中共华东局常委兼社会部部长等。自幼喜爱书法，数十年潜心书艺，集历代书法名家之长，取法求新，独创一体，称为“舒体”。1980 年，发起成立中国书法家协会，被推选为第一届主席。著有《舒同书法集》《舒同字帖》《舒同书法艺术》等。作为当代书法事业的主要奠基人，为中国书法艺术的传承和创新作出了贡献。1949—1954 年在上海工作，任中共华东局常委兼宣传部部长、华东人民革命大学校长、华东党报委员会主任等。1954 年后，历任山东省委第一书记、陕西省委书记、中国军事科学院副院长、中共中央顾问委员会委员。

“马背书法家”的“七分半”

舒同 5 岁就学书法，曾系统地临过古代碑帖，但师古而不泥古，尊法而求新变，并取其精华，大胆尝试，逐渐形成了自己的书法风格。

1930 年，舒同加入中国工农红军后，一直在团部和师部搞宣传工作。紧张战事之余，他潜心书艺，寄情翰墨。他随红一军团长征到陕北时，一路上书写大幅标语，弄得身上全是石灰，衣服上也烧了好多洞。行军途中，没有纸笔，舒同就捡树枝在地上划拉。骑在马上，他也用手指头在裤腿上比画。有一天，被毛泽东看到了，就笑着说：“舒同，你成了马背书法家啦。”这“马背书法家”的美名由此传开。到了延安后部队转战较少，舒同就到处寻找古代碑帖临摹，书艺日有精进。舒同在担任红四师政治部主任一职后，有一次给当地老百姓做报告，台下的群众一看，这不就是昨天写大字的红军干部吗，于是到处宣传，红军队伍里有秀才。

经数十年不懈努力，舒同的书法慢慢自成一体，世人称之“舒体”，被评价为宽博端庄，圆劲婉通，用笔老重，藏头护尾，点划润厚通畅，别具风格。他自己说过，自己的书法是“七分半”，即真草隶篆行各一分，颜真卿、柳公权各一分，何绍基半分，足见其广纳百川之严谨态度。据舒同之子王征回忆：“老爷子即使卓然成一代大家后，在平时还坚持临池不辍，写楷书、隶书，偶尔画点梅兰竹菊，认真得像个小学生，可以说直到生命的最后一刻。”

舒体浑圆有力，外柔内刚，深为人们珍爱。如今，舒体已被输入电脑，广泛用于图书、报刊、电影、电视，更显出其独特的魅力。

虽然被赞为书法改革大家，在中国书法艺术发展史上具有重要的地位，但舒同一直泰然处世，甚至视自己一生钟爱的书法为“余事”，并不怎么当回事。然而如此淡然超脱，大象无形地造就了一代宗师。

建筑简介：湖南路20弄

舒同旧居位于湖南路20弄福园。福园在湖南路20弄1至12、14、16、17、20至22号，位于湖南路北，永福路西，武康路东，占地1.72公顷。1940年后，在此建造砖木结构花园住宅楼13幢，其中3层楼房5幢，假3层楼房4幢，2层楼房4幢。中华人民共和国成立后又增建3层新村住宅楼3幢及瓦平房3间，建筑总面积9690平方米。每幢楼前均有小花园，环境幽静。中华人民共和国成立前出入口设在西侧福开森路（今武康路），以其首字命名，"福"也是吉祥语。中华人民共和国成立后出入口设在湖南路。

SHU Tong

SHU Tong (1905–1998) has his ancestral family from Dongxiang County in Jiangxi province and makes his fame as calligrapher and politician. In 1926 he became a member of the Communist Party of China. In 1930 he joined the Chinese Red Army of Workers and Farmers and participated in the Long March. During the War of Resistance against Japanese Invasion and the War of Liberation, he served as Secretary-General of the Headquarters of the Eighth Route Army, as well as member of the Standing Committee of the CPC East China Bureau and minister of Social Affairs. Since his childhood he loved calligraphy and decades of painstaking practice in Chinese calligraphy found him integrating the strength of calligraphy masters of generations, absorbing their essence and seeking novelty, and creating an original style known as the "SHU Style". In 1980, he initiated to establish the China Calligraphers Association and was elected as the first president. He also authors such books as *Collection of SHU Tong's Calligraphy, Calligraphy Copybook by SHU Tong* and *Calligraphy Art of SHU Tong* and so on. As one of the main founders of contemporary Chinese calligraphy, he has contributed to the heritage and innovation of the Chinese calligraphy. Between 1949 and 1954 he worked in Shanghai, serving in succession as member of the Standing Committee of the CPC East China Bureau and minister of Publicity Department, president of East China People's Revolutionary University, and director of East China Party Newspaper Committee. After 1954, he served successively as the first secretary of Shandong Provincial Party Committee, secretary of Shaanxi Provincial Party Committee, vice president of China PLA Academy of Military Sciences, and member of the CPC Central Advisory Commission.

"Seven and a Half Style" of "A Calligrapher on Horse Back"

SHU Tong started Chinese calligraphy practice at the age of five and once systematically copied from models of ancient calligraphy masters. Though he learned from the ancient masters, he was not bound with them. Respecting the laws of calligraphy, he also sought new changes, took the essence and made brave attempts. Gradually he formed his own calligraphy style.

In 1930 after he joined the Chinese Red Army of Workers and Farmers, he had been engaged in publicity in the military regiment and division headquarters. In his spare time after tense war, he devoted himself to the calligraphy art and dedicated his sentiment to brush and ink. When he reached the north of Shaanxi with the First Corps of the Red Army, he was all lime from head to

下笔如有神
Creation with a gifted brush.

foot and his clothes were also corroded with a lot of holes since he wrote banner slogans all along the way. On the way of the march, he had no brush and paper, but he picked up tree branches to draw lines on the ground. Riding on the horse back, he also gesticulated with his fingers on his trousers. One day Mao Zedong saw him and said with smile, "SHU Tong, you've become a horse back calligrapher". This reputation spread ever since. After he arrived at Yan'an, his troops transferred and fought less from place to place. Consequently, he searched everywhere to find the ancient rubbings for copy so that his calligraphy improved day by day. After he served as political department director of the Fourth Division of the Red Army, he once delivered a report to the local people. When the audience found that he was the very person from the Red Army who did calligraphy the day before, they passed from mouth to mouth that there was a learned scholar in the Red Army.

After decades of unremitting efforts, his calligraphy gradually formed its own style. Known as "SHU Style", it is evaluated as being broad and dignified, round and powerful, graceful and flexible, and steady and sober. In his style of calligraphy, the tip of the brush is concealed at both ends in each stroke and his strokes are thick and smooth to form a unique style. He said to himself that his calligraphy is of a "seven and a half style", with one portion from each of the five styles of Chinese calligraphy including regular, grass, official, seal and running styles, one portion from each of the two calligraphers YAN Zhenqing and LIU Gongquan of Tang Dynasty, as well as one half portion from the well-known calligrapher HE Shaoji of Qing Dynasty, which shows his rigorous attitude to absorb from various former masters. According to the recall of his son WANG Zheng, "After my father became an outstanding master, he still adhered to copy and practice in his spare time to practice regular and official styles. Occasionally he practiced painting of such four flowers as plum, orchid, bamboo and chrysanthemum. He did all this as seriously as a pupil, until the last moment of his life".

His calligraphy is characterized by roundness and power with softness in appearance and stoutness in essence, which is deeply cherished and valued by people. Today, his style has been imported into the computer and widely used in books, newspapers, movies and television, demonstrating its unique charm all the more.

Although praised as a master of calligraphy reform and enjoying an important position in the history of the development of Chinese calligraphy, he had kept a calm attitude in his life. He even regarded calligraphy as a "hobby", not taking it too seriously, though he loved it in his lifetime. But such an attitude of being indifferent and detached has helped to invisibly create a grand master.

The former residence of SHU Tong is located at Happiness Garden in Alley 20 on Hunan Road. The garden includes buildings with numbers from 1 to 12, 14, 16, 17 and numbers from 20 to 22 in the alley on Hunan Road. It is situated on the north of Hunan Road, the west of Yongfu Road, and the east of Wukang Road, covering an area of 1.72 hectares. After 1940, thirteen garden residential buildings were constructed with brick and wood structure, of which five buildings are of three floors, four enjoy nominally three floors and another four are of two floors. After the founding of the People's Republic of China, three residential buildings with three floors and three bungalows covered with tiles were added in a new residence village with a total construction area of 9,690 square meters. In front of each building, there is a small garden, with peaceful environment. Before the founding of the People's Republic of China, the gate of the garden was at the west side on Ferguson Road (now Wukang Road) and the garden was named after the first character of the road, which is also a lucky word. After the founding of the People's Republic of China, the garden gate was on Hunan Road.

舒同 （钱定华画） SHU Tong （By QIAN Dinghua）

福开森
（1866—1945）

美国人。出生于美国马萨诸塞州牧师家庭。1886 年毕业于波士顿大学，并受美国美以美会派遣到南京传教。1888 年在南京创办汇文书院，自任监督（校长）。1897 年盛宣怀在上海创办南洋公学，受聘为外国语文教习，后升任监院。1899 年从英国人丹福士手中购得《新闻报》，在其经营下成为与《申报》并驾齐驱的报纸。因参加镇压四明公所事件，拓展公共租界、法租界界址，法租界当局将一条新辟的马路（今天的武康路）以他的名字命名。义和团运动爆发后，参与策划“东南互保”。1903 年协助吕海寰和盛宣怀同美国签订《中美通商行船续订条约》。先后担任亚洲文会会长，华洋义赈会会长，中国红十字会董事、副会长等职。还担任过刘坤一、张之洞的顾问。1921 年以中国代表团成员身份参加华盛顿会议。1917—1928 年任北洋政府顾问。国民党统治期间，担任故宫博物院鉴定委员，利用“庚子赔款基金”和“哈佛—燕京学社基金”的津贴，聘请中国古文物学家，助其编著《历代著录吉金目》《历代著录画目》《艺术综览》等著作。1936—1938 年任国民党政府顾问。太平洋战争爆发后，被遣送回国。在中国居留 60 年，对中国美术和瓷器有研究，著有《中国绘画》《中国美术大纲》《历朝瓷器》等书。

南洋公学第一届田径运动会

1899 年冬天，南洋公学举办了第一届田径运动会，这在当时的学校是从来没有过的事情。而这个创新的举动就是时任监院兼西文总教习（相当于今天的副校长和教务长）的美国人福开森发起的。

当时的福开森不过 30 来岁，他发现中国的学生热衷于读书却忽视体育运动，于是，他先是将足球、棒球和网球等西方的文体活动引进了南洋公学，鼓励学生参与。可是，学生们始终对这些体育项目没有什么意识，锻炼起来很是被动。为了刺激学生的兴趣，福开森终于想出个主意，他要在这一年的冬天举办学校第一届田径运动会，并且要求全校学生人人参与。

什么叫运动会，学生不懂，家长不懂，老百姓更是当作稀奇事。这个消息一传十，十传百，运动会那天，附近的居民纷纷赶来学校看热闹，甚至于连松江、青浦和昆山都有乡民摇着船前来观战，把整个南洋公学挤得满满当当。

由于是第一次举办运动会，很多事缺少经验，为此闹出了不少笑话。

当天，学校邀请来一些清廷官员，请他们既观战又做裁判，还在跑道终点的前十余米处设了座位观赛。哪里料到，比赛开始后，运动员奋力奔跑，到达终点时那股惯性让人无法收住脚步，冲得裁判人仰椅翻，根本看不清谁先谁后。不得已只得重新来过，这回裁判老爷的座椅被摆在了跑道终点的两侧，比赛才算顺利完成。

在福开森的努力之下，南洋公学在 1900 年还成立了足球队，他们第一次与沪上劲旅圣约翰学院比赛时输得很惨，可这一来反倒激起了学生们对足球的兴趣，他们自发地进行训练，福开森还请来教练传授技艺，当他们再与圣约翰比赛便势均力敌了。

建筑简介：福开森路（今武康路）

19世纪末，在南洋公学教书的教授大都住在市区公共租界，他们前往南洋公学都要先租一辆人力车从租界到静安寺南面的善钟马房，然后在那里再雇上一辆马车沿徐家汇路（今华山路）到徐家汇的南洋公学，交通十分不便。美国传教士福开森当时负责公学的教学管理工作，目睹此种情况，捐出自己的薪水，修筑了从徐家汇南洋公学到静安寺善钟马房的马车道。当时附近居民将其称作"福开森路"。今为武康路。

John Calvin Ferguson

John Calvin Ferguson (1866–1945), an American, was born in a family of priest in Massachusetts, the United States. In 1886 he graduated from Boston University and was sent to Nanjing as a missionary by Methodist Episcopal Church in the United States. In 1888 he founded Huiwen College (The Nanking University) in Nanjing and served as president. In 1897, SHENG Xuanhuai founded Nanyang Public School in Shanghai and employed him as a foreign language teacher, who was later promoted to supervisor. In 1899, he purchased *Newspaper* from the British businessman A. W. Danforth and became a newspaper which kept pace with *Shenbao* in his operation. For his participation in the crackdown of Siming Country Guild Office to expand the boundaries of the International Settlement and the French Settlement, the authority of the latter named a newly constructed road (now Wukang Road) after his name. After the outbreak of the Boxer Movement, he involved himself in the planning of the "Southeast Mutual Protection". In 1903, he assisted LÜ Haihuan and SHENG Xuanhuai in signing with the United States "Sino-US Trade Relations and Navigation Renewal Treaty". Once he served successively as president of Asiatic Society, president of China International Famine Relief Committee, as well as director and vice president of China Red Cross Society. Also he once served as consultant of LIU Kunyi and ZHANG Zhidong. In 1921, he attended the Washington Conference in the capacity of one of the representatives of the Chinese delegation. From 1917 to 1928, he served as consultant of the Northern Warlord Government. During the reign of the KMT, he served as member of the appraisal committee of the Palace Museum, when he made the use of his allowances from the "Boxer Indemnity Fund" and the "Harvard-Yenching Institute Fund" to employ Chinese ancient cultural antique experts to help with his compilation of works including *A Catalogue of the Recorded Bronzes of Successive Dynasties*, *A Catalogue of the Recorded Paintings of Successive Dynasties*, *Art Survey* and other works. From 1936 to 1938 he served as consultant of the KMT government. After the outbreak of the Pacific War, he was repatriated back to his country. Staying in China for 60 years, he made researches on Chinese art and porcelain and authored and got published works such as *Chinese Painting, An Outline of Chinese Art*, *Porcelains of Successive Dynasties* and others.

The First Track and Field Games in Nanyang Public School

In the winter of 1899, Nanyang Public School held the first track and field games, which had never been done in schools at that time. This innovation was initiated by Ferguson, an American who was then the supervisor and chief of western languages (equivalent

1903 年，福开森（左上）和盛宣怀（右下）合影
A photo of Ferguson (upper left), SHENG Xuan huai (bottom right) and others in 1903.

to today's vice president and provost).

At the time, he was no more than 30 years old. He found that Chinese students were fond of reading and neglecting sports, so he first introduced Western sports activities such as football, baseball and tennis to Nanyang Public School and encouraged students to participate in these sports. However, the students always had no awareness of these sports and their exercise was only passively aroused. In order to stimulate the interest of students, Ferguson finally came up with an idea that he would hold the first track and field games in the school in the winter of that year and asked all students to participate in them.

What were the Games? Students did not understand, parents did not know and the common people took them as surprising things. The news of the games spread fast from one to ten and then from ten to one hundred. On the day of the games, residents nearby came in crowds to school to take a look. Even people from remote places like Songjiang, Qingpu and Kunshan took boat to come over to watch the activities, which only found Nanyang Public School packed to the full.

Because the Games were held for the first time and also because of lack of experience in many aspects, a lot of jokes were made.

On the day, the school invited some officials of the Qing government, asking them to watch the sports and act as referees. Also seats were set up ten meters before the finish of the runway for their inspection. But it was out of expectation that the athletes struggled to run after the start of the games and, when they reached the end, the inertia only found them out of control of their step with the result that the official referees together with their chairs were turned up. Therefore, it was impossible to see who was the first to get to the finish. The last resort was that the whole process had to be repeated. This time the chairs of official referees were placed at both sides of the end of the runway so that the games were completed successfully.

With the efforts of Ferguson, Nanyang Public School also set up a football team in 1900. When they had a match with the team from Shanghai St. John's College for the first time, they were beaten bitterly. But this actually stirred up the interest of students in football so much that they organized training spontaneously. Ferguson also invited the coach to teach them football skills. When they had another competition with the team from St. John's College, the two teams were well-matched.

At the end of the nineteenth century, most of the professors in Nanyang Public School lived in the International Settlement in the downtown areas. Therefore for their commutation between the settlement and the school, they had to rent a rickshaw to go from the settlement to the Good Bell (Say-Zoong) Stable to the south of Jing'an Temple and then rent another carriage to travel along Xujiahui Road (now Huashan Road) to reach Nanyang Public School at Xujiahui district. Evidently the traffic was very inconvenient. Ferguson, the American missionary, was in charge of the teaching management of the public school at that time. As a witness to this situation, Ferguson donated his own salary and built a carriageway from Nanyang Public School to the Good Bell Stable at Jing'an Temple. At that time, residents in the vicinity named the road after his name and called it "Ferguson Road". It is now Wukang Road.

福开森（叶雄画） John Calvin Ferguson （By YE Xiong）

蔡昌
（1877—1953）

广东香山（今广东中山）人。生于贫苦农民家庭，只读过三年私塾。1891年随兄蔡兴到澳洲，在雪梨（今译悉尼）开小商店，经营水果、百货。1900年回国在香港先施公司任职。1912年，他集资四百万港元，在香港德辅道闹市区开设了大新百货公司，担任经理。1918年，在广州西堤创办大新公司，即著名的南方大厦。1929年，参加以唐绍仪为首的中山训政委员会，被推为九委员之一，并被选为常委与财务委员会主任及中山县民众实业公司董事长，为建设模范县献策出力。1930年，在老家外沙村新建礼和小学，免费招收附近村童入学；创办"慈善福寿帛金会"，捐资救助年老贫穷乡亲。1934年集六百万港元巨资，于上海南京路西藏路口，建造上海大新公司大厦。自此，商界巨子蔡昌及其大新公司驰名于海内外。1947年，蔡昌携全家定居香港。1950年后，曾先后任香港慈善机构保良局局长、东华三院董事长、香港中山海外同乡济难总会委员等职。1953年夏在香港病逝。

大新公司的孕育人

蔡昌是20世纪初中国商界中赫赫有名的人物。怀着做大做强大新公司连锁业的雄心，他于30年代初来到了上海，准备拓展新型的商业理念。

南京路的十里洋场是蔡昌看中的风水宝地，然而，当时的南京路已经有了永安公司、先施公司以及新新公司这三大公司了，如何后来者居上？蔡昌觉得公司的选址是他首先需要考虑的问题。

1934年初春，在南京路一家叫日升楼的茶馆附近，连着几天，有两个男人隔着一条马路面对面站着，从清晨一直站到深夜戏院散场。他们显然是为了某种目的而来的。这目的就是以豆子计数南京路上行人的数量以及各种车辆的流量。两个男人中的一位就是年近六旬的蔡昌。

深夜回家的蔡昌顾不上劳累，要做的第一件事就是倒出豆子数数。街道两边哪边的豆子多，就说明人气旺，他要根据豆子的数量来确定大新公司的选址。最终，蔡昌把公司定在了西藏路和六合路的交汇处。

1936年1月10日，上海大新公司正式开张。为了吸引顾客，公司安装了2台每小时可供4000人上下的自动扶手电梯。上海人素来喜欢"轧闹猛"，因为要尝新鲜，公司刚开张时真可谓人山人海，自动电梯前更是被挤得水泄不通。为安全起见，蔡昌不得不决定每天下午四点钟就提前关门，对外的理由是公司内部需要整顿。

从1936年到1939年是大新公司的黄金岁月，真正谱写了一段商业百货的传奇。从此，上海的大新公司以面积大、设备先进、管理新颖而后来者居上，一跃成为当时中国百货公司之冠。

蔡昌旧居位于五原路212弄16号。五原路212弄大华新村，为新式里弄，1947年建造，共有17幢，占地面积5420平方米，总建筑面积7226平方米。建筑略具现代派风貌，三层砖混结构。平屋顶四周设置女儿墙，立面简洁，极少装饰。南部二层设有悬挑的阳台，下部为底层门廊。素色水泥砂浆外墙面均布钢窗，窗裙板仅以网格细槽略作装饰。楼内布局紧凑，功能齐备，原用锅炉水汀供暖。大华新村居住过社会各界名人，有国民党将领张发奎、大新公司创始人蔡昌、画家汪观清、大中华橡胶厂经理洪念祖、指挥家陈传熙、歌唱家周碧珍等。

CAI Chang

CAI Chang (1877–1953) has his ancestral family from Xiangshan (now Zhongshan) in Guangdong province. Born in a poor peasant family, he only had schooling for three years. In 1891, he went with his brother to Sydney in Australia to run a small shop, doing business of fruit and general merchandise. In 1900, he returned to China and served in Sincere Company in Hong Kong. In 1912, he raised four million Hong Kong dollars and founded Dah Sing Department Store in the downtown area on Des Voeux Road in Hong Kong and served as its manager. In 1918, he founded Dah Sing Company at Xidi in the city of Guangzhou, i.e. the famous Southern Building. In 1929, he participated in the Zhongshan Political Tutelage Committee led by TANG Shaoyi and was elected as one of the nine committee members. Also he was elected member of the standing committee and director of the finance as well as board director of the People's Industrial Company of Zhongshan County. He contributed his efforts and ideas to the building of a model county. In 1930, he built a primary school in a village of his hometown and enrolled children free of charge from nearby villages; he also founded "Charity Fund for Happiness and Longevity", donating to help those elderly and those in poverty. In 1934, he raised a huge sum of capital of six million Hong Kong dollars to construct the building of Dah Sing Company at the crossing of Nanjing Road and Tibet Road in Shanghai. Since then, CAI Chang, the business tycoon, and his Dah Sing Company became well-known inside and outside the country. In 1947, he settled together with his family in Hong Kong. After 1950, he was appointed in succession as director of Po Leung Kuk which was a charity organization in Hong Kong, chairman of Tung Wah Group of Hospitals, and member of Hong Kong-Zhongshan Overseas Countryman Relief Association. In the summer of 1953, he passed away of illness in Hong Kong.

The Founder of Dah Sing Company

CAI Chang was a very famous person in the businessmen field in China in the early 20th century. With the ambition to become bigger and stronger in the chain Dah Sing Company, he came to Shanghai in the early 1930s and prepared to develop new business concepts.

20 世纪 40 年代大新公司内的上海第一部自动扶梯（右二为蔡昌）
The first escalator in Shanghai installed in Dah Sing Company in the 1940s. (CAI Chang second from right).

The district infested with foreign adventurers on Nanjing Road in Shanghai was a rich wonderland in a favorable geographic location which he took a fancy to. However, along the then Nanjing Road there had already been three big companies including Yongan Company, Sincere Company and Xinxin Company. How could he catch up from behind? He thought the company's site was his first consideration.

In the early spring of 1934, there were two men near a teahouse called the Sunrise Building on Nanjing Road who stood face to face across the road for a few days continuously, standing there from the early morning until shows at the theater were over late at night. They evidently came for some purpose. The purpose was to count the number of pedestrians with beans on Nanjing Road and the volume of flow of various vehicles. One of the two men was CAI Chang, nearly sixty years old.

Regardless of his fatigue after coming back home late, the first thing he did was to pour the beans out and counted the number. For either side of the road, the more beans illustrated the popularity of flourishing. Then he should base it on the number of beans to determine the location of Dah Sing Company. In the end, he located his company at the crossing of the Tibet Road and Luhe Road.

On January 10, 1936, the Shanghai Dah Sing Company officially opened. In order to attract customers, the company installed two escalators with the capacity for 4,000 people going up and down per hour. The natives of Shanghai had always liked "bustling with noise and excitement" for the purpose of tasting fresh. In the beginning when the company had just opened, there were mountains and seas of people and escalators were so crowded that not a drop of water could have trickled through. For safety reasons, CAI Chang had to decide to close the door in advance at four o'clock every day and the explanation to the outside world was the need to rectify the company.

The time from 1936 to 1939 was the golden age of Dah Sing Company, when it really composed a legend of commercial department stores. Since then, Dah Sing Company in Shanghai caught up from behind to be the first for its large area, advanced equipment and new management, becoming the top department store in China at that time.

The former residence of CAI Chang is located at No. 16 in Alley 212 on Wuyuan Road, which was Dahua Village, a new-style alley. Built in 1947, it has a total of 17 buildings, covering an area of 5,420 square meters with a total construction area of 7,226 square meters. With a little bit of modern style, it has three stories of mixed structure of brick and cement. Around the flat roof are constructed parapets with a concise facade of very little decoration. On the second floor of the south, there are cantilevered balconies and under them is the ground floor porch. The outside walls coated with plain cement mortar are evenly covered by steel windows and window skirts are only slightly decorated with grids of thin grooves. The layout in the building is compact with all functions available, which was originally heated with steam from water boiler. Dahua Village once accommodated celebrities from various circles of the society, including ZHANG Fakui, the KMT general, CAI Chang, founder of Dah Sing Company, painter WANG Guanqing, HONG Nianzu, manager of Greater China Rubber Factory, conductor CHEN Chuanxi and singer ZHOU Bizhen.

蔡昌 （陆小弟、陆旻画）　CAI Chang （By LU Xiaodi and LU Min）

罗伯特·赫德
（1835—1911）

英国人，生于北爱尔兰，字鹭宾。1853 年于贝尔法斯特女王大学毕业后入英国外交部。1854 年奉派来华。初在香港，为英国驻华商务监督署翻译学生，后调任宁波领事馆副翻译。1858 年转任广州领事馆副翻译，并充当英法联军占领广州时“三人委员会”的秘书。1859 年任广州海关副税务司。1861 年曾代理中国海关总税务司职。1863 年 9 月任上海海关税务司，同年 11 月继李泰国为中国海关总税务司。1908 年请假回国，至死始卸任。任中国海关总税务司长达 48 年之久。著有《“这些从秦国来”：中国问题论集》。

清朝海关的外籍掌门

1863 年 11 月，年仅 28 岁的赫德在上海正式担任海关总税务司，兼管长江各口关务。在沪任职期间，赫德建立中国海关关署，并在附近的毕勋路（今汾阳路）9 弄 3 号，建造了中国海关关署俱乐部，内设舞厅、酒吧、棋牌室、会客厅等设施。来自异国他乡的外籍海关员工下班后，纷纷聚集在这里，喝酒、跳舞、打牌，排遣寂寞、放松身心，第二天继续迎接紧张而繁忙的工作。

赫德非常重视人才，他通过全球招考公开选拔海关雇员。为调动员工的工作积极性、防止腐败，赫德建立了科学、严密的管理制度。他在中国政府机关内首创养老储金制度，忠诚的海关雇员将获得丰厚的福利待遇。

赫德每天在办公室十余小时，为了提高工作效率，他坚持站着办公。这位脑不停、手不停、腿不停的“三不停”工作狂在任海关总税务司的 48 年漫长岁月中，运筹帷幄，始终思考如何完善海关各项制度。他常亲自向各口岸布置工作并走访巡查，总税务司通令均为他亲笔撰写，他和总税务司伦敦办事处往来的书信和电文据统计有上千万字。

独在异乡为异客，内心孤独的赫德几乎天天写日记，他曾这样写道：“我们不曾忘怀一丝乡音，气息和影像都会唤起儿时的回忆和甜蜜的故乡景致，走笔至此，泪水已湿了双眼。”他还经常给亲友写信，每封信都写得非常细致具体，仿佛在与对方面对面聊天。

在赫德的打理下，1887 年海关税收由 1861 年的 496 万两跃升至 2000 万两，占清廷财政收入的 24.35%。1908 年 4 月 13 日，73 岁的赫德在他的中国海关总税务司办公室内留下一张写着“罗伯特·赫德，走了”的便条。休假离职回国的他仍保留总税务司的头衔，直到三年后去世。

建筑简介：汾阳路9弄3号

海关俱乐部旧址位于汾阳路9弄3号，建于1898年，建筑面积478平方米，属英国早期殖民地式建筑风格的花园住宅。建筑为二层砖木结构，平面呈正方形，底部被架空1米左右，近似干栏式。南面设方柱敞廊，柱头有类似中国古典建筑的斗拱和雀替，方锥台式瓦楞板屋面，檐角翘起，四面开老虎窗。外墙采用宽14厘米、厚8厘米的木板条，以水平向铺，故有“木屋”之称，门窗均用木材制成。西北角有一方形攒尖小塔。1994年2月15日上海市人民政府公布其为市优秀历史建筑。

Robert Hart

Robert Hart (1835–1911), an Englishman, was born in Northern Ireland. He had a courtesy name of Lubin. In 1853, he graduated from Queen of Belfast University and got into the Ministry of Foreign Affairs of the United Kingdom. In 1854, he was sent to China. At the beginning he was in Hong Kong, working as an apprentice translator for the British Business Supervision Office in China. Later he was transferred to Ningbo Consulate to serve as deputy translator. In 1858, he was transferred to Guangzhou Consulate to serve as deputy translator and acted as secretary of the “three person committee” when the Anglo-French allied forces occupied Guangzhou. In 1859, he served as deputy director of the Guangzhou Customs. In 1861, he served as acting general commissioner of the China Customs. In September 1863, he served as general commissioner of Shanghai Customs. In November of the same year, he served as general commissioner of the China Customs following LI Taiguo. In 1908, he asked for a leave to go back home. He did not retire from the position until he died, serving as general commissioner of the China Customs for forty-eight years. He authors one book with the title of “*These from the State of Qin*”: *Collection of China Problems*.

The Foreign Head of Qing Dynasty Customs

In November 1863, at the age of only twenty-eight, Hart officially served as general commissioner of the Shanghai Customs and was also in charge of taxation affairs along the Yangtze River. During his tenure in Shanghai, he established the office building of China Customs and built its club at No. 3, in Alley 9 on the nearby Bixun Road (now Fenyang Road), which included a ballroom, bar, chess room, reception room and other facilities. After work, foreign customs officers from other countries gathered here to drink, dance and play cards, diverting themselves from solitude and getting to be relaxed. In the next day they continued hard and busy work.

He attached great importance to pooling of talents, openly selecting customs employees through global recruitment. To mobilize the enthusiasm of the staff and prevent corruption, he established a scientific and strict management system. He took the initiative in

1905年赫德与中国海关欧籍职员合影（第二排中坐者为赫德）
A group photo of Hart (middle in second row) and staff members of European nationalities in China Customs in 1905.

founding the pension fund system in the Chinese government agencies and loyal customs employees could enjoy generous benefits.

Hart worked for over ten hours in the office every day. In order to promote work efficiency, he insisted on standing in office. Serving as general commissioner of the China Customs for as long as forty-eight years, the "three non-stop" workaholic, i.e. non-stop of brain, hands and legs, devised strategies, always thinking about how to improve the customs system. He often personally arranged work to all ports and made visits of inspections. All the commands of the customs were written by himself. According to statistics, his correspondences and messages with the London Office of the customs added up to tens of millions of words.

Cast as a stranger in a foreign land, he felt lonely and wrote diaries almost every day. Once he wrote, "We never forget a trace of hometown accent, breath and image, which could evoke memories in the childhood and sweet scenery in the hometown. Writing to this point, my eyes have been filled with tears." He often wrote letters to friends and relatives, each of which was very detailed and specific, as if chatting with each other face to face.

Under the careful management of Hart, the revenues of the customs leaped from 4.96 million of tael in 1887 to 20 million, accounting for 24.35% of the total fiscal revenue of the Qing government. On April 13, 1908, the 73-year-old Hart left a note in his office of the general commissioner of China Customs, which read "Robert Hart, gone." He returned home on leave, but he still retained the title of general commissioner until his passing away three years later.

The former place of the Customs Club is located at No. 3 in Alley 9 on Fenyang Road. Built in 1898, it has a construction area of 478 square meters. It is a garden house with the British style in its early colonies. The building has a two-story structure of brick and wood with a square plane. The bottom is raised about one meter above the ground, similar to the stilt style architecture. At the south side is a gallery supported with square pillars, at the top of which there are structures similar to bucket arches and decorated brackets in the Chinese classical architecture. The roof is shaped like a square truncated cone and coated with corrugated sheets and its eaves have tilted angles. On four sides of the roof there are tiger windows. The outer walls adopt wood laths with a width of 14 cm and a thickness of 8 cm which are paved horizontally on the roof, hence the name of "wooden house". All doors and windows are made of wood. In the northwest corner there is a small square pyramidal tower. On February 15, 1994, it became a Heritage Architecture issued by the Shanghai Municipal People's Government.

罗伯特·赫德 （钱定华画）　Robert Hart （By QIAN Dinghua）

潘汉年
（1906—1977）

江苏宜兴人。1924 年加入创造社，主编刊物《洪水》。1925 年加入中国共产党。曾任《革命军日报》总编辑、国民革命军总政治部宣传科长、中共中央宣传部文化工作委员会书记、左翼文化总同盟中共党团书记、中共江西苏区中央局宣传部长、中国工农红军总政治部宣传部长兼地方工作部部长等。1927 年后还曾代表中共同鲁迅建立联系，组织左翼作家联盟。1936 年和 1937 年被中共中央正式任命为与国民党谈判的代表。1937 年 9 月任八路军驻上海办事处主任。抗日战争和解放战争期间，在上海等地领导对敌隐蔽斗争和开展统战工作。1949 至 1955 年，先后任中共华东局和上海市委社会部部长、统战部长、上海市委副书记和第三书记、上海市副市长。1955 年 4 月 3 日因“内奸”问题被判刑。1977 年含冤病逝。1982 年 8 月，中共中央为其平反昭雪，公开恢复名誉。

他把我们凝聚在党的周围

1950 年初，国民党飞机轰炸上海，不少工商企业遭受重创，市民争先恐后地抢购物资，人心惶惶。过年在即，荣氏企业却因原料、动力、资金等问题，无法及时向工人发放年关双薪，工人们怨声载道，劳资矛盾一触即发。

2 月的一天，申新六厂多位职工来到荣府，将荣毅仁围在客厅，情绪激烈地交涉领取薪资事宜，双方陷入了僵局。时任上海市副市长的潘汉年闻讯后在第一时间赶赴荣家，安抚群情激愤的工人们，承诺会为他们做主。潘汉年见荣毅仁神情焦虑尴尬，便走上前恳切地握着他的手，表示工人们的思想工作由他来做，请荣毅仁相信上海的工人阶级是通情达理的。当一位年长的工人埋怨“市长太官僚，不知市面上的东西全抢光了”时，潘汉年并未动怒责怪他，反而微笑着对他说：“全国都在支持上海，上海国营公司货源不断，投机商的钱快用光了，他们的仓库堆满了，物价开始下跌，这下他们可吃够投机的苦头了！”深入浅出的阐释缓解了工人们的恐慌心理。他诚恳地劝慰工人们顾全大局，可派遣工人代表到市委开会，与市委书记和总工会负责人商议解决方案，并建议他们投入生产，因为“工厂开起工来，恢复和发展生产，不只是对资本家有利，对工人也有利”。

离开荣家后，潘汉年立即召集有关部门开会研讨，从公私关系、劳资关系到原料供应、成品收购以及银行贷款，都逐一做出了综合部署，使申新六厂在短时间内恢复了正常的生产与运作。

潘汉年顺利平息这场年关风波，使荣毅仁和其他工商人士认识到共产党真诚帮助私营企业渡过难关、雪中送炭的执政理念，深切体悟并衷心拥护共产党“发展生产，繁荣经济，公私兼顾，劳资两利”的政策。后来，荣毅仁回忆潘汉年的文章便是以“他把我们凝聚在党的周围”为题。

建筑简介：淮海中路1350弄5号

潘汉年旧居位于淮海中路 1350 弄 5 号。1 至 15 号建于 1941 年，16 号稍晚，总建筑面积 5877 平方米。建筑由 4 排 16 幢三层砖混结构住宅组成，入口上方书“愉园”两字。单幢正立面左侧入口以爱奥尼克式柱支承二层阳台，右侧三层退为阳台，钢窗，缓坡红瓦屋顶，水泥拉毛外墙，用红砖砌窗框和窗间柱，房前为花园。1949 年前，潘汉年曾住愉园 5 号，那里同时也是中共地下党机关所在地。2005 年 10 月 31 日上海市人民政府公布其为市优秀历史建筑。

PAN Hannian

PAN Hannian (1906–1977) has his ancestral family from Yixing in Jiangsu province. In 1924, he joined the Creation Society and worked as editor of *Flood*. In 1925, he joined the CPC. Once he severed as editor-in-chief of *Revolutionary Army Daily*, section chief of the publicity division of the General Political Department of the National Revolutionary Army, secretary of Cultural Affairs Working Committee of the Publicity Department of the CPC Central Committee, Party secretary of the CPC in Left-Wing Culture General Union, minister of the Publicity Department of the Central Soviet Area in Jiangxi province, and minister of publicity of the General Political Department as well as minister of Local Work Department of the Chinese Red Army of Worker and Farmer. After 1927, he also established contact with LU Xun on behalf of the CPC and organized the Left-Wing Writers Union. In 1936 and 1937, he was officially appointed as one of the representatives by the CPC Central Committee to negotiate with the KMT. In September 1937, he started to serve as director of office of the Eight Route Army in Shanghai. During the War of Resistance against Japanese Invasion and the War of Liberation, he led underground struggle against enemy and carried out united front work in Shanghai and other places. From 1949 to 1955, he served in succession as minister of Social Affairs Department and United Front Department of the CPC East China Bureau and the Shanghai Municipal Committee, deputy secretary and the third secretary of the Shanghai Municipal Committee and deputy mayor of Shanghai. On April 3, 1955, he was sentenced to imprisonment due to the issue of "traitor". In 1977 he died of disease with grievance. In August 1982, the CPC Central Committee redressed the fabricated case and publicly restored his reputation.

He United Us around the Party

In early 1950, the KMT airplanes bombed Shanghai so that many industrial and commercial enterprises suffered from heavy losses. The public scrambled to buy supplies and people were disquieted and rushed into panic. The Chinese New Year was approaching, but the Rongs' business could not double pay workers in a timely manner at the eve of the New Year because of raw materials, power and capital. In his case workers complained everywhere and labor-capital conflicts could be triggered at any moment.

One day in February, a number of employees of Shenxin No. 6 Factory came to the house of the RONG family and surrounded him in the living room. They negotiated for the matters of salary indignantly and intensively and the two sides reached an impasse. At

1938 年春，潘汉年（后排左一）与文化界人士合影
A group photo of PAN Hannian (first from left in the back raw) together with people from the circle of culture in the spring of 1938.

that time PAN Hannian was vice mayor of Shanghai. At the news he rushed to the RONG family in the first time, appeased the crowd of angry workers and promised to call the shots for them. Seeing that RONG Yiren looked worried and embarrassed, he walked forward and earnestly held his hand to confirm that he would pacificate workers. In addition he asked RONG to believe that the working class in Shanghai was reasonable. When an older worker complained that "the vice mayor is too bureaucratic, but he does not know that the market emptied", PAN did not get angry or blamed him. Instead he smiled and said to him, "The whole country is in support of Shanghai. Moreover the supplies of goods for the state-run companies in Shanghai are incessant. When the speculators run out of money and their warehouse are filled with goods, the prices will begin to fall. In the event, they will suffer a lot because of their speculation." The clear and plain interpretation relieved all the panic of workers. He persuaded the workers to take the overall situation into consideration and asked them to select representatives of workers to attend the meeting held by the municipal committee of the CPC to discuss for solution with the party secretary and head of the trade union. Also he suggested that they should renew production because "the factory starts to restore and develop production, which is not only beneficial to capitalists, but to workers as well."

After leaving RONG's home, PAN immediately held a meeting of relevant departments to make a discussion. The meeting made a comprehensive deployment, including public-private relations, labor-capital relations, raw material supply, finished product purchase and bank loans, so that Shenxin No. Six Factory restored normal production and operation in a short period of time.

PAN successfully calmed down this crisis at the eve of the Chinese New Year, which enabled RONG Yiren and other businessmen to realize the governing philosophy of the Communist Party who helped with good faith the private enterprises pull through difficulties with timely assistance, so that they deeply understood and sincerely supported the policy of the Communist Party "development of production, economic prosperity, consideration of both public and private and win-win of both labor and capital". Later, RONG recalled him in his article which took as its title "He United Us around the Party".

The former residence of PAN Hannian is located at No. 5 in Alley 1350 on Middle Huaihai Road. Buildings No. 1 to 15 were built in 1941 and No. 16 later, with a total construction area of 5,877 square meters. There are four rows of 16 three-storey residences with a structure of brick and concrete. Above the entrance are two Chinese characters which mean "Happy Garden". At the left side of the entrance in the front of a single facade the Ionic pillars are used to support the second floor balcony, while the right side at the third floor retreats to form the balcony. These buildings have steel windows, roofs with gentle slope and red tile, and cement napped walls. Red bricks are adopted for window frames and window columns. In front of them is a garden. Before 1949, PAN lived at No. 5 in Happy Garden, which was also the office of the underground Communist Party. On October 31, 2005, it became a Heritage Architecture issued by the Shanghai Municipal People's Government.

潘汉年 （钱定华画） PAN Hannian （By QIAN Dinghua）

潘序伦
（1893—1985）

江苏宜兴人。1921年毕业于上海圣约翰大学，获文学学士学位。1923年，获美国哈佛大学企业管理硕士学位。1924年，获哥伦比亚大学政治经济学博士学位。当年回国，受聘于上海商科大学，任教务主任兼会计系主任，后又担任暨南大学商学院院长。1927年，开设潘序伦会计师事务所，从事会计师业务。1928年后，在上海及全国多地创办会计补习学校。1937年，筹办立信会计专科学校，抗战期间，迁重庆办学。抗战胜利后，潘序伦回到上海，恢复、重建上海立信会计专科学校。上海解放后，任立信会计专科学校名誉校长。1952年，组建立信会计编译所，从事著作和编译工作，曾出版《苏联会计述要》和《国营企业会计概要》。著有《基本会计学》《劳氏成本会计》等。被誉为“中国现代会计之父”。

捐房办校的“中国现代会计之父”

潘序伦认为社会发展离不开会计这一科学的经济核算法，1937年，决心筹办立信会计专科学校。他把编著的《立信会计丛书》版权（每年可收版税四万余银元）及自己在立信会计师事务所工作数年积累的六万银元工资，全数捐献给立信会计专科学校作为建校基金。然而抗日战争的全面爆发打断了潘序伦在上海的办校计划，他只得将立信会计专科学校迁往重庆办学。

1945年抗日战争胜利后，潘序伦从重庆回到上海，决定将立信会计专科学校从重庆迁回上海并扩建。在徐家汇立信会计专科学校校舍筹建期间，潘序伦把自己在长乐路（当时名为蒲石路）434弄3号的五开间三层楼的一所住宅捐赠给立信会计专科学校作为临时校舍。

潘序伦为扩建立信会计专科学校的校舍殚精竭虑。为了让学生们在学习会计专业知识之余能有强健体魄的场所，潘序伦捐资一万美元在新校舍中建造了一座体育馆。他不仅无私捐献自己历年的积蓄，还积极动员社会各界共同资助办学。为表诚意，潘序伦亲自前往各单位洽谈，然后委托女儿潘屺瞻到各家同意赞助的单位签署书面赞助文书。

在潘序伦的奔走感召下，许多实业家纷纷慷慨解囊、捐资助学。仅申新纺织总公司和荣氏兄弟就捐助法币达一亿八千万元。历时近两年，耗资十亿二千五百多万元法币，立信新校舍于1947年2月在徐虹路圆满竣工。长乐路434弄3号的临时校舍后被辟为立信高级会计职业学校及立信会计专科学校夜校部。

潘序伦克勤克俭，致力于发展中国的会计事业，视立信会计如子，多次捐房出资办学，自己却长期蜗居旧式里弄的斗室，除一床、一几、一柜、一桌、四椅外，屋内别无他物，唯有成堆的书籍。20世纪80年代初，潘序伦四次谢绝上海市政府分配给他的住房，表示“学校新厦未完工，绝不为个人安适作打算”。

建筑简介：淮海中路1285弄

潘序伦旧居位于淮海中路1285弄上方花园，占地面积26634平方米，建筑面积13674平方米。原地为英籍犹太人沙发的私家花园，1933年浙江兴业银行购买后建造，马海洋行设计，至1941年共建成74幢三层砖木结构花园住宅，仍名沙发花园。建筑群为行列式布局，有独立式、两户联立式、多户联立式等户型，既有装饰简洁的现代式，也有缓坡筒瓦的西班牙式。栅门、窗栅、阳台、栏杆都用铸铁精制而成，室内宽敞明亮，硬木打蜡地板，各种生活设施一应俱全，园中布有草坪、喷水池和小别墅。商务印书馆董事长、上海文史馆首任馆长张元济于1939—1959年在24号居住。20世纪50年代，沙发花园改名为上方花园，寓有幽静美好之意，由张元济题名。1992年6月1日上海市人民政府公布其为市文物保护单位。1994年2月15日上海市人民政府公布其为市优秀历史建筑。

PAN Xulun

PAN Xulun (1893–1985) has his ancestral family from Yixing in Jiangsu province. In 1921, he graduated from Shanghai St. John's University with a bachelor degree of arts. In 1923, he went to the United States to study at Harvard University, obtaining a master's degree of enterprise management. In 1924, he attended Columbia University and received his Ph.D. degree in political economy and in the same year he returned to China. He was recruited by the Shanghai University of Commerce as both director of teaching affairs and head of the Accounting Department. Later he held the post of dean of the Business School in Jinan University. In 1927, he established PAN Xulun Accounting Office, specializing in accounting business. After 1928, he founded several accounting tutorial colleges in Shanghai and other places in China. In 1937, he made preparations for Shanghai Lixin University of Commerce, which was moved to Chongqing during the War of Resistance against Japanese Invasion. After the victory of the war, he returned to Shanghai to restore and rebuild the Shanghai Lixin University of Commerce. After the liberation of Shanghai, he became the honorary president of the university. In 1952, he established Lixin Accounting Compilation and Translation Institute with compilation and translation of books as its scope of business which compiled and published books including *An Outline of Accounting in Soviet Union* and *An Outline of Accounting for State-owned Enterprises*. Also he authored such books as *Basic Accounting, Lloyd's Cost Accounting* and so on. He is honored as "Father of Modern Accounting in China".

Father of Modern Accounting in China: Donating His House to Run the School

PAN Xulun believed that accounting, the scientific method of economic calculation, was indispensable to social development. Therefore he was determined to start up Shanghai Lixin University of Commerce in 1937. He donated all his savings to the university as its initial fund, including his earnings from the copyright of the series of books named *Lixin Accounting Series* (their annual royalties were over 40,000 silver yuan) and his salary of 60,000 silver yuan from the accounting office accumulated for several years. However, the outbreak of the War against Japanese Invasion interrupted his plan to run the school in Shanghai, so he had to move the

中国现代会计之父、立信创始人潘序伦
PAN Xulun, father of modern accounting in China and founder of Shanghai Lixin University of Commerce.

campus of the university to Chongqing.

After the victory of the War in 1945, he came back to Shanghai from Chongqing and decided to move the campus of the university back from Chongqing to Shanghai and expand it. During the construction of the university in Xujiahui, he donated a three-storeyed residential building of his own to it as a temporary school building, which was located at No. 3 in Alley 434 on Changle Road (then Pushi Road).

He spared no effort to expand the university. In order to provide students with a place to strengthen their health apart from learning expertise in accounting, he donated 10,000 US dollars to building a gymnasium on the new campus. He not only selflessly donated his savings over the years, but also actively mobilized people from all walks of life to sponsor the university. To express his sincerity, he negotiated personally with various individuals and establishments and then entrusted his daughter PAN Qizhan to sign written sponsorship documents with those willing to sponsor.

Inspired by him, many industrialists donated money to sponsor the university generously. For instance, Shenxin Textile Company and the Rong Brothers donated 180 million yuan, to name just a few. The new campus of the University of Commerce was completed on Xuhong Road in February, 1947, which took nearly two years and over 1.025 billion yuan. The temporary campus at No.3 in Alley 434 on Changle Road was then turned into the campus for both Lixin Senior Accounting Vocational School and the Night School of the university.

As an industrious and frugal man, he committed himself to developing the cause of accounting in China. He cherished the Lixin University of Commerce from the bottom of his heart and donated houses and money to sponsor it for several times. However, he himself lived in a small cubicle in an old-fashioned alley all the time. In his cubicle there was nothing but a bed, a teapot, a cabinet, a table, four chairs and piles of books. In the early 1980s, he refused to live in the house allocated to him by the Shanghai Municipal Government for four times. As he often said, "I will not live in comfort until the new campus of Lixin University of Commerce has been completed."

The former residence of PAN Xulun is located in the Shangfang Garden in Alley 1285 on Middle Huaihai Road, which covers an area of 26,634 square meters and a construction area of 13,674 square meters. It was originally the private garden of Sofa, a British-Jew, which was purchased and then built in 1933 by Zhejiang Industrial Bank and was designed by Moorhead & Halse. Up to 1941, a total of 74 garden residences of three-storied structure of brick and wood were built, which still took the name of the Sofa Garden. The building complex has a layout of lines and rows and different types of house, including independent type, two-house type, and multiple-house type, embracing modern style with simple decoration and Spanish style as well as gentle slopes and pantile. The fence gate, window grilles, balconies and railings are all made of cast iron. The inside is both spacious and bright and the floor is of waxed hardwood. In addition, all living facilities are available. Moreover, there are lawns, fountains and small villa in the garden. From 1939 to 1959, ZHANG Yuanji, the chairman of the Commercial Press and the first curator of Shanghai Research Institute of Culture and History, lived at No. 24. In the 1950s, the Sofa Garden was renamed as the Shangfang Garden with the meaning of being quiet and beautiful, whose title was written by ZHANG Yuanji. It became the Cultural Relics Protection Unit and the Heritage Architecture issued respectively on June 1, 1992 and on February 15, 1994 by the Shanghai Municipal People's Government.

潘序伦 （钱定华画） PAN Xulun （By QIAN Dinghua）

颜惠庆
（1877—1950）

上海人，字骏人。早年毕业于上海同文馆，后留学美国。辛亥革命后历任北洋政府外交部次长和总长、内务部总长等职。1922 年曾署理国务总理。1926 年以国务总理摄行总统职权。南京国民政府成立后，先后任驻英、苏大使和出席国际联盟大会首席代表。1937 年后，在上海从事慈善和教育事业。1949 年，曾赴北平（今北京）、石家庄与中国共产党商谈和平事宜。中华人民共和国成立后，历任华东军政委员会副主席、中央人民政府政治法律委员会委员等。1950 年病逝于上海。

战火中的拯救者

1937 年 7 月 7 日，卢沟桥事变爆发。迫于局势严峻，颜惠庆决定举家南迁。当他们乘火车辗转到达上海的第二天，“八一三”淞沪抗战爆发。这是颜惠庆平生中第一次亲历发生在身边的战争。

在随后长达三个月的淞沪抗战中，大批中国民众在日军的炮火下沦为难民，流离失所。此时，上海的租界成了中国民众的避难场所。据上海《申报》等媒体记载，当时聚集在上海的难民总数不下 130 万人，逃入租界的难民最多时超过 70 万人（租界当时总人口数不过 140 万余人）。

大批难民举目无亲，缺衣少食，只得露宿街头。租界当局不顾难民死活，无所作为。中方的慈善机构力不从心，且寒冬将临，解决难民的食物、住所和医疗问题已成燃眉之急。于是，在中国红十字会特许下，中国红十字会上海国际委员会于 10 月 2 日正式成立，办事处设在静安寺路（今南京西路）的国际饭店，颜惠庆出任名誉主席和执行委员会主席。

当时，有数以千计的服务人员参与了救助伤员和难民的工作，不取分文报酬。但是，这两项工作本身需要大量的经费。颜惠庆和一位同仁去拜访当时国民政府的财政部长，建议政府通过拨出第一笔经费以树立一个榜样，使下一步民间募捐顺利开展。终于，他从政府新发行的国债中，争取到了 100 万元的拨款。随后的募捐工作不仅在国内，也在海外各地大张旗鼓地开展起来。据统计，国际委员会总共募集到 3500 万美元，足够维持大约 4 万伤员和 20 万难民 12 个月的开销。

南市难民区是“八一三”淞沪抗战后期，在中国红十字会上海国际委员会发起下，专事收容、安置中国难民的特定区域。这种在战争中设立非战区收容战争难民的模式，不仅成为日后中国抗战期间被反复援引和复制的救援范例，还在一定程度上促进了国际人道法的订立。

终颜惠庆先生一生，虽以外交家称名于世，但他同时还是一位杰出的英语教育家、实业家，更是一位大慈善家。

建筑简介：淮海中路1285弄

颜惠庆旧居位于淮海中路1285弄上方花园，占地面积26634平方米，建筑面积13674平方米。原为英籍犹太人沙发的私家花园，1933年浙江兴业银行购买后建造，马海洋行设计，至1941年共建成74幢三层砖木结构花园住宅，仍名沙发花园。建筑群为行列式布局，有独立式、两户联立式、多户联立式等户型，既有装饰简洁的现代式，也有缓坡筒瓦的西班牙式。栅门、窗栅、阳台、栏杆都用铸铁精制而成，室内宽敞明亮，硬木打蜡地板，各种生活设施一应俱全，园中布有草坪、喷水池和小别墅。商务印书馆董事长张元济于1939—1959年在24号居住；被誉为“中国现代会计之父”的潘序伦曾在16号居住。20世纪50年代，沙发花园改名为上方花园，寓有幽静美好之意，由张元济题名。1992年6月1日上海市人民政府公布其为市文物保护单位。1994年2月15日上海市人民政府公布其为市优秀历史建筑。

YAN Huiqing

YAN Huiqing (1877–1950) has his ancestral family from Shanghai and has a courtesy name of Junren. He graduated from Shanghai Tongwen College in his early years and later pursued studies in the United States. After the 1911 Revolution, he successively served as vice minister and minister of the Ministry of Foreign Affairs and minister of the Ministry of Internal Affairs of the National Warlord Government. In 1922, he once served as acting premier of the National Warlord Government. In 1926, he acted temporarily as premier for the role of president. After the establishment of the National Government in Nanjing, he served as ambassador of China to Great Britain and the Soviet Union and chief representative attending the meeting of the League of Nations. After the outbreak of the War against Japanese Invasion, he was engaged in charity and education in Shanghai. In 1949, he went to Beiping (now Beijing) and Shijiazhuang to negotiate for peace with the Communist Party of China. After the founding of the People's Republic of China, he served successively as vice chairman of the East China Military and Political Commission and member of Political and Law Committee of the Central People's Government. He passed away of illness in Shanghai in 1950.

The Savior during the War

On July 7, 1937, the Lugou Bridge Incident broke out. Forced by the severe situation, YAN Huiqing decided to move the whole family to the South. The “August 13” Battle of Shanghai broke out the next day after they arrived in Shanghai by train. This was the first time in his life that he personally experienced the war around him.

Later, during the Battle of Shanghai which lasted for three months, a large number of Chinese people were reduced to homeless refugees under the bombs of Japanese invaders. Under this circumstance, Shanghai settlement became the shelter for the Chinese people. According to the reports in *Shenbao* (*Shanghai Newspaper*) and other media, no less than 1.3 million refugees gathered in Shanghai at that time and the maximum number of refugees fleeing to the settlement hit over 700,000. (The settlement had a total population of less than 1.4 million then)

颜惠庆
YAN Huiqing.

A large number of refugees were left homeless, lacked clothing and food and had to sleep on the streets. The settlement authorities did nothing to prevent them from dying. China's charities were unable to deal with the situation, while with the winter approaching, it was extremely urgent to solve the problems of food, shelter and medical care for refugees. As a result, under the special approval of the China Red Cross Society, the Shanghai International Committee of the China Red Cross Society was formally established on October 2 with the office in the Park Hotel on Jing'an Temple Road (now West Nanjing Road). He was appointed as honorary chairman and chairman of the Executive Committee.

At that time, thousands of service staff involved themselves in the rescue of the wounded and refugees, refusing to take any reward. However, these two tasks themselves required substantial funding. YAN Huiqing, together with one of his colleagues, visited the then minister of the Ministry of Finance of the National Government, suggesting that the government should set an example by allocating the first fund so that the next step of social donation could be carried out smoothly. Finally, he secured 1 million yuan of appropriate fund from the national bond newly issued by the government. Subsequently, large-scale fundraising was carried out not only at home, but also in foreign countries. According to the statistics, the International Committee raised a total of 35 million US dollars, enough to support the living of about 40,000 wounded and 200,000 refugees for 12 months.

The South Refugee Zone, initiated by the Shanghai International Committee of the China Red Cross Society, was a specific area for the hosting and the resettlement of Chinese refugees in the latter period of the Battle of Shanghai. The model of establishing demilitarized zones in warfare to host war refugees not only became an example of relief that was repeatedly cited and replicated later in China during the War against Japanese Invasion, but also promoted the establishment of international humanitarian law to a certain extent.

Although Mr. YAN Huiqing was world-renowned as a diplomat in his entire life, he was also an outstanding English educator, industrialist and a great philanthropist.

The former residence of YAN Huiqing is situated in Shangfang Garden in Alley 1285 on Middle Huaihai Road, which covers an area of 26,634 square meters with a construction area of 13,674 square meters. It was formerly the private garden of Sofa, a British Jew, which was designed by Moorhead & Halse and was built in 1933 by Zhejiang Industrial Bank. Up to the year 1941, a total of 74 garden residences of three-storied structure of brick and wood were built, which still took the name of the Sofa Garden. The building complex has a layout of lines and rows and different types of house, including independent type, two-family type and multiple-family type and embracing modern style with simple decoration and Spanish style as well as gentle slopes and pantile. The fence gate, window grilles, balconies and railings are all made of cast iron. The inside is both bright and spacious and the floor is of waxed hardwood. In addition, all living facilities are available. Moreover there are lawns, fountains and small villas in the garden. From 1939 to 1959, ZHANG Yuanji, chairman of the Commercial Press, lived in the Shangfang Garden at No. 24. PAN Xulun, known as "the father of Chinese modern accounting", once lived at No. 16. In the 1950s, the Sofa Garden was renamed as the Shangfang Garden, with the meaning of being quiet and beautiful. The title was written by ZHANG Yuanji. It became a Cultural Relics Protection Unit and a Heritage Architecture issued respectively on June 1, 1992 and on February 15, 1994 by the Shanghai Municipal People's Government.

颜惠庆 （邬海佳画） YAN Huiqing （By WU Haijia）

颜福庆
（1882—1970）

上海人，字克卿，医学教育家、公共卫生学家。1904 年毕业于圣约翰大学医学院。1906 年被选送到美国耶鲁大学深造，1909 年获医学博士学位，是在耶鲁大学获得博士学位的第一位亚洲人，同年至英国利物浦热带病医院继续深造，获热带病学学位证书（D.T.M）。回国后任长沙雅礼医院外科医生。1911 年在京汉铁路沿线开展鼠疫防治工作。先后创办了第四中山大学医学院（上海医学院）、上海中山医院、澄衷肺病疗养院，曾任教于北京协和医院、中央大学医学院、中国红十字会上海总医院（现华山医院）、长沙湘雅医学院。1937 年任上海市救护委员会主任委员，积极发动并组织志愿医疗手术队进行救护工作。1938 年去武汉任卫生署署长。抗战胜利后，重返上海医学院工作。中华人民共和国成立后，被选为第一、二、三届全国人民代表大会代表，中国人民政治协商会议全国委员会委员，九三学社中央委员兼上海分社副主任委员。他倡导“公医制”和预防医学，影响深远，为培养我国医学卫生人才作出重要贡献，著有《我国医学卫生事业发展》《中国医学教育的现状和过去》等。

心系医学秉公严明

1943 年 3 月 21 日，颜福庆夫人曹秀英在福开森路 24 号颜府因突发中风去世，老年丧偶的颜福庆悲痛万分。家中少了女主人，颜福庆按照习俗，遂要求已过而立之年的长子颜我清尽早结婚。经小女儿颜湘清牵线，这年冬天，颜我清迎娶了沪上著名留日牙医高长顺之女高舜华。翌年，高舜华产下一对双胞胎女儿，却由于早产不幸双双夭折。屡失至亲的颜福庆肝肠寸断，但仍不忘毕生为之奋斗的医学事业。他强忍悲痛，请医学界同仁将这对匆匆辞世的小生命精心制成标本，安放在上医解剖教研室里供师生们学习研究。

1945 年初，再度怀孕的高舜华在上医待产。颜福庆很关心媳妇的身体状况，天天前去探望。有一天晚上，忙碌了一整天的颜福庆照例去医院看望儿媳，然而，他到达医院大门时已经过了探望时间。新入职的印度门卫以“一夫当关，万夫莫开”之势说什么也不让颜福庆进医院大门。万般无奈之下，颜福庆只能遥望媳妇病房的方向寄托牵挂之情。

第二天，颜福庆来到上医，让下属找到了那位印度门卫，和蔼亲切地望着这位浓眉大眼的外籍员工。惊悉原来昨晚被自己严词拒之门外的那位衣着简朴、平易近人的老人就是上医的副院长，这位印度门卫诚惶诚恐、局促不安地低下头。然而，颜福庆非但没有责备他，反而赞扬他忠于职守、兢兢业业的工作态度，当场褒奖他一双皮鞋。深受鼓舞的印度门卫钦佩颜副院长秉公严明的作风与宽广博大的胸襟，越加勤勤恳恳地守卫上医。

1945 年 2 月，颜府喜事临门，颜福庆的长孙健健康康地呱呱坠地。成为爷爷的颜福庆不胜欣喜，亲自为其取名“志渊”，意在希望长孙“志在颜渊”，长大后像孔子的弟子颜渊般德才兼备。

建筑简介：武康路40弄4号

颜福庆旧居位于武康路40弄4号，建于1923年，砖木结构假三层，英国乡村别墅式花园住宅。屋面覆盖红色机平瓦，南北皆设置高耸的老虎窗。建筑外墙为淡黄色水泥拉毛，窗边框以隅石形红砖贴面装饰。1943—1950年间，颜福庆曾在此居住。1956年起由上海市委行政处租用。现由徐房集团管理。

YAN Fuqing

YAN Fuqing (1882–1970), medical educator and public health expert, has a courtesy name of Keqing and has his ancestral family from Shanghai. In 1904, he graduated from Medical College of Saint John University. In 1906, he was sent to Yale University for further education and got a PhD degree there in 1909. For that he was the first Asian who got such a degree from Yale University. In the same year he went to Liverpool Tropical Disease Hospital in Britain to continue his study and obtained the diploma in tropical medicine (DTM). After returning home, he served as a surgeon in Changsha Yali Hospital. In 1911, he carried out the prevention and cure of plague along the railway from Beijing to Wuhan. Successively he founded the Fourth School of Medicine of Sun Yat-sen University (Shanghai Medical College), Shanghai Sun Yat-sen Hospital and Chengzhong Hectic Sanatorium. He once worked as a teacher in Beijing Union Medical College Hospital, School of Medicine of the Central University, Shanghai General Hospital (now Huashan Hospital) of the Red Cross Society of China, and Xiangya School of Medicine in Changsha. In 1937, he served as chairman of the Shanghai Rescue Committee, actively mobilizing and organizing volunteer medical and surgical teams to do rescue work. In 1938, he went to Wuhan to serve as director of the Department of Health. After the victory, he returned to work in Shanghai Medical College. After the founding of the New China, he was elected as member of the first, second and third sessions of the National People's Congress, member of the National Committee of the CPPCC, as well as member of the Central Committee of Jiusan Society and vice chairman of its Shanghai Branch. He advocated "public medical system" and preventive medicine, whose influence was far-reaching. In addition he made important contribution to the training of professionals for China's medicine and health. Under his name were published such books as *The Development of China's Medicine and Health and The Present* and *Past of Medical Education in China*.

Dedication to Medicine and Strict Medical Justice

On March 21, 1943, YAN's wife passed away due to a stroke at No. 24 on Ferguson Road, which left him deeply grieved. In this case, there was no mistress in the family. According to the custom, he asked his eldest son at the age of thirty to get married

1940—1941 年颜福庆（左一）全家在香港合影
A family photo of YAN Fuqing (first from left) in Hong Kong during the period between 1940 and 1941.

as soon as possible. His youngest daughter acting as the go-between, his son married that winter in Shanghai the daughter of a famous dentist who once studied in Japan. In the following year, the new wife gave birth to twin daughters, who unfortunately died young due to premature birth. For the repeated loss of his beloved ones, YAN was overwhelmed by grief, but he still did not forget the cause of medicine for which he had worked for his lifetime. Gulping back his tears, he asked medical colleagues to carefully make specimens of the twins, which were placed in the teaching and research section of Shanghai Medical College for teachers and students to do research.

At the beginning of 1945, the wife was pregnant again and waited for delivery in the Medical College. Concerned about her physical condition, YAN went to visit his daughter-in-law every day. One day in the evening, he went to hospital as usual after a busy day. However, when he arrived at the gate of the hospital, the time for visit had passed. The newly recruited Indian doorkeeper did not allow him in whatever he said. In desperation, he could only look into distance in the direction of the ward of his daughter-in-law.

The next day when he came to hospital, he asked people to find the Indian doorkeeper and looked kindly at the foreign employee with bushy eyebrows and big eyes. Astonished to know that the elderly man who was simply dressed and easy-going and who was sternly blocked at the gate of the hospital turned out to be the vice president of the hospital, the Indian doorkeeper was really afraid and awkwardly bowed his head. However, instead of blaming him, YAN praised him for his devotion to duty and his proper attitude to work. In addition a pair of leather shoes was given to him on the spot as a token of praise for him. Admiring the vice president for his strict style of work and his broad-mindedness, the inspired Indian doorkeeper guarded the hospital diligently all the more.

In February 1945, a big blessing visited his family for his first grandson was born. Now a grandfather, he felt pleased very much and personally found for his grandson the name “Zhiyuan”, intending to hope that his grandson would “have aspiration as that of YAN Yuan” and grow up like him, one of the disciples of Confucius who has both virtue and ability.

The former residence of YAN Fuqing is located at No. 4 in Alley 40 on Wukang Road, which was built in 1923. A countryside residential villa garden of British style, it has a three-storied structure of brick and wood with an interlayer. The roof is covered with red flat tile made with machine and there are high dormers at both north and south sides. The exterior walls are napped with light yellow cement and window frames are decorated with coign-shaped red brick veneer. Between 1943 and 1950, YAN Fuqing lived here. Since 1956, it has been rented by the administration office of the CPC Shanghai Committee. It is now managed by Xufang Group.

颜福庆 （杨宏富画） YAN Fuqing （By YANG Hongfu）

瞿维
（1917—2002）

江苏常州人，原名瞿世雄，作曲家。1933 年就读于上海新华艺术专科学校师范系。1938 年加入中国共产党。翌年 10 月赴陕甘宁边区。1940 年起，任教于延安鲁迅艺术学院音乐系。抗战胜利后到东北解放区。中华人民共和国成立后，历任东北电影制片厂和中央新闻纪录电影制片厂作曲、上海交响乐团作曲、中国音乐家协会副主席、上海音乐家协会主席。第一部重要作品是与马可、张鲁等合作的歌剧《白毛女》。另有代表作品：钢琴曲《花鼓》、交响诗《人民英雄纪念碑》、歌曲《工人阶级硬骨头》、电影音乐《革命家庭》、舞剧音乐《白毛女》等。

寄明
（1917—1997）

江苏淮安人，原名吴亚贞，作曲家。早年毕业于上海国立音乐专科学校。1939 年赴延安。1942 年加入中国共产党。曾任延安鲁艺、东北鲁艺教员，牡丹江鲁艺文工团副团长。中华人民共和国成立后从事电影音乐创作。1955 年调任上海电影制片厂，先后为《李时珍》《凤凰之歌》《春满人间》《金沙江畔》《燕归来》等 20 余部影片作曲。由她作曲的还有电影《英雄小八路》主题歌《我们是共产主义接班人》（后定为《中国少年先锋队队歌》）以及《给解放军叔叔洗衣裳》《少年，少年，祖国的春天》等少儿歌曲。

《中国少年先锋队队歌》的由来

1955 年，寄明从北京调到上海电影制片厂，先后担任音乐创作室副主任、作曲组组长。期间，她为《李时珍》《平凡的事业》《凤凰之歌》《鲁班的故事》《金沙江畔》等多部电影创作了主题歌。

1958 年，厦门和金门之间发生了炮战，它让全国人民知道了厦门何厝小学 13 名小学生穿行炮火中支前的故事。一年后，厦门第三中学语文老师王添成根据他们的故事，创作了话剧《英雄小八路》。这引发了上海影剧作家周郁辉的关注，他把话剧改编成同名电影剧本。上海天马电影制片厂决定拍摄此片，把谱写影片主题歌的任务交给了寄明。

那天，在复兴西路 34 号寓所里，寄明与同为作曲家的丈夫瞿维商讨起来。为让主题歌能真正反映影片所依据的事实和片中人物的思想感情变化，瞿维建议寄明到实地采风，以丰富素材。寄明采纳了瞿维的意见，专程到厦门，寻找到那些已经升入初中的“支前小英雄”们，听他们讲述当时冒着炮火上阵地，给解放军送饭、送开水的英勇故事。寄明不时被孩子们那种奋不顾身、勇往直前的精神所打动。她一边听，一边寻找最能体现影片主题的旋律。

采风快结束了，一个热情奔放、节奏和起伏度较大的曲调在寄明耳边萦绕，她连忙挥笔疾书，主题歌《我们是共产主义接班人》一气呵成。寄明带着曲子回到家中，马上哼唱给孩子们听。孩子们一边学唱，一边连说好听。

1961 年，电影《英雄小八路》正式上映，主题歌以其鲜明、朝气蓬勃的音乐形象，受到孩子们的喜爱。1978 年，共青团中央在征求群众和专家的意见后，将《我们是共产主义接班人》正式确定为《中国少年先锋队队歌》。1980 年，歌曲荣获第二次全国少年儿童文艺创作一等奖。

建筑简介：复兴西路34号

瞿维、寄明旧居位于复兴西路 34 号卫乐公寓，原名卫乐精舍，建于 1934 年，赉安洋行设计，占地面积 1720 平方米，建筑面积 3797 平方米，汽车间附屋 802 平方米，属现代点式建筑风格的公寓住宅。建筑为十三层钢筋混凝土结构，两翼跌落一层，立面对称，竖三段布置，中间凸出，设一串挑出的半圆阳台为构图中心，两边为卧入式阳台形成竖向线条。水泥砂浆外墙，立面中部竖线条及突出的半圆阳台为暗红色粉刷，其余部分为浅黄色粉刷，山墙顶部及南侧有重复线条装饰，楼前有小花园。中华人民共和国成立后，吕蒙与黄准夫妇、陈鲤庭、吴强、赖少其、峻青、王西彦等一批文化人在此居住。1994 年 2 月 15 日上海市人民政府公布其为市优秀历史建筑。

QU Wei and JI Ming

QU Wei (1917–2002), music composer, has his ancestral family from Changzhou in Jiangsu province and had a former name of QU Shixiong. In 1933, he studied at the Department of Teachers of New China Art College in Shanghai. In 1938, he joined the CPC. In October in the next year, he went to the Shaanxi-Gansu-Ningxia Border Region. In 1940, he worked as a teacher at the Music Department of LU Xun Art Academy at Yan'an. After the victory of the War against Japanese Invasion he went to liberated areas in the Northeast. After the founding of the People's Republic of China, he served in succession as music composer of Northeast Film Studio and Central News Documentary Film Studio, composer of Shanghai Symphony Orchestra, vice chairman of Chinese Musicians Association, and chairman of Shanghai Musicians Association. His first major work is the opera with title of *The White-haired Girl*, completed in collaboration with others. His other representative works include a piano music *Flower Drum*, a symphonic poem *Monument of the People's Heroes*, a song *The Working Class Have Hard Bones*, film music *A Revolutionary Family*, and dance drama music *The White-haired Girl*.

JI Ming (1917–1997), music composer, has her ancestral family from Huaian in Jiangsu province and she was formerly known as WU Yazhen. In the early years, she graduated from Shanghai National Academy of Music. In 1939, she went to Yan'an. In 1942, she joined the CPC. Once she worked as teacher in both LU Xun Art Academy at Yan'an and Northeast LU Xun Art Academy as well as deputy head of Mudan River LU Xun Art Group. After the founding of the People's Republic of China, she engaged herself in the creation of film music. In 1955, she was transferred to Shanghai Film Studio and composed music in succession for over 20 films such as *LI Shizhen*, *Song of the Phoenix*, *Spring Reigns Everywhere*, *Along the Jinsha Rive*r and *Swallow Coming Back*. She is also the composer of the theme song *We Are the Successors of Communism* (later identified as *China Youth Vanguard Team Song*) of the film *A Little Hero of the Eighth Route Army*, as well as *Washing Clothes for the PLA Uncles* and *Youth as the Spring of the Nation*. All these songs are for children.

The Origin of the "China Youth Vanguard Team Song"

瞿维、寄明夫妇在家中研究创作

The couple of QU Wei and JI Ming were discussing creative work.

In 1955, JI Ming was transferred from Beijing to Shanghai Film Studio and served in succession as deputy director of the music creation office and team leader of music composer. During this period, she created theme songs for many films, including *LI Shizhen*, *Ordinary Cause*, *Song of the Phoenix*, *Story of Luban* and *Along the Jinsha River*.

In 1958, artillery battles took place between Xiamen and Jinmen, which allowed people to know the story that 13 pupils from Hecuo Primary School in Xiamen ran through the fire to support the front. A year later, WANG Tiancheng, a teacher of Chinese language in the Third High School of Xiamen, wrote the drama *A Little Hero of the Eighth Route Army* according to their stories. This attracted the attention of the ZHOU Yuhui, a drama writer, in Shanghai. He adapted the drama into the script of a film with the same title. Shanghai Tianma Film Studio decided to produce this film out of it and gave the task of composing the theme song to JI Ming.

One day, she and her husband, another music composer talked together about the theme song at home at No. 34 on the West Fuxing Road. In order to create one which can truly reflect the facts on which the film was based on and the ideological and emotional changes of the characters, the music composer suggested she should go to collect materials on the spot to enrich materials. She adopted the suggestion and made a special trip to Xiamen so that she found those "little heroes supporting the front" who had been studying in junior high schools, listening to their heroic stories at that time when they braved gunfire to go to the battlefields and send food and boiled water to the PLA. She was moved from time to time by the children for their selflessness and the courage to march forward. While listening, she was looking for the melody which best embodies the theme of the film.

Towards the end of material collection, a passionate, rhythmic and highly undulating tune lingered in her ears, so she picked up pen to write quickly and the theme song *We Are the Successors of Communism* was accomplished in a breath. Bring the music back home, she immediately hummed it to her children. While they were learning to sing, they also commented that it was nice.

In 1961, the film *A Little Hero of the Eighth Route Army* was officially released. The theme song, with its distinctive and vibrant music image, was favored by children. In 1978, the Central Committee of the Communist Youth League officially identified this song as *China Youth Pioneer Team Song* after seeking the views of the masses and experts. In 1980, this song won the second national award of children's literature and art creation award.

The former residence of QU Wei and JI Ming is located at Willow Apartment at No. 34 on West Fuxing Road, formerly known as Willow Court. Designed by Leonard-Veysseyre-Kruze Architects and built in 1934, it covers an area of 1,720 square meters with a construction area of 3,797 square meters and attached rooms of 802 square meters for garage. It is an apartment house of point construction and modern architectural style. The building has thirteen floors with a reinforced concrete structure. Its facade is symmetrical with three sections with the middle standing out and the two wings being one floor lower than the middle. A series of projected semi-circular balconies form the center of the composition. At both sides the receding balconies form vertical lines; exterior walls are coated with cement mortar; the vertical lines and prominent semi-circular balconies in the middle section have color of dark red, and the remaining parts are of light yellow. At the top and south side of the gable repeated lines are used for decoration. In addition, a small garden is in front of the building. After the founding of the People's Republic of China, a number of intellectuals once lived here. On February 15, 1994, it became a Heritage Architecture issued by the Shanghai Municipal People's Government.

瞿维、寄明 （钱定华画） QU Wei and JI Ming （By QIAN Dinghua）

湖南街道

后记

湖南路街道因缘际会存留了厚实的历史底蕴和丰富的文化资源。这几年街道党工委和办事处为了进一步挖掘历史资源、传承历史文化，专门成立了编委会并组织人员收集整理历史资料，为众多曾经生活在这一地区的政治、经济、文化界等人物，以“人物简介、人物故事、人物旧居、人物画像”，勾勒一幅幅人物剪影。经过漫长艰苦的努力，克服了人物住址难找、旧居资料难查、故事情节难写的重重困难，最终编撰成这套《200031——一个历史街区的文化记忆》。

在资料收集过程中，目前已发现曾经居住于湖南路街道的各界人物300余位。由于资料翔实程度不同，现整理出111位人物及其旧居的资料，按照人物姓氏笔画排序，先行出版两册，其余的我们将继续充实资料，抓紧编撰，分批出版。

这套书的出版，首先要感谢上海文史馆馆员、上海民盟书画院院长、上海梧桐画社名誉社长汪观清先生及其他参与的画家。汪老是居住在这个区域，对湖南路街道有着深厚感情的一位德高望重的艺术家。他非常关心支持社区公共文化事业，不顾八十七岁高龄，不仅组织上海梧桐画社众多画家为本书配画，还亲自为巴金一篇创作题为《真爱》的画像，并对所有绘画作品把关。这些佳作为本书内容增光添彩。

对建筑作介绍是一项专业性要求极高的工作。我们参考书籍、调阅档案，并邀请上海市房地产科学研究院李占鸿、周云、代红超、李承根，以及上海石库门文化研究中心娄承浩等专家现场勘查，撰写部分建筑介绍，并请同济大学钱宗灏教授审阅部分内容。感谢他们从专业的角度，为本书出版付出的辛勤劳动。

还要感谢上海教育出版社原社长包南麟、中国中福会出版社副总编辑陈苏，他们不仅在体例规划、内容编写、稿件统筹上给予指导，还以湖南路街道老居民的真实情怀提供了很多有益的帮助。感谢上海大学上海美术学院汪大伟院长、上海市档案馆冯绍霆老师、上海市档案局郭红解老师、上海书店出版社完颜绍元老师的热心指教。感谢参与此书资料收集、资料整理、照片拍摄、文章撰写、稿件翻译等工作的所有人员，感谢上海图书馆、上海教育出版社、上海市徐汇区档案馆、众多人物的家属以及社会热心人士，不仅为我们提供了许多宝贵的线索和建议，还帮助我们查找资料和图片。书中引用的许多资料、图片，出自众多作者之手，难以一一详述，只能在此一并致谢。

本书编写历经数年，其间我们对资料反复调查、核实、修改、筛选，数易其稿，力求事实可靠、内容可读，具有艺术欣赏价值。然而，毕竟许多人和事年代久远，当事人大多已不在人世，虽经努力，难免挂一漏万。加之编者水平有限，书中错误和疏漏之处在所难免，敬请广大读者指正。也希望曾生活在这个区域的各界人士给我们提供有益的线索，以便再版时修正及使后续编撰工作进一步完善。

Postscript

Thanks to chances and opportunities, the Hunan Road Residential Subdistrict has accumulated handsome historical information and rich cultural resources. In order to further dig up historical resources and inherit the history and culture, the Party working committee and the subdistrict office specially set up an editorial board and organized personnel to collect and sort out historical documents and sketch the silhouettes for many people in the fields of politics, economy and culture who have lived in this area. The silhouettes have been materialized in the forms of "profile, story, former residence and portrait". After long and arduous efforts we have overcome various difficulties in looking for the addresses of people, searching for information about their former residences and writing the plots of their stories. Finally we have finished the compilation of this series with the title *200031—Cultural Memories of A Historical District*.

In the process of material collection, we have found at present over 300 celebrities from all walks of life who once lived in Hunan Road Residential Subdistrict. Due to the different degrees of fullness of information, we have now sorted out materials of 111 people and their former residences and put them in the order of stroke numbers of their surname. Two volumes are to be published first. We will continue to enrich the information of other people and lose no time in the compilation and writing. In the future more volumes will come out.

For the publication of these books, we are first of all indebted to Mr. WANG Guanqing, librarian of the Shanghai Research Institute of Culture and History, president of the Painting and Calligraphy Academy affiliated to Shanghai Committee of the China Democratic League and honorary president of Shanghai Wutong Painting Society, and our thanks also go to other artists involved. Mr. WANG is a highly respected artist who lives in this area and has a deep feeling for the Hunan Road Residential Subdistrict. He has much concern about and support for the public cultural undertakings of the community area. Regardless of his age of eighty-seven, he has not only organized many artists from the Shanghai Wutong Painting Society to prepare paintings for the books, but also personally created a portrait with the title of "True Love" for the passage BA Jin. In addition he has also made the final examination of all the paintings, which are the highlights of the books.

Writing introductions of architectures is a highly demanding job as far as professional knowledge is concerned. We have referred to books and read archives. Also we have invited such experts as LI Zhanhong, ZHOU Yun, DAI Hongchao and LI Chenggen from the Shanghai Real Estate Science Research Institute, and LOU Chenghao from Shanghai Stone-frame Gate Culture Research Center to make on-site investigations and write part of introductions of the architectures. In the meanwhile we have asked Professor QIAN Zonghao from Tongji University to read and approve part of the content. Therefore thanks go to all of them for their hard work for the publication of the books from a professional point of view.

We would also express our thanks to BAO Nanlin, former president of the Shanghai Educational Publishing House and CHEN Su, deputy editor-in-chief of China Welfare Institute Publishing House. They have not only given us guidance in the style and planning, content preparation and overall planning of manuscripts, but also provided a lot of useful help with the authentic feelings of the old residents of Hunan Road Residential Subdistrict. Our thanks still go to WANG Dawei, dean of Shanghai Academy of Fine Arts of Shanghai University, FENG Shaoting from Shanghai Archives, GUO Hongjie from Shanghai Archives Administration and WANYAN Shaoyuan from Shanghai Bookstore Publishing House for their warmhearted advice and instructions. We would also like to express our thanks to all people who have participated in the information collection, sorting out of documents, photo shooting, article writing, manuscript translation and so on. We would further like to extend our thanks to Shanghai Library, Shanghai

Educational Publishing House and Shanghai Xuhui District Archives, as well as family members of many public figures and warm-hearted people, who have not merely provided a lot of valuable clues and suggestions for us, but also helped us find information and pictures. A lot of the information and pictures cited in the books come from the hands of many writers, while it is difficult to elaborate one by one. We cannot help but express our thanks once for all.

The compilation of the books has lasted for several years, during which we have repeatedly investigated, verified, modified and sifted and the manuscripts have been revised for several times in order that the contents are reliable and readable along with values for artistic appreciation. However, many people and things are of the remote past and most people concerned are no longer alive. With all of our efforts, it is inevitable that the information is far from being complete. In addition editors are limited in one aspect or another. Therefore errors and omissions in the book are unavoidable. We sincerely invite all readers to point out mistakes so that they can be corrected in the future. Also we hope that people who have lived in this area provide us with useful clues so that revisions are to be made at the time of reprinting and that the subsequent compilation can be further improved.

图书在版编目（CIP）数据

200031：一个历史街区的文化记忆. 2 / 中共上海市徐汇区湖南街道工作委员会，上海市徐汇区人民政府湖南路街道办事处组织编写. — 上海：上海教育出版社, 2017.12
ISBN 978-7-5444-7859-5

Ⅰ.①2… Ⅱ.①中… ②上… Ⅲ.①城市道路—介绍—徐汇区 Ⅳ.①K925.13

中国版本图书馆CIP数据核字（2017）第285561号

责任编辑 隋淑光 严 岷 林 翘
装帧设计 王 捷 金一哲
封面设计 陈世东
封面绘画 钱定华
插页设计 邬海佳

200031：一个历史街区的文化记忆（2）

中共上海市徐汇区湖南街道工作委员会
上海市徐汇区人民政府湖南路街道办事处 **编**
陈世东 主编

出版发行 上海教育出版社有限公司
官 网 www.seph.com.cn
地 址 上海市永福路123号
邮 编 200031
印 刷 上海盛通时代印刷有限公司印刷
开 本 890×1240 1/16 印张 15.25 插页2
版 次 2017年12月第1版
印 次 2017年12月第1次印刷
书 号 ISBN 978-7-5444-7859-5/G·6473
定 价 （精装）148.00 元